THE

EVERYTHING

SHARE PRICE

ONLINE
INVESTING
BOOK

Get the latest stock tips, make quick trades,
and manage your portfolio like the pros

Harry Domash

Adams Media Corporation
Holbrook, Massachusetts

ACKNOWLEDGMENTS

Thank you to my loving wife, Norma, who read every word of this book more than once; to Carol Roth, who made it happen; to Laura and Jeffree Lee, who made so many helpful suggestions; and to my neighbor, Gary Schilling, who not only read chapters and made valuable suggestions, but also mowed my lawn while I was writing this book.

An Everything Series Book.
The Everything Series is a trademark of Adams Media Corporation.

Published by Adams Media Corporation
260 Center Street, Holbrook, MA 02343 U.S.A.
www.adamsmedia.com

ISBN: 1-58062-338-7

Printed in the United States of America.

J I H G F E D C B A

Library of Congress Cataloging-in-Publication Data available upon request from the publisher.

This publication is designed to provide accurate and authoritative information with regard to the subject matter covered. It is sold with the understanding that the publisher is not engaged in rendering legal, accounting, or other professional advice. If legal advice or other expert assistance is required, the services of a competent professional person should be sought.
— From a *Declaration of Principles* jointly adopted by a Committee of the American Bar Association and a Committee of Publishers and Associations

Many of the designations used by manufacturers and sellers to distinguish their products are lcaimed as trademarks. Where those designations appear in this book and Adams Media was aware of a trademark claim, the designations have been printed in initial capital letters.

Illustrations by Barry Littmann

This book is available at quantity discounts for bulk purchases.
For information, call 1-800-872-5627.

Contents

CHAPTER EIGHT: A QUICK LOOK AT ANALYZING STOCKS / 111

CHAPTER NINE: PROFILING THE COMPANY / 123

CHAPTER TEN: ANALYZING THE ANALYSTS / 129

CHAPTER ELEVEN: CASHING IN ON INSIDER INFO / 143

CHAPTER TWELVE: GETTING THE MOST OUT OF QUOTES AND CHARTS / 155

CHAPTER THIRTEEN: DECODING FINANCIAL STATEMENTS / 167

CHAPTER FOURTEEN: SECOND OPINIONS / 177

CHAPTER FIFTEEN: FORECASTING THE FUTURE / 187

CHAPTER SIXTEEN: WHAT THE SECTORS SAY / 201

CHAPTER SEVENTEEN: FINDING THE FUNDS / 213

CHAPTER EIGHTEEN: SCREENING FOR TOP MUTUAL FUNDS / 243

Introduction

These are exciting times to be an investor. We are in on the beginning of a major transformation.

Long-established firms, the so-called "old economy," are quickly adopting new technologies to improve their efficiency and to better respond to their customer's needs. The technology producers are racing to meet demands for newer and even better products. It's a revolution of massive proportions.

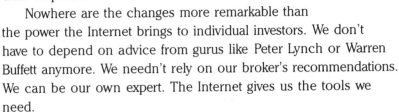

The benefits of the technological revolution aren't limited to large corporations. They affect you and me just as much. We can watch the news 24 hours a day. We can buy books, computers, perfumes, even lingerie, at 2:00 A.M. if we desire. We can dash off e-mail to someone halfway around the globe, and get an almost-immediate response.

Nowhere are the changes more remarkable than the power the Internet brings to individual investors. We don't have to depend on advice from gurus like Peter Lynch or Warren Buffett anymore. We needn't rely on our broker's recommendations. We can be our own expert. The Internet gives us the tools we need.

We can see fact-filled reports from companies the day they're filed with the Securities and Exchange Commission.

We can learn news about a company as soon as it happens, see stock market analysts' buy, hold, and sell advice and earnings forecasts, and read their research reports. We can find out if "in-the-know" insiders are buying or selling shares of their own company's stock.

We can scan the entire stock market in seconds to find stocks with attributes we've determined to be critical to beating the market.

The Internet opens new opportunities for the individual to be a better investor.

Yet, few of us are harnessing more than a tiny percentage of the power the Internet affords us.

I started teaching investment classes because I saw that although they were online, most people were still picking stocks the same way they did in the "old days," following tips and hunches.

We've all heard that the secret to success in almost any endeavor is to follow a systematic approach, then evaluate your results, and modify your approach if necessary, and keep following your plan. This process assures continual improvement the longer you do it. This fundamental principle applies fully to the stock market.

I teach my students the strategies I've discovered for finding and analyzing stocks and mutual funds. I didn't make them up, I stole them! That's right, I filched them from Warren Buffett, Peter Lynch, William J. O'Neil, Martin Zweig, David Dreman, James P. O'Shaughnessy, David and Tom Gardner, Alexander Elder, and many others who were careless enough to leave their time-proven winning strategies unguarded on bookstore shelves and on Web sites waiting for me to swipe.

The systems I teach are an amalgamation of these great investors' ideas, modified and tailored to harness the fantastic resources offered by the Internet.

This book, my first, by the way, is intended to teach you the same strategies I teach my students. Like them, most of you probably won't follow my system exactly, and that's good. I hope you will take my ideas and adapt them to your investing style. I expect some of you will discover better ways of searching out winning investment candidates, and better methods of analyzing them. When you do, I hope you'll tell me about it. My e-mail address is *hdomash@winninginvesting.com*.

All of the resources described in this book, although extremely valuable, and hopefully profitable, are available to you free.

You probably realize if you're already online, that everything on the Internet changes all the time. That's certainly true for financial Web sites. Layouts of some of the Web sites described in this book will undoubtedly have changed by the time you access them. The information will probably still be available, only the path to it will have changed.

Not a problem! We'll post known changes to sites described here on our own Web site: *www.winninginvesting.com*. Drop us a note if you've uncovered changes we haven't posted.

I wish you good health and profitable investing.

Harry Domash

CHAPTER ONE

Choosing an Online Broker

Best Investment Sites for:

Analysts' Ratings and Forecasts

Quicken
(*www.quicken.com*)
and **Yahoo! Finance**
(quote.yahoo.com):
Best display of analysts'
recommendations, earnings
forecasts, earnings sur-
prises, etc.

Analysts' Research Reports

Internet Stocks
(*www.internetstocks.com*):
Robertson Stephens's site
publishes an extensive
weekly analysis of Internet
stocks.

Multex Investor
(*www.multexinvestor.com*):
A hub for distribution of
research reports from a
variety of brokerage houses.
Some require payment, but
many are free. An excellent
research resource.

Wit Capital
(*www.witcapital.com*):
Research reports on about 80
Internet-related companies.

Trading on the Internet has caught on with the investing public. Every month sees an increasing percentage of market trading conducted on the Web. Established brokers have gotten the message and most, if not already online, are planning to offer Web trading. Many new brokers have sprung up to offer trading services exclusively on the Web. There are currently hundreds of brokers offering Web trading services, and the list continues to grow.

Your Investing Style

When choosing the right Web broker a lot will depend on your investing style. Ask yourself these questions:

- How often do you trade and how long do you hold stocks or mutual funds once you own them?
- Do you make your entire investment in each stock or fund all at once, or do you prefer to test the waters with a small position and add to it if the market goes your way?
- Do you mainly buy mutual funds, stocks, or a mixture of both?
- Do you do your own fundamental research, or do you make your decisions based on tips you've heard on TV or the buzz on online message boards?

Here are descriptions of types of investors that will help you decide where you fit in:

ACTIVE TRADERS

If you're making dozens of transactions monthly, sometimes holding your positions for only a few hours, or one or two days, you're an active trader. You watch real-time quotes and jump on a stock when it starts its move. Failure to make a timely buy because your broker's Web site is down could mean a lost opportunity, or even a major loss if you're trying to get out of a rapidly deterio-rating position. Even a minute's delay in executing your trade could turn profit into loss. Commissions add up fast and saving $10 on every trade makes a big difference to your bottom line. You need absolute site reliability, rock bottom commissions, and lightening-fast trade executions.

LONG-TERM INVESTORS

Long-term stock investors have different priorities. They don't worry much about trade execution speed. What difference does an extra minute make to someone who is planning on holding a stock for years? Same thing with commissions. Nobody likes to waste money, but saving $10 on a commission isn't top priority on a long-term investment. What is important is picking the right stock. Online research tools helpful in accomplishing that goal are an important consideration.

MUTUAL FUND INVESTORS

If you invest mainly in mutual funds, neither stock trading commissions nor execution speed mean anything. Mutual fund transactions only happen once a day, after the market closes. What's important is choice, minimum purchase requirements, and transaction charges. You need a broker with the widest possible selection of funds, with as many as possible available with no transaction fees.

If you buy shares in a *no-load fund,* you can purchase the shares directly from the fund or through a discount broker. If you buy through a broker, the fund doesn't have to handle your paper-work, keep track of your balance, mail out statements, answer your phone calls, etc. Instead, the broker does all that, incurring costs along the way. Some funds recognize the value of letting your broker handle the paperwork and reimburse the broker accordingly. If that's the case, and it's a no-load fund, your broker will probably handle your purchases and sales of those funds' shares with no trans-action charges. If your broker and the fund haven't come to an agreement for the fund to cover the transaction and maintenance costs, your broker will charge a fixed fee, ranging from $9.99 to over $100.

Brokers in General

But what exactly is a *Web broker,* as opposed to other kinds of brokers? Here are the different types of brokers and what they do:

Full-service brokers offer financial planning and advice on market timing, advice on selecting mutual funds, stocks, and other investment vehicles. Trading commissions are high compared to conventional discount and Web brokers, but it's well worth it to individuals who don't have the time or the expertise to manage their own portfolios.

Clients of full-service brokers have an individual broker at the firm, someone they've probably met in person and who is familiar with their financial circumstances and needs, and who understands their investment temperament and risk tolerances. All trades result from conversations between the client and broker and commissions typically run in the $200 to $300 range, varying with the share price and the number of shares traded.

Discount brokers are the bare-bones, no-frills alternatives to full-service brokers for investors willing and able to make their own investment decisions. They make a point of not offering advice on anything other than the mechanics of trading. If you want to know how to place a stop order—fine—they'll be glad to explain the difference between stop limits, stop losses, and so on. But don't bother asking whether the market's heading up or their views on Microsoft's prospects for the coming year, they're too busy making trades—volume is how they make money.

Clients usually don't have a specific broker at the firm, they place their trades with whoever answers the phone. Discount broker commissions run in the $30 to $100 range, again depending on the share price and number traded.

A **Web broker** is any brokerage house, discount or full-service, accepting trades through their Web site. Accepting trades via the Internet defines them as a Web broker, regardless of their commission schedule. In practice, though, most brokers charge less to trade on the Web than if you place your trade on the phone or in person.

Some Web brokers are traditional brick-and-mortar firms such as Charles Schwab and TD Waterhouse. If need be, you can show up at a local office and transact business face-to-face. Other brokers were born with the Web, accept trades via the Internet exclusively, and have no real offices for clients to visit. E*Trade is a good example of an exclusively cyber/broker.

Trading commissions typically range from $5 to $30 and are fixed, that is, they don't vary with the number of shares traded or the share price, at least in the range traded by most individual investors. Some brokerages charge higher commissions for trades exceeding a specified minimum, typically 2,000 to 5,000 shares.

How to Get Background on Brokers

Let's start our hunt for the best Web broker for you with some online sites that will help you in your selection process.

GOMEZ.COM (*www.gomez.com* > Brokers)

Gomez is in the business of rating all online services. It could be banks, music sites, airlines, or toy stores. You'd think their ratings for brokers would be superficial, since brokers are just another category, but in fact they do a good, responsible job. Just click on "Brokers" on their homepage. (The > in the Web address indicates a menu selection to click.)

Gomez ranks broker sites in five categories:

1. **Ease of use:** rating of the site's ease of navigation and availability of tutorials and demos.
2. **Customer confidence:** rates phone response time, customer service, staff willingness to disclose information about rules, etc., patience, and ability to answer questions.

Firm	Score
1. E*Trade (review)	7.66
2. Charles Schwab (review)	7.39
3. Fidelity Investments (review)	7.37
4. DLJdirect (review)	6.84
5. TD Waterhouse (review)	6.43
6. NDB (review)	6.32
7. My Discount Broker (review)	6.24
8. A.B. Watley (review)	6.13
9. Morgan Stanley Dean Witter Online (review)	6.08
10. Suretrade (review)	6.06
11. Ameritrade (review)	6.05
12. Siebert (review)	5.99
13. Web Street (review)	5.95
14. Wingspan Investment Services (review)	5.90
15. Quick & Reilly (review)	5.81
16. Datek (review)	5.77
17. WallStreet Electronica (review)	5.72
18. Empire (review)	5.72
19. American Express Brokerage (review)	5.71
20. Freeman Welwood (review)	5.64
View All Firms ...	

Ratings as they appear on Gomez.com.

The Still-Almighty Telephone

Whether you're an active trader or a buy-and-hold investor—experienced or beginner—take my advice and pick an online broker with readily available telephone support and telephone trading capability. E-mail is useful for a lot of things, but it can be exasperating when you wait hours to receive a response that could have been generated by a computer, and that doesn't answer your question. At times an old-fashioned telephone conversation with a real person is the best solution.

Things frequently go wrong on the Internet. It could be your broker's Web site, or problems having nothing to do with your broker. Your computer could lock up, you might have a power failure, your Internet Service Provider could go down, you name it. Eventually something will happen to keep you from entering a trade through your computer. An alternate trading approach is essential when the Internet fails.

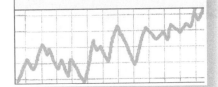

3. **On-site resources:** research and screening tools, market commentary, etc.
4. **Relationship services:** updating of account balances, site security, educational content, etc.
5. **Overall cost:** commission and margin rates.

Gomez computes an overall score for each broker site and rates the broker's suitability for four different trading styles:

- Hyper-Active Trader: low commissions, simple interface, and fast execution times are the main criteria for this sort of trader.
- Serious Investor: investment analysis and research tools are rated.
- Life Goal Planner: mutual fund availability, financial planning, and portfolio optimization tools are most important.
- One-Stop Shopper: breadth of offerings and ease of use are the primary concern.

On the Brokers page, pick the category that interests you to see a list of the 20 highest rated brokers. You can read a detailed discussion of each broker's strengths and weaknesses by clicking on review next to each name. You can also compare two broker's ratings side-by-side.

The ratings are done by Gomez analysts and do not include customer feedback. However, they do provide a message board for each broker. You can find it under "Consumer ratings & reviews" on the main Broker page, or by selecting "Read what consumers are saying . . ." on each individual broker's report page.

Gomez is a good start, but some of their ratings are limited in scope. For instance, they don't evaluate the quality of investment research offerings. A site offering simple company profiles—available free on dozens of other sites—ranks just as high as a broker offering complete Standard & Poor's company reports. Nonetheless, Gomez is a good resource for getting you up to speed on who's out there. For a more in-depth look at broker features and offerings, check out XOLIA.com.

XOLIA.COM (*www.xolia.com*)

XOLIA, the brainchild of Anas Osman and Azhar Usman, makes comparing Web brokers easy. When I checked in January '00, you could compare up to three brokers side-by-side, but they plan to expand that limit later in 2000.

Using the site is simple. Select "Comparison Tool" from their homepage, and select the brokers you want to compare from the list on the left. You can choose Basic, Advanced, or Custom comparisons. Basic lists fewer categories than Advanced, and Custom lets you pick the categories to compare. (You may as well select Advanced and see everything.) The categories are the following:

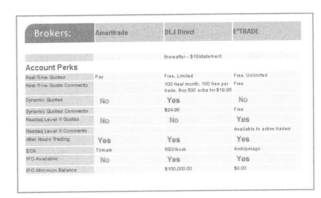

Brokers:	Ameritrade	DLJ Direct	E*TRADE
		thereafter – $10/statement	
Account Perks			
Real-Time Quotes	Pay	Free, Limited	Free, Unlimited
Real-Time Quote Comments		100 free/ month, 100 free per trade. Buy 500 extra for $19.95	Free
Dynamic Quotes	No	Yes	No
Dynamic Quotes Comments		$24.95	Free
Nasdaq Level II Quotes	No	No	Yes
Nasdaq Level II Comments			Available to active traders
After Hours Trading	Yes	Yes	Yes
ECN	Trimark	REDIbook	Archipelago
IPO Available	No	Yes	Yes
IPO Minimum Balance		$100,000.00	$0.00

Xolia.com compares other Web brokers.

- *Broker Information:* Includes the number of walk-in offices, service hours, and whether foreign accounts are allowed. (I prefer companies with real offices within driving distance—just in case.) Also shown is the amount of the account insurance carried by the broker. The figure represents the maximum account value covered. Usually it's in the millions, but not always, so check it.
- *Account Types:* Shows allowable account types such as individual, corporate, money market, margin, etc., and the required opening balances for each account type. Also shows the sweep frequency; that is, how often your extra cash is moved into an interest-bearing account.
- *IRA:* Availability and fees for traditional IRAs and Roth IRA accounts. Look for zero fees if you're planning on opening an IRA account.
- *Stocks:* Commissions for stock transactions, varies depending on the market where the stock is listed, number of shares, and transaction type; market or limit order. Pay attention to limit order fees. Sometimes they're much higher than the advertised "market order" fees. This is important because you could very well find yourself placing limit orders in the future, even if you're not sure what that means now.

- *Options:* Commissions for put and call option trades.
- *Mutual Funds:* Availability and charges associated with mutual fund transactions. If you're planning on buying mutual funds, be sure to check Online No-Load commissions, which are the transaction fees the broker charges for purchases and sales of funds not participating in their no-fee program; it varies substantially between brokers.
- *Other Stocks:* Availability of, and commissions for trading penny, Canadian, bulletin board, and foreign stocks.
- *Other Securities:* Availability of bond trading and short sales.
- *Fees:* Some brokers charge low commissions but get you on the fees for miscellaneous services such as account transfers, returned checks, wire transfers, and duplicate statements. All such fees are listed here.
- *Account Perks:* Availability of real-time quotes, checking accounts, NASDAQ Level II quotes, after-hours trading, and a variety of ancillary features.

One thing I appreciate about XOLIA is they don't try to squeeze important details into a predetermined space. They use as much room as necessary to explain features and charges.

Gomez and XOLIA are good at what they do, but much of their information is about features and charges. What about the real world? What's actually happening in the trenches? OnLine Investment Services is a place to find out.

ONLINE INVESTMENT SERVICES *(www.sonic.net/donaldj)*

Don Johnson, a retired history professor and former publisher of the *Online Investment Letter,* a stock advisory newsletter, created this site listing over 150 Web brokers. Each listing includes a detailed report including fees, commissions, and charges, number of mutual funds offered, research options, speed of the Web site, etc.

There's a lot of detail there, as much or more than XOLIA provides, but what's more important is the down and dirty practical stuff, which is mostly based on customer experience.

For example, using a fictitious brokerage name, *"We are raising XYZ to 4½ stars. For a brief period, there was a flurry of com-*

plaints that XYZ could not be reached quickly by phone. We suggest that all prospective customers call XYZ a few times with questions about this and that, just to check on how good/bad their phone service might be," or *"Customers complain that brokers are rude and do not understand the intricacies of IRA and Keogh accounts,"* or *"I've discovered that staff in their options department are undertrained, misinformed, and reluctant to take responsibility for their mistakes,"* or *"The Web page remains slow, and market orders generally take three to four minutes to be executed."*

This is hard information you can use, and you won't find it anywhere else, on or off the Net.

Johnson maintains several lists rating brokers according to specific investment needs:

- *For active investors:* Johnson compiles his assessment of the best brokers for active investors in a section called "Best Online Discount Brokers for Experienced Investors—A Special Report." These ratings give most emphasis to low commissions, low margin rates, good customer service, availability of real-time quotes, speed of the Web site, and rapid confirmation of executed orders.
- *For beginners:* You need plenty of patient, readily available help on the telephone when you're learning how to invest online. Johnson's "Best Brokers for Beginners, and/or Investors New to the Internet" gives its heaviest ratings to brokers with excellent customer service, but doesn't neglect overall quality. High ratings in this category also require brokers rated "very good or excellent overall."
- *For penny stocks investors:* Stocks selling for less than $2 per share, or stocks listed on the Bulletin Board or Pink Sheet trading systems are classified as "penny stocks." Stocks not available for purchase on margin also fall into this category. Most Web brokers discourage trading of penny stocks. There's not enough profit, and too many headaches. This list rates brokers that offer penny stock trading.
- *For day traders:* Day traders are rapid-fire traders who often buy and sell a stock in less than one hour. These traders

Buying on Margin

Buying on margin means you are borrowing part of the money needed to purchase your shares from your broker. The standard margin requirements are 50 percent, meaning you have to put up half of the purchase price in cash, and your broker puts up the rest. Sometimes brokers require more cash (higher margin), especially on volatile Internet stocks.

Your broker collects interest on the money you owe, and you can't sell your shares without repaying the loan to your broker. If the share price on margined stock drops close to the amount you borrowed—typically within 25 percent—your broker can "call the margin." When that happens you have to add more cash to your account or sell the stock and repay the broker. You cannot buy on margin in retirement accounts such as IRAs, nor can you buy stocks selling for less than $5 per share on margin.

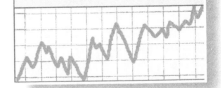

Transferring Your Stocks to a Web Broker

Suppose you already own stocks or mutual funds and want to move them from your account with Broker Old to a new account on the Web with Broker New. It's easy to do, assuming you've already opened your account with Broker New. Download and print out a transfer form from Broker New. Fill it out detailing the stocks or funds you want to move and mail it, along with a copy of a recent statement from Broker Old, to Broker New.

That's all you have to do. Broker New will take care of making it happen. The transfer usually takes about two weeks.

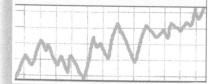

need special services such as NASDAQ Level II quotes, very reliable trading sites, and the fastest possible trade executions. Johnson's "Special Report on Day Trading" rates the best brokers in this specialized field.

- *For options trading:* The "Special Report on Options Trading" lists the brokers with the lowest commissions for various types of options trades.
- *For commodities trading:* "Commodity Brokers Ranked" lists the best brokers for commodities trading.

If you don't fall into one of these specialized categories, scroll down the main page until you see "Discount Stock Brokers Ranked," and click on that. This will take you to a listing of all 150 plus brokers rated by Johnson.

If you're interested in a particular broker, select the alphabetical listing and scroll until you find your broker of interest. Click on the name to display a complete report. The site displays additional lists on this page including:

Deep discounters (less than $15), listed in order of lowest commissions
Deep discounters, listed in order of best overall service
Middle-cost discounters ($15 to $19.95), listed in order of lowest commissions
High-cost discounters, listed in order of lowest commissions

The site is a bit confusing to navigate, and Johnson scatters investing and broker selection advice in various places. I've found navigating the site is easiest if you always go back to the home page. There is much good information here, and it's well worth spending the time to ferret it out. Johnson updates the reports twice a month, so the information is current.

What Is a Share of Stock?

COMMON STOCK

Shareholders are the owners of a public corporation. If a corporation has sold 100,000 shares, and you own 100 shares, you own

1/1,000 of the whole corporation. You get one vote on corporate matters for each share you own. If you own enough shares, you can decide who sits on the board of directors, and through them, who runs the company. Theoretically, if the company goes out of business, shareholders divide the assets after liquidation, but in the real world, companies go out of business because they've gone bankrupt. Companies go bankrupt when they owe more than they have, and stockholders typically get nothing. Some investors don't realize that and buy shares in bankrupt companies because they're cheap. They believe they're getting a bargain because they're getting shares that used to trade at, say $25.00, and are now going for $0.50. These shares eventually become worthless.

Sometimes corporations issue multiple classes of stock, for instance, Class A shares and Class B shares. Often they do this so the original owners can maintain control by giving one class more votes than the other. For instance, Class A shares have 10 votes, compared to one vote for each Class B share.

PREFERRED STOCK

Preferred shares are debt instruments, they collect interest, and eventually the principal is repaid, but they have no voting rights. They're called "preferred" because preferred shareholders have priority over common shareholders if the assets of the corporation are liquidated. Convertible preferred shares can be converted into common shares under certain predetermined conditions.

Opening an Account

Of course, you won't be *really* ready to open an account until you've finished this book(!). But when you are, you may be surprised to find that despite the amazing progress of communications via the Internet, setting up a new account with most Web brokers is still done the old-fashioned way. Most broker's sites have application form blanks you can print out on your laser or inkjet printer. Some allow you to fill in your personal information before you print out the form, saving the broker from having to read your handwriting. You still have to sign the form, enclose a check, and mail the package to the broker.

How Fast Is Your Web Broker?

Keynote Systems (www.keynote.com)

Keynote Systems measures Web site performance, and provides diagnostic and consulting services, mostly to companies with e-commerce sites. When they decided to measure Web broker performance, they did it right. Here's how they do it:

A transaction begins by connecting to a broker's site and logging on. Keystone then gets a stock quote, creates an order to buy stock, then logs out, ending the transaction. They repeat the process every 15 minutes from 10 major metropolitan areas. They do this between 9:00 A.M. and 4:00 P.M. every trading day.

Select "Broker Trading Index" on their site to see the performance ratings for the last two weeks. Keynote sorts the list with the fastest brokers on top, and shows the average transaction time and success rate for each broker. The ratings are updated on Wednesdays.

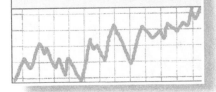

Robert's Online Commissions Pricer!

*(www.intrepid.com > **Robert's Financial Page > Commissions Pricer!**)*

Robert is Dr. Robert Lum, a computer science professor with a doctorate in math. His site contains several financial calculators. His Commissions Pricer! calculates the commission that any of the 100 brokers covered would charge for a specific trade. You enter a stock price and number of shares, then select the exchange where the stock trades. The Commissions Pricer! lists the commission each broker on the list charges for the trade. You can also see trading commissions if you enter your trade via a phone touchtone entry or by calling a broker (broker-assisted trade), instead of using the Web.

The site is updated only twice yearly, so the information can be up to six months old.

Web brokers require a minimum balance to open an account, typically in the $1,000 to $5,000 range. After you've deposited that money—either by credit card or sending them a check or money order—you're still not automatically ready to start trading. Most brokers require you to call customer service to activate your account. They'll give you a temporary password when you call, then you'll usually be prompted to change it when you log on for the first time.

Give some thought to choosing a password. Someone could do plenty of damage to your financial health if they know your account number and password. Make it something easy to remember, but not easy for someone else to guess. Don't use your favorite color (I bet it's blue), your children's name, or your birthdate, etc. Experts say passwords containing a combination of at least six letters and numbers are best.

Now, before jumping in to make your first million, let's learn about trading.

CHAPTER TWO

All about Trading

B rokers on the Web provide four main types of stock transactions:

1. *Buy:* An order to buy a specified number of shares either at the market price at the time the trade is executed, or at a specified maximum price.
2. *Sell:* An order to sell shares that you own, either at the market price at the time the sale is executed, or at a specified minimum price.
3. *Sell-Stop:* An order to sell shares you currently own if the share price drops to a designated level.
4. *Sell Short:* An order to sell shares that you do not currently own (but borrow from your broker) because you're expecting the stock to drop in price, at which time you can buy shares back and repay the broker.

Let's look into these transactions and what they entail.

Buy

To identify shares of a company you wish to buy (or sell), you need to know the ticker symbol. You can look up the ticker symbol on your broker's site, usually in the "quote" section, or on almost any financial site. Take care when you do this. It's easy to buy the wrong stock because two companies have similar names. For instance, Applied Micro Circuits (ticker symbol AMCC) could easily be confused with Applied Microsystems (APMC). Some companies have two or more separate types of stock with different symbols. General Communications, Inc., has ticker symbols GNCMA and GNCMB.

Many Web brokers display the full company name when they ask you to confirm your order. If you're unsure of the ticker symbol, call or e-mail your broker before you buy.

CHECK THE QUOTE

Before buying or selling stock, check the current quote. Prices change quickly, and the current price may be much different than

last night's close, or even the quote you saw a few minutes ago. Make sure you get a "real-time" quote, not a delayed quote. Most Web brokers provide, at the very least, a limited number of free real-time quotes to account holders.

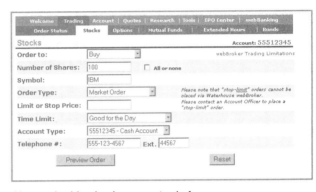

Always double-check your entry before you process.

Quotes usually include a bid price, ask price, last transaction price, and price change. The *bid price* is the price buyers are offering to pay for your shares. *Ask price* is the amount you'll have to pay to buy shares. The *price change* is the difference between the *last transaction price* and yesterday's closing price. Quotes also include the day's high and low transaction prices, and the volume (number of shares traded) as the day goes on.

Quote prices may be shown in dollars and fractions of a dollar, or as a decimal. If it's shown in dollars and fractions, a quote of 16 27/64 means the price is $16.42 per share. The difference between the bid price and the ask price is called the *spread.* The spread for actively traded stocks is usually less than 1/8 of a point ($0.125 per share). Lightly traded stocks could have spreads of as much as $1.00. Seasoned investors avoid stocks with spreads exceeding $0.50 (1/2).

ENTER THE BASIC TRADE INFORMATION

If you're satisfied with the current quote, you'll now be ready to enter your transaction, which involves several steps.

- If your account is approved for margin transactions, you may have to specify whether you're buying the stock on margin or using your cash account.
- Enter the ticker symbol and the number of shares you want to buy.

In the past, you were penalized with an extra commission if you bought less than 100 shares, which is called an "odd lot" transaction. But no longer—you can buy any number of shares, even one, if you desire, without penalty. Of course, if you buy too few shares, the commission could be a large percentage of the transaction cost. For instance, say you buy two shares of a stock selling for $10 per share, and the commission is $10. The total cost of the transaction is $30, or $15 per share. Your stock would have to increase 50 percent in value before you break even, and you'd lose another $5 per share when you sold.

- *All or None:* You will be asked to specify how you want the transaction to be executed. Selecting "All or None" prevents the order from being executed in pieces. For instance, if you haven't selected "All or None," and you're buying 300 shares, the trade could conceivably be executed as three separate orders at three different prices. If it's a limit order, possibly only an order for 100 shares of the 300 requested would be executed. Orders of less than 200 shares are always executed in a single transaction.
- *Market Order or Limit Order:* You have a choice of how you want the trade price to be determined by choosing market order or limit order. If you select *market order,* you'll pay the current ask price when your order is executed. If you don't want to pay more than a certain amount, you can set the maximum price you're willing to pay by choosing *limit order,* and entering a limit price. Your trade will not be executed if no one is willing to sell shares at your limit price.

When you place a limit order, you choose whether you want your order to expire at the close of today's trading if it isn't filled (good for the day) or kept active indefinitely (good until canceled). "Good until canceled" orders are not necessarily in force indefinitely. Some brokers cancel them if they're not executed within a specified time, say 60 days.

- *Submit and Confirm:* When you're satisfied with your order, push the "Submit" button. Most Web brokers give you a chance to review your order before sending it off for execution. Often they'll show you an updated real-time quote at the same time. Check the information carefully. Computers can make anyone careless, so read the screen carefully, so you don't end up buying the wrong stock, the wrong number of shares, or selling instead of buying.

Once you give the OK, your order is on its way. If it's a market order, it will probably be confirmed within 30 to 60 seconds. Limit orders take longer. You have to wait for someone willing to do the trade at your price.

BUY STOP

The opposite of a buy limit order is a buy stop. Instead of setting a maximum price, you're saying you don't want to buy the stock unless it's at or **above** your set price, called the *stop price*. Why would you do that? Technical analysts (chartists) look at a stock's price chart to determine if and when to buy. A popular strategy is to follow a stock that is in a "consolidation pattern," meaning it's trading within a narrow price range. Chartists wait until the stock price breaks out—that is, moves up above the trading range—and then they buy. For instance, say a stock is trading in a range between $40 and $50 and you want to buy it if it breaks out to $52. Entering a buy order with a stop price of $52 would accomplish that by converting to a market buy order if the price hits $52.

Sell

Most brokers use the same Web page for buying and selling, and the transactions are similar. As with a buy, get a quote before starting your transaction, then enter the ticker symbol, number of shares, and select "Sale" from the dropdown action menu.

When selling, the limit order specifies the **minimum** price you're willing to accept for your shares.

Sell Stop

Sell stops are used to instruct your broker to sell your shares if the stock goes down to a specific price or lower. For

instance, say your stock is currently trading at $50, and you want to sell it if it goes down to $45.

You could simply keep an eye on the stock and manually enter a sell order when it hits $45. That's termed a "mental stop." One problem with using mental stops is our lack of self-discipline. If the stock does go down to $45, we're tempted to give it a little slack and say, "Let's wait and see what is does tomorrow." The next day we're likely to be looking at a market price of $44, and we're praying for it to hit $45 again so we can sell it.

Setting a sell stop gets us out of that bind by making the process automatic. If you set the stop at $45, it becomes a market sell order when the stock trades at $45 or lower. Setting a stop at $45 doesn't mean you will get $45 for your shares. It just means you've placed a market sell order. Your order could be filled at a lower price if nobody wants to pay $45.

STOP LIMIT

A stop-limit order is a combination of a stop order and a limit order. The stop order sets the trading price when the limit order becomes active. Say a stock is trading at $50 and you want to put in a sell order if it hits $45 but you don't want to take less than $42. You would place a stop-limit order at $45 with a stop-limit price of $42. That means your order becomes active when the price hits $45, though the sell will not be executed if the price drops below $42 before the trade can be executed. For NASDAQ stocks, not all brokers accept stop limit orders.

Selling Short

Short-sellers sell stocks they don't own. They borrow them from the broker, thinking that the share price will drop and they'll be able to buy the shares and pay the broker back at a lower price later.

Short-selling requires the establishment of a margin account. A margin account is, in effect, a credit account. You can borrow 50 percent of a stock's value on margin on a regular purchase. When selling short, you must have 50 percent of the stock's current value in your account to cover the cost of buying shares. Your broker

---

Avoid Costly Typos: Trade When the Market Is Closed

It's embarrassing, frustrating, and sometimes very expensive to make a keyboard error and buy 1,000 shares of a stock when you only intended to buy 100 shares. Sounds silly, but it could happen if you don't read the order confirmation screen carefully enough before clicking "Confirm." By the time you realize your mistake, it's too late, the order has already been executed. You can, however, change or cancel any order if it hasn't been executed yet. That's why I advise entering trades when the market is closed. That way, you have time to print out a list of pending orders and correct any errors.

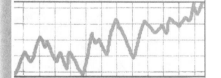

---

may ask you to deposit more funds if the stock goes up instead of down and you don't have enough cash in the account to satisfy the margin requirement.

The mechanics of selling short online are the same as for selling stock you own, except you select a "short sale" instead of "sale" for the transaction type.

Why would you want to sell shares of a stock you don't own? Say XYZ's shares are selling for $50 per share. You've done your homework and are convinced XYZ's earnings will come in below forecast and the share price will tumble on the news, probably down to $30 or so. You could make $20 per share if you could sell XYZ now, and buy the shares back when they hit $30.

Selling short allows you to do just that. Since you don't own the shares, you "borrow" them from your broker, who then sells them to another buyer at $50. Say 100 shares are involved. At this point, you're short 100 shares, because you've sold 100 shares you don't own. The money from the sale—in this case, $5,000—goes into your account.

Let's say XYZ does report lower than expected earnings, and the share price sinks to $30. That was your goal, so you cover your short—that is, buy back the shares you borrowed. You're only paying $3,000 for the 100 shares you've already sold for $5,000, so you've made $2,000, not counting commissions and bid/ask spreads. Your broker has the 100 shares he loaned you back, so the transaction is closed.

There is no time limit on how long you can borrow the shares, as long as the trade is going your way—that is, XYZ's share price is going down, not up.

But what happens if your analysis is wrong, and XYZ reports blockbuster earnings and their share price goes up to $70? You've already sold 100 shares at $50 and the resulting $5,000 is sitting in your account. The problem is, you owe your broker 100 shares, and at the current price, it will cost you $7,000 to buy the shares to redeem your marker. If the shares go to $100, it would cost you $10,000 to get out of the deal!

Meanwhile your broker is doing the same calculations and wondering if you'll be able to come up with the cash to cover if

Short Tips

- It's difficult to make money selling short in a strong market when even stocks with poor fundamentals rise with the tide. Your best bet is to wait for a down market or, at the very least, a market moving sideways, that is, bouncing around without making progress either up or down.
- Always use stops to limit your exposure, just in case you short a stock at $20 that ends up going to $200.
- Mutual funds such as Rydex Ursa or Potomac US/Short short-sell the S&P 500 index. You can buy these funds if you think the entire market is about to tank.

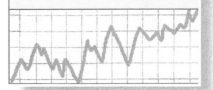

Much of the information in this section is derived from the SEC publication, "Trade Execution: What Every Investor Should Know." It is available online from the SEC at *www.SEC.gov/ consumer/tradexec.htm.*

worst comes to worst. At some point your broker will call you and ask you to either add more cash to your account or cover your short. Therein lies the risk in shorting. You can be right on with your analysis, but it may take six months or a year before the pigeons come home to roost and XYZ shares come tumbling down. By that time, you've probably been forced to cover at a loss. Just as buyers can set limit orders to curb losses if share prices drop, short-sellers can set buy stops to automatically cover them before losses get too high.

The whole premise of short selling is based on borrowing shares from another of your broker's accounts. What happens if the shareholders you borrowed from sell their stock? Whoops! You borrowed their shares, but you can't give them back because you sold them. Normally your broker can simply replace the shares by borrowing from another account. But what if everybody is thinking like you, and shorting XYZ? There could be a shortage of shares available to borrow, and your broker can't come up with any more. Guess what? You'll have to cover your position by buying shares on the open market. You're forced out of your short position whether you're ready or not, whether you're ahead or behind. The term for that is being "called away."

Since you must have a margin account to sell short, your broker may charge you the margin interest rate on your short balance. If a company pays a dividend while you're shorting its stock, your broker deducts the dividend from your account because it has to be paid to the buyer of your shares. Profits made from selling short are taxed as regular income, regardless of how long you had the position. You can't sell a stock short while its share price is dropping, you have to wait for an uptick.

What Happens When You Place a Trade Order?

What happens to your buy or sell order after you give the go-ahead by clicking "Submit" or "Confirm"? You probably think the information goes directly to a securities market. It doesn't. Your order goes to your broker's trading desk.

If it's a New York Stock Exchange stock, your broker can direct the order to the NYSE itself, a regional exchange such as the Pacific Coast Stock Exchange, or a "third market maker." Third market makers trade stocks off the floor of traditional exchanges, but at publicly quoted prices. Why would your broker send trades to a regional exchange, or to a third market maker? Money! Sometimes the regional exchanges, or third market makers, pay your broker for sending them the order. This "payment for order flow" may amount to a penny or so per share, but it adds up.

Orders for NASDAQ-listed stock transactions are always sent to a market marker, unless your broker fills the order from his own inventory. NASDAQ market makers frequently pay your broker for order flow.

"Limit orders" are orders to buy or sell a stock at a specific price. Market makers do not pay for order flow on limit orders. That's why some brokers charge higher commissions for limit orders than for market orders. Your broker sometimes routes limit orders to electronic communication networks (ECNs), such as the Island Network.

In theory, your broker is supposed to route your order where you get the "best execution," meaning the lowest possible price if you're buying, and the highest available price if you're selling. Often the best execution is not the fastest execution. Investors and broker rating services measure and compare broker's trade execution times. Brokers with the fastest execution times are rated higher than slower brokers. Measuring trade execution time is a snap. Gauging which brokers get you the best execution price is much more difficult, if not impossible, so nobody tries to in any meaningful way.

Stockbrokers aren't dummies. They know they're being graded on execution speed, and they know in practice, they can't be compared on execution price. Which factor do you think they give the highest priority to when routing your order, speed or price?

TRADING AT THE NEW YORK STOCK EXCHANGE

If the stock you're buying is listed on the New York Stock Exchange (NYSE), your order is relayed by your Web broker to a

Short vs. Put

An alternative approach to selling short is to buy "put options" instead. Holders of puts make money if the underlying share prices drop, but their losses are limited to the price of the option if the share price goes up instead of down.

Missing Dividends?

Dividends are paid to shareholders on a preannounced date. The day after the dividend payment is called the "ex-dividend date," meaning investors buying shares on that date or later do not receive the dividend. You can see the ex-dividend date by requesting a quote for your stock on Yahoo! (*quote.yahoo.com*).

trader on the floor of the exchange, which is on Wall Street in New York City. Every stock traded on the NYSE has an individual called a "specialist" who is responsible for maintaining an orderly market in the stock. The specialist tries to keep buy and sell orders balanced by adjusting the stock price. For instance, if there are more buy orders than sell orders, the specialist will move the price up until he finds enough sellers. If there's more stock for sale than buyers want to buy, the process is reversed—the specialist will keep moving the stock price down until he attracts enough buyers. The specialist is expected to buy and sell shares for his own account, if need be, to maintain an orderly market.

If you place a limit order, the specialist adds the order to his list, and when he finds someone willing to take the other side of the trade at your price, he executes your order. If the specialist has more than one pending limit order at the same price, he executes them in the order received.

TRADING AT THE NASDAQ

The NASDAQ market has no central trading floor. It's just a network of computer terminals sitting on the desks of traders across the country.

Unlike the NYSE, where you buy from a seller, or sell to a buyer, trading NASDAQ stocks involves a middleman, called a "market maker." When you place a trade, your broker sends your order to a market maker. If you're buying, the market maker sells you the stock out of his inventory. When you sell, you're selling to the market maker.

Each market maker posts a "bid" and "ask" quote. If you're buying, you pay the ask price. If you're selling, you get paid the bid price. The ask is always higher than the bid. The difference between the bid and the ask is the "spread." If the market maker buys a share of stock at the bid price from you, and sells that same share to me at the ask, the spread is his profit. Since the market maker holds stock in inventory to facilitate trading, he makes money if the stocks in his inventory go up in value, and loses if they go down.

ELECTRONIC COMMUNICATION NETWORKS

Individual investors were, until recently, limited to trading stocks during standard market hours, from 9:30 A.M. until 4:00 P.M. Eastern Standard Time. Institutional investors could, however, trade around the clock using Reuters' Instinet, an electronic communication network, or ECN. In this system, there is no specialist or market maker involved. The ECN matches buyers' and sellers' orders directly.

Now, new ECNs catering to individual investors are popping up, and extended hours trading is quickly becoming available through a variety of Web brokers. Reuters Instinet is developing their own brokerage service catering to individual investors, which should be available by the time you read this.

Currently, several ECNs are competing for Web brokers' business. The front-runners are Instinet, Island ECN and MarketXT, but there are many more out there. Each ECN handles trades from affiliated brokers, and none of the ECNs talk to each other. When you place an order, it's only displayed on the ECN it came in on. If your order is matched and executed, the trade is only reported on that ECN.

Electronic communication networks operate by matching customer orders, there is no market maker involved. For that reason, you cannot place market orders on an ECN. All orders are limit orders. For instance, if you enter an order to buy XYZ at $50.50, your order will only be executed if someone has entered an order to sell at the same, or lower price, and on the same electronic network. Also, you can't specify "all or none," you have to accept partial fulfillment of orders, known as partial fills.

Let's look at an example. Say you place a buy order for 300 shares of XYZ at $50, meaning you're offering to buy as many as 300 shares at a maximum price of $50 per share. Seconds later, a sell order for 100 shares at $49 hits the network. So the ECN has your order saying you'll pay $50 or less, and a sell order for $49. Assuming these are the only orders on the network for XYZ, the trade executes at $50 because the first order received is executed at its limit price. So far, you've only bought 100 shares. Your order for the remaining 200 shares will be displayed until executed or canceled.

The Trading Clock

Not long ago, stock trading started at 9:00 A.M. and ending promptly at 4:00 P.M.

Here's the current schedule; all times are Eastern.

8:00 A.M. Trading opens on electronic communication networks (ECNs)

9:30 A.M. Regular trading starts on NYSE, NASDAQ, and other markets

4:00 P.M. Regular trading closes on NYSE, NASDAQ, and most other markets

4:30 P.M. Late-trading session opens on Chicago Stock Exchange

5:00–5:15 P.M. Trading closes on some ECNs

6:30 P.M. Closing time of trade reporting and price quotation systems for NASDAQ, Chicago Stock Exchange late session, and another group of ECNs

6:35 P.M. Closing of pricing data systems for NYSE stocks

8:00 P.M. Trading closes on third group of ECNs, but two systems remain open overnight

For an up-to-date list of after-hours brokers, go to Internet Investing (www.internetinvesting.com).

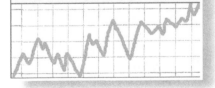

NASDAQ Ticker Symbols

NASDAQ-listed stocks generally have four-letter ticker symbols. NASDAQ adds a fifth letter to indicate special conditions. Be especially wary of C, E, and Q suffixes.

A or B Class A or B shares

C Exempt from NASDAQ listing requirements for a limited time

D A new issue of an existing stock, often the result of a reverse split

E Company is delinquent in filing SEC required reports

F Foreign-based company

G, H, I Convertible bond

J Voting shares

K Nonvoting shares

L, Z Miscellaneous special situations

M, N, O, P Preferred stock

Q In bankruptcy proceedings

R Rights

S Shares of beneficial interest

T With warrants or rights

U Units

V When-issued and when-distributed

W Warrants

X Mutual fund

Y ADR (American Depository Receipts representing shares of foreign-based companies)

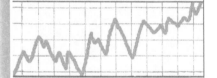

All open orders are canceled when trading closes for the session; "good-until-canceled" and stop orders are not accepted. Trades executed during extended hours are considered traded during regular hours on the same day for settlement purposes.

Market makers maintain an order book listing all open buy and sell orders, usually listing the buys with the highest bids, and sells with the lowest asks at the top. Many ECNs display their order book on their Web site. Viewing their order book helps you assess the balance of buying and selling interest in a stock.

Trading rules vary among ECNs. MarketXT limits stocks traded to members of the S&P 100, or NASDAQ 100 indexes. Island trades only NASDAQ-listed stocks, while Instinet and MarketXT trade NASDAQ and NYSE listings. MarketXT accepts short sellers, while Island and Instinet do not.

Trading, whether during extended hours or regular market hours, works best when there is plenty of liquidity, that is, an abundance of buyers and sellers bidding against one another. Without sufficient liquidity, sellers may not find enough buyers when a company announces bad news after the close of regular trading, and the stock price will drop farther than if the trading were conducted on the traditional exchanges. Conversely, a scarcity of sellers could result in ECN buyers paying too much when good news, such as greater than expected earnings, is announced.

Sufficient liquidity will be difficult to achieve with the ECN trading market so fragmented. Either the individual ECNs will have to start talking to each other—meaning that offers to buy and sell from all networks will be displayed universally—or ECNs representing a major percentage of total trading will have to merge. It's not certain at this time whether ECNs will be able to complete a satisfactory percentage of orders on their own without the aid of market makers.

Trading Mutual Funds

Mutual fund trading is somewhat different from stock trading. You can trade all the stocks listed on major exchanges through any broker. Not so with mutual funds. No broker makes all existing mutual funds available to its customers.

Most Web brokers provide a means on their site for determining available mutual funds. It may take the form of a list, or you may search for a fund on their "fund finder" and see a "not found" response. Sometimes you have to call the broker to find out if they offer a particular fund.

Brokers offer both *load* and *no-load* funds. Loads are fees, similar to sales commissions. Most loads are front-loads, meaning the fees are collected when you buy the fund, although some are deferred, meaning they're paid when you sell your shares. Often, the amount of deferred fee declines the longer you hold the shares. A no-load fund has no fees or commissions but your broker may charge a commission called a transaction fee on the purchase or sale of a no-load fund. It depends on the deal your broker has with the fund.

There is no rule of thumb to determine which funds incur transaction fees, but the amount of a specific broker's transaction fee typically will not vary from fund to fund. A fund either has a fee or it doesn't. Transaction fees apply equally to purchases and sales and range from $9.95 to more than $100.

Mutual funds all establish minimum purchase requirements, but brokers sometimes establish their own minimums. For instance, the Rydex OTC fund requires a $25,000 minimum investment if you purchase shares directly from the fund. TD Waterhouse requires only a $5,000 minimum, but Charles Schwab will let you buy the fund with only $2,500. On the other hand, the Gabelli Growth fund only requires a $1,000 opening balance if you buy direct, but Charles Schwab requires $2,500.

Redemption Fees

Some funds charge redemption fees if you sell before a predetermined holding minimum. Brokers assess their own redemption fees. For instance, Charles Schwab charges a redemption fee on all funds held less than 180 days.

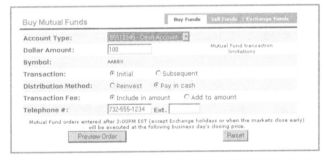

Sample Buy and Sell Screens for mutual funds.

Settlement

Settlement is the process of paying for stocks you purchased, or receiving credit for stock you sell. U.S. government regulations require stock transactions to be settled with three business days. Brokers send a confirmation of your trade including the total dollar amount by U.S. mail on the day of the transaction. Some online brokers also send an e-mail confirmation.

ENTERING A MUTUAL FUND PURCHASE

Mutual fund orders differ from stock trades because you typically enter the dollar amount of your purchase, rather than the number of shares, as you do for stocks.

You first must identify the fund by its ticker symbol. Looking up a mutual fund's ticker symbol can be tricky. Different funds in the same family often have similar names. For instance, Weitz funds include the Weitz Value and the Weitz Partners Value, Vanguard has the Vanguard Growth & Income, Vanguard Growth Index, and Vanguard Growth Index Institutional funds, etc. So be sure you know the exact title of the fund when you look up the ticker symbol and enter it on your order.

The second step is specifying if you want the dividend and capital gains distributions credited to your account in cash, or reinvested in additional fund shares. Most investors choose to reinvest distributions for stock funds. Investors often select cash payments if the funds are purchased for income, such as bond funds or real estate investment trusts (REITs).

The next step is to enter your dollar purchase amount. You'll also need to indicate if you want the broker's transaction fees, if any, included in, or added to your specified purchase amount.

Let's take an example. Say you invested $5,000 in a mutual fund with a $14.00 share price (NAV). You would receive 357.14 shares (mutual fund shares don't have to be purchased in even share amounts) if your broker does not charge a transaction fee on that account.

Now assume the broker does charge a $25 transaction fee. Your account would be debited $5,025 if you elected not to include the fees in your $5,000 specified purchase amount. Your account would only be debited $5,000, but you would receive fewer shares (355.36) if you elected to have the fee included in the purchase amount.

As with stock purchases, you're given a chance to review your transaction before confirming, but you needn't be concerned about the transaction being executed before you have a chance to correct errors. Mutual fund buy and sell orders are not executed during the trading day. They're executed after the close of trading based on the fund's "net asset value" as of that day's close. Orders entered after a predetermined cut-off time will not be executed until after the close of trading on the following day. The cut-off time varies; for instance, it's 2:00 P.M. Eastern Standard Time for TD Waterhouse, and 4:00 P.M. Eastern for Charles Schwab.

SELLING AND EXCHANGING FUNDS

When selling mutual funds, you can usually enter the number of mutual fund shares you want to sell on the Web site, or you can instruct your broker to sell your entire holdings in the fund. You can determine the number of shares you own by looking at your account holdings list, typically available from the fund's trading screen on the Web site.

Some brokers make it easy for you to sell one fund and put the entire proceeds into a new fund by providing a trading screen specifically for that purpose.

As with purchases, fund sales and exchange transactions are executed after the close of trading on the same day, or the following day, depending on the time you entered the transaction.

Short Squeeze

Short sellers eventually have to "cover" their positions by buying the stock they've borrowed, preferably at far lower share prices. Unexpected good news, a short seller's worst nightmare, can abruptly drive share prices higher and force short sellers to cover their positions early to avoid major losses. Short sellers cover by buying back the stock they originally borrowed. Their buying forces the share prices higher, inducing additional short sellers to cover, driving prices even higher, etc. Rapid upward movements in share prices caused by short sellers covering their positions is termed a "short squeeze."

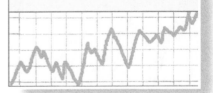

CHAPTER THREE

Managing Your Portfolio Online

The collection of stocks and bonds you own is called a portfolio. Web portfolio trackers are handy devices. You can use them to see how your investments are doing, keep up with the news, insider trading, and a host of other factors affecting your stocks.

One thing Web portfolio trackers don't do very well is taxes. Some try, but their reports are primitive compared to those created by computer programs such as Quicken or Microsoft Money.

Just about every major financial Web site offers a portfolio tracker. Most work in more or less the same way. You have to register so the tracker knows which portfolio belongs to you. Then you enter the pertinent data for each of your investments. Most sites let you maintain several portfolios. They may set a limit on the number of stocks allowed in a single portfolio and on the total number of portfolios, but the limits are so high, you'll probably never run up against them.

A limitation of most portfolio trackers involves their ability to handle stock splits. Most don't even try. When one of your stocks splits, you're supposed to edit the portfolio manually. Say your stock splits 3 for 2. You then have to adjust the number of shares in your portfolio by 1.5. For instance, if you started with 30 shares, you now have 45. Then you'll have to change your share cost by dividing the original cost by 1.5. Got it?

You'd be amazed how often stocks split. If you're following a lot of stocks, it seems like one is always splitting. It's easy to forget about the split until you glance at your portfolio one day and go into shock when it looks as if you lost half of your investment in that stock. That's why automatic handling of stock splits can be a big issue if you're using the tracker to monitor gains and losses.

CNET Investor has an easy-to-use portfolio manager that automatically adjusts for splits.

Web Portfolio Trackers

CNET INVESTOR (*investor.cnet.com* > My Portfolio)

CNET's portfolio manager doesn't present you with an overwhelming number of choices. You don't have to decide what it's going to display or where it's going to display. In fact, CNET doesn't display, or even know, your date of purchase. CNET does, however, display other details on your original purchase, including the number of shares, purchase price, and the total purchase amount. The purchase price is automatically adjusted for stock splits that occur after the date you entered the stock in your portfolio.

CNET shows you today's close and price change, the current value of your holdings, and how you're doing in terms of percent and actual dollar change since purchase. CNET also displays recent news headlines on the same page, below your portfolio.

When you select "Portfolio" from CNET's homepage, you'll be asked to register. After registering, click on "Create New Portfolio," give your portfolio a name, click "Submit," then click "Add stocks to your new portfolio," enter the ticker symbols, and you're on your way.

Click "Edit Portfolio" from the portfolio display to enter the purchase information. However, if you don't want to enter the purchase information, you don't have to.

That's all you have to do. CNET is fast, it's simple, and automatically adjusts for splits. It's a good place to start and if you decide you need more features later, you won't have wasted much time.

If you conclude you do need more features, you might as well go for the best, Microsoft's MSN MoneyCentral.

MSN MoneyCentral

(*moneycentral.msn.com* > Investor > Portfolio)

MoneyCentral's portfolio tracker is considerably more sophisticated and powerful than other Web portfolio trackers I've experienced. It reminds me a lot of using a regular computer program such as Quicken. In fact, I prefer it to Quicken for keeping track of stock performance because of its flexibility and ease of use. It's worlds more accommodating when it comes to customizing displays and printouts. It tells me what I want to know, not what it *thinks* I should know. It quietly updates prices when I'm online on a schedule I've chosen.

The only downside is getting started. The registration process is confusing and Microsoft wants to know more than they need to know about your life. After you've registered, the program is supposed to remember your login name and password, but every so often, it will make you log in again.

Best Investment Sites for Charts

Big Charts (*www.bigcharts.com*): A good site for technical analysis charts.

ClearStation (*www.clearstation.com*): Simplified technical analysis charts, with associated message boards. Caters to short-term investors. The message boards make it a hangout for chartists.

Live Charts (*www.quote.com*): Quote.com's live charts are mesmerizing. Check it out, even if you don't use charts.

Metastock Online (*www.equis.com*): The only place on the Net I know of that charts relative strength of a stock compared to a user-selected index. You can also draw trendlines on the charts. Find it under Free Stuff.

MSN MoneyCentral (*moneycentral.msn.com*): Easy-to-use charts with the most popular technical indicators.

Quicken (*www.quicken.com*) and **Yahoo!** (*quote.yahoo.com*): Best sites for easy to use, and quickly accessible charts.

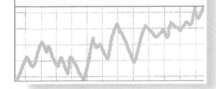

Before you use the MSN tracker you have to download software into your computer. Since it only takes 5 or 10 minutes, it's not a big deal, but for reasons known only to Microsoft, once in a while you're told you have to download the software again to open your portfolio. This can be annoying, especially if you're in a hurry, but don't be dissuaded—just say yes. The program soon realizes its mistake, and the delay is minimal.

▼File	▼Edit	▼Analysis	▼Accounts	▼Columns	▼Help					Last Updated 11:20 AM	
Symbol	Name		Last Tran.	Avg. Cost	Last	Change	ROI All Dates	ROI YTD	%Gain	Qu..
☐ Science & Technology											
LXK	Lexmark International Group, Inc.	2/16/1999	51.09	106⅛	¹⁵/₁₆ ↑	107.7%	17.3%	107.7%	
NT	Nortel Networks Corporation	3/16/1999	30.94	104¾	⁷/₁₆ ↑	239.0%	3.7%	239.0%	
SLR	Solectron Corporation	10/18/1999	35.38	42	1⅜ ↑	18.7%	-11.7%	18.7%	
	Total Account Value						121.8%	4.2%	121.8%	

MSN MoneyCentral has the Web's best portfolio tracker.

Sometimes the portfolio tracker doesn't work with my Netscape browser, although, coincidentally, I suppose, there's never any problem when I'm using Microsoft's Internet Explorer!

Using the MSN portfolio manager is a snap. The program is operated by controls within the portfolio tracker window, not your browser controls. For instance, if you want to print your portfolio, use the File dropdown menu just above your portfolio display to select "Print." Don't use the file dropdown menu at the very top of your browser.

Before you enter stocks or mutual funds, you have to set up at least one account. MoneyCentral supports three different types of account:

1. **Regular accounts** are intended to track actual accounts with a cash balance.
2. **Watch accounts** are designed to track stocks you are following (watching) but don't own in an actual account. A watch account doesn't handle cash balances. Otherwise, you can add stocks and funds the same way you do in a regular account.

   Or you can use the model portfolio feature, which lets you set up an entire portfolio without entering the individual details for each stock. All you do is enter the ticker symbols and the starting date for the portfolio. The starting date can be today, or any date in the past. Then you choose how you want to set up your starting holdings: with 100 shares of each stock; with $10,000 in each stock; or with a starting dollar amount for the entire portfolio with the money equally divided among the stocks. MoneyCentral sets up the portfolio. You can enter new purchases or sales individually after the initial setup.

3. **Import accounts** are designed to import portfolio data directly from your existing accounts at Charles Schwab, E*Trade, DLJ Direct, TD Waterhouse, Fidelity, and other Web brokers. Once set up, you can instruct it to retrieve updates from your broker's account at any time.

Create a new account: Select New from the portfolio manager File dropdown menu (not from your browser's File dropdown menu). Select the account type and name, and you're done. You can enter stocks then, or at any time.

Enter new stock transactions: Highlight the account name and then select "Record a Buy" or "Record a Sell" from the Edit dropdown menu. Enter the ticker symbol and security type (usually stock or mutual fund). The "Find Symbol" function works amazingly fast if you need to look up the ticker symbol.

Next enter the date of purchase and number of shares purchased. The current date is the default, but you can either type in another date or click on the calendar icon to enter a different trade date. Type in the share price if you're entering actual transactions. If you're not entering real transactions, you can let the program look up the closing price for the date you entered. Type in the commission and you're done. Don't select "reinvest income" for stocks unless you have a dividend reinvestment plan.

You can change anything you've entered at any time by double clicking on the security or account name you want to modify. Like CNET, the program automatically adjusts your holdings for stock splits.

Display: The Columns dropdown menu gives you a choice of several display options. Try selecting different column formats to see the possibilities.

It's easy to create your own display format by selecting Customize Column Set from the Columns dropdown menu. Use the pop-up panel to pick items you want to display using the Add and Remove buttons. If you're not sure of an item definition, highlight it, and the program will display a description in the Column

Other Features

To see an interesting analysis of your portfolio select Portfolio Review from the Analysis dropdown window. The program opens a separate window showing, among other things, your allocation among small, medium, and large-cap companies, your best and worst investments (who needs to be reminded about the worst?), your largest holdings, and recent transactions.

MSN MoneyCentral can be used for mutual funds, but I prefer Morningstar's portfolio for that purpose.

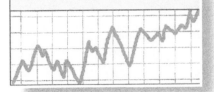

Definitions window on the lower left. Once you're satisfied with your selections, highlight a displayed item and use the Move Up and Move Down buttons to control the column display order.

When you're done select OK to go back to the portfolio display. When you do, don't be surprised when you don't see the column format you so painstakingly designed. Use the Columns dropdown menu to select "Your Customized Column Set." Now, every time you access the portfolio manager, your custom column format will be used.

MORNINGSTAR *(www.morningstar.com* > Portfolio)

Morningstar's portfolios can be used for mutual funds or for stocks. It's nothing special for stocks, but I use it for mutual funds because it shows the fund's year-to-date fund returns.

Getting accurate year-to-date returns on mutual funds in a portfolio tracker is tricky because of distributions. Most funds make dividend and capital gains distributions at least once each year, sometimes more often.

If a fund pays you $1.00 in capital gains, they turn right around and reduce the share price of the fund (the Net Asset Value, or NAV) by the same amount. If you've told them to reinvest distributions, they give you additional shares to make up for the price decline and you end up even.

That process creates a problem. You can't simply look at your fund's share price to see how much money you're making because the share price drops when a fund makes a distribution. And you usually don't know about a fund's distribution until you receive your statement. Interpreting distribution information on many statements is a daunting task. In the meantime, the fund returns displayed by conventional portfolio trackers are wrong.

Morningstar's display of year-to-date returns is not a total solution, especially if you're interested in the return since you purchased the shares. Yet it gives you a feel for how the fund's doing without having to worry about distributions.

As with most portfolio trackers, you have to register before you set up your portfolios. After you register, click on Portfolio and then select Create New Portfolio. You can choose between Quick Portfolio and Transaction Portfolio. Choose Quick Portfolio if you just want to track how the funds are performing, and Transaction Portfolio if you want to enter buy and sell transactions. If you do that, though, you'll have to manually enter all the distributions.

Type in a portfolio name and click Continue to display the Edit screen. Type in the fund's ticker symbols, one per line, and click Save Portfolio when you're finished. You don't have to enter a number of shares or purchase price unless you want to.

Your Morningstar portfolio can be displayed in five different formats, called views.

1. **Snapshot View** shows today's price change for each fund.
2. **Performance View** shows the year-to-date returns and data pertaining to the original cost and gain or loss since purchase. These columns aren't used if you selected the Quick Portfolio.
3. **Intraday View** displays today's dollar value and price change, as well as the 52-week high and low. The 52-week data is (is not) corrected for distributions.
4. **Fundamental View** shows the fund style, price/earnings and price/book valuation ratios, and dividend yield for each fund. The style indicates whether the fund holdings are large-, medium-, or small-cap companies, and whether the fund is characterized as a value, blend, or growth fund. The price/earnings ratio is an important indicator of future risk. (See Chapter 8 for instructions on interpreting price/earnings ratio.)
5. **Custom View** allows you to create your own display by selecting Custom View and then clicking Edit Custom. You can pick what you want to display from a menu of 28 data items. For instance, I've combined day change, price/earnings ratio, year-to-date return, and fund category into a single view. You can also choose whether you want the display to show the ticker symbol or the fund name.

Click "Save Changes" when you're done. Click "Set Default View" if you want to see this view when you first access the portfolio tracker.

Up to now, we've talked mainly about using portfolio trackers to keep up with your stock and mutual fund performance. Portfolio

Yahoo!
(finance.yahoo.com)

You can use Yahoo!'s tracker to program your personal finance page so you can see at a glance how your stocks are performing, and to keep up with the news on your portfolio. Yahoo's tracker is explained in Chapter 20.

trackers are also useful for keeping up with the news, and other factors affecting stocks of interest. Yahoo!'s portfolio tracker is a good example. See Chapter 20 for more information.

CNBC (*www.cnbc.com* > Portfolio)

CNBC's portfolio tracker is an exceptional tool for quickly evaluating important fundamental factors affecting your stocks. It's also designed to track financial performance, but it doesn't automatically update for splits.

You can select from seven different portfolio views:

1. **Current Quotes** displays the day's open, high, low, close, change, and volume. The view displays a news icon if there is recent news on the stock. Click on the icon to display the headlines; read the complete story by clicking on the headline. You can program this tracker to display an "alert" icon when the stock price goes above or below the breakout limits you've set. You can also choose to be alerted when a company executive makes an on-air appearance on CNBC.

2. **Insider Trading** shows you a graphic display of each company's "Insider Rank," a measure of insider buying and selling activity. The screen also displays the details: number of buys, sells, option exercises, and the 3-month, 6-month, and 12-month changes in those numbers. The insider rank is important, because it alerts you to trading activity, even though it doesn't show you important details such as who's buying or selling, number of shares traded, and so forth. It's up to you to investigate further. (See Chapter 11 for information on how to interpret insider trading.)

3. **Current Valuation** shows you how you're doing by comparing current values to what you paid.

4. **Today's Events** lists the current and previous day's news headlines for each stock in your portfolio. You can click on the headlines to read the full story.

5. **+/- Valuation Ratio** displays CNBC's assessment of each of your stock's valuation based on price/sales rank. It's an effective graphic display that clearly shows how each stock ranks. The screen also displays ratios for P/E (price/

earnings), relative P/E, projected P/E (P/E based on this year's forecast earnings), price to book, price to cash flow, debt to equity, and current ratios. Price/sales rank doesn't mean much by itself, but this screen gives you a good picture of your portfolio's valuation using a variety of measures.

Symbol	Insider Rank		Net Insdr	No. Buys	No. Sells	Exer. Options	3Mo. Chg	6Mo. Chg	12Mo. Chg
PORTFOLIO	STRONG SELL	STRONG BUY	-15.0	1	16	12	-2.0%	-0.3%	1.2%
CPQ	STRONG SELL	STRONG BUY	0	0	0	1	-1%	-2%	11%
C	STRONG SELL	STRONG BUY	-4	1	5	4	1%	-1%	3%
AES	STRONG SELL	STRONG BUY	-8	0	8	5	-5%	3%	-7%
BA	STRONG SELL	STRONG BUY	-3	0	3	2	-3%	-1%	-2%

CNBC Portfolio Tracker Insider Trading Rank shows you insider trading activity at a glance.

6. **Analyst Ratings** display the average analysts' buy/hold/sell ratings on each stock along with details such as a breakdown of the buy/hold/sell ratings, and recent positive or negative surprises. (See Chapter 10 to learn how to evaluate analysts' ratings and forecast information.)

7. **Technical Rankings** displays composite values for a variety of fundamental and technical ranking factors for your combined portfolio. More valuable in my view are the individual rankings for each stock. All ranking values range between 1 and 99, and higher is better. Some ranking indicators are powerful and quite useful.

Ranking indicators are described in detail in Chapter 16.

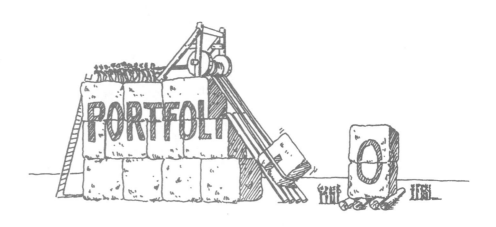

CHAPTER FOUR

The Financial Gurus

Wouldn't it be great if you could snap your fingers and financial geniuses like Peter Lynch or Warren Buffett would sit down next to you and help you pick stocks? You can. All you have to do is "click" instead of "snap."

There's no point in going it alone, when the world's best stock pickers are standing by, ready, willing, and eager to help.

Tapping into Genius

VALIDEA (*www.validea.com*)

I've read many excellent books by market gurus describing their favorite stock selection methods. Usually I was excited about trying their ideas when I finished the book. But as with a lot of things, I rarely got around to it, or by the time I did, I'd forgotten the details. Someday, I told myself, I plan to go through those books again and take better notes this time.

Fortunately, thanks to Validea, I don't have to. It seems that John Reese and his crew read the same books I did, and they took better notes for me and came up with Guru Analysis.

The Validea program emulates the stock-picking strategies of many of the best gurus you could ask for. They're grouped here by their investment styles.

Value

- Benjamin Graham—Along with David Dodd, wrote *Security Analysis,* the first book ever published on fundamental analysis. Graham is considered the founder of value investing and is said to be a mentor of Warren Buffett.
- Kenneth Fisher—The first to suggest using price/sales ratio instead of P/E to evaluate stocks. He authored the best selling *Super Stocks*, and his columns appear regularly in *Forbes* magazine.
- David Dreman—Mutual fund manager and author of several books on value investment strategies.
- James P. O'Shaughnessy—Fund manager and author of several books, including one of my favorites, *What Works on Wall Street.* The book reported the results of O'Shaughnessy's

groundbreaking research comparing stock selection strategies.

Growth

- Peter Lynch—Former manager of top-ranked Magellan fund, best-selling author, and columnist for *Worth* magazine.
- Martin Zweig—Highly respected analyst, fund manager, and author of another of my favorites: *Winning on Wall Street*.

Momentum

- William J. O'Neil—Publisher of *Investor's Business Daily* and author of *How to Make Money in Stocks*. O'Neil is probably the inventor of momentum investing.

Validea also emulates two newer selection strategies, one based on strategies published by the Motley Fool (*www.fool.com*), the other Olympic Internet, a Validea proprietary method applicable only to Internet stocks.

Validea's analyses are based on their interpretation of each guru's stock-picking style. The real gurus aren't making these picks and may not agree with Validea's conclusions.

You can use Guru Analysis two ways: 1) pick a guru, and see a list of stocks meeting their criteria, or 2) enter a stock's ticker symbol, and see how each guru would rate the investment. We'll show you how to have the gurus rate your stocks in Chapter 14. Right now we're looking for tips, so let's see what stocks they're suggesting.

GURU LISTS

Start by clicking on "Guru Stock Screener" in the New Investment Ideas section of Validea's main page. You will see a list of stocks meeting each guru's requirements by selecting "Strong Interest" or "Some Interest." on the dropdown menus on the right. Strong Interest means the stock meets all of the guru's requirements, while Some Interest means the investment meets most but not all requirements. "None Selected," the default, means you don't want to use that guru's strategy.

You usually end up with too many stocks on the list by picking Some Interest, so stick with Strong Interest unless you don't get enough potential candidates.

Styles of Investing

Value Value investors, a.k.a. contrarians, take advantage of the stock market's tendency to overreact to bad news which usually drives a stock price lower than justified by the events. Good news often impels a stock's price much higher than the news warranted, and conversely, bad news drives a stock price lower than justified by the events.

Growth Growth investors seek out companies with substantial future sales and earnings growth prospects. They prefer fundamentally solid companies with competitive advantages in growing industry sectors.

Momentum Momentum investors look for companies with two major characteristics: high relative strength and strong earnings growth.

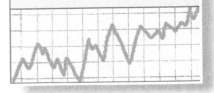

When I selected Strong Interest from Peter Lynch, Validea listed more than 600 stocks. That's too many. Here's a strategy I used to narrow the list:

Sort the list of stocks meeting the guru's requirements by clicking on any one of the column headings: ticker, company name, price, market capitalization, sales, relative strength, EPS growth, PEG, P/E, or projected P/E.

If you know which variables are most important to a guru's selection strategy, you could sort the list on that variable. Here's how you can find out what the variables are: Click on the company name (not the ticker symbol) for any stock on the list. It doesn't matter which company you pick. The program will then display the guru's—in this case, Peter Lynch's—analysis of the company.

Validea describes the variables employed in the analysis and how each is applied to the selected company. By reading the analysis, you'll learn about the guru's selection strategy. Sometimes the criterion for acceptance of the same variable is explained differently in the analysis of different companies, so read over the guru's analysis for at least two or three companies.

Once you understand the guru's selection process you'll be able to decide how to sort the list of strong interest stocks so the best prospects come out on top. For instance, when I went through this short process for Peter Lynch, I concluded that earnings growth is an important factor in his strategy. He favors companies with several years of fast, but not too fast (50 percent maximum), earnings growth.

Armed with that information, I used my browser's Back button to return to Lynch's Strong Interest stocks. I clicked on the EPS Growth (three-year) column heading to sort the list. Now I had Peter Lynch's Strong Interest stocks arranged with the fastest earnings growers at the top.

I find it compelling to find stocks favored by more than one guru in a category. For instance, if you're a growth investor, it would be an advantage to know which stocks are favored by both Peter Lynch and Martin Zweig. Same thing with value stocks. I'll pay more attention to stocks with interest from both Kenneth Fisher and James P. O'Shaughnessy than I will to stocks favored by only one value investor.

How about this idea? See if you can find stocks favored both by value guru Benjamin Graham and momentum guru William J. O'Neil!

Invest Like Warren Buffett

A lot of us wish we could invest like Warren Buffett—and for good reason. Buffett and his partners acquired control of Berkshire Hathaway, then a textile company, in 1965. Since then, Buffett has transformed Berkshire into a conglomerate, and in effect, a closed-end mutual fund, by outright acquisition of a variety of businesses, and purchases of stock in other publicly traded companies. If you had invested $10,000 in Berkshire in 1965, it would be worth about $49 million today.

Naturally, anyone who hears about Buffett's investment success wants to get in on the action. You can buy Berkshire stock—Class A shares are going for about $63,000, and the newer Class B stock is around $2,000. What's the difference? Besides representing less ownership, the Class B shares have limited voting rights.

Despite the fantastic track record, some investors don't see Berkshire shares as a good deal today. They worry that Buffett's fabulous reputation has created enormous demand for Berkshire stock, driving the share price to a hefty premium compared to the value of the holdings. Others say Berkshire Hathaway itself has become heavily dependent on the insurance business (about 70 percent of revenues), and the outlook for that industry is clouded.

For these investors, it makes more sense just to buy the same publicly traded stocks Berkshire owns, thereby avoiding the questions surrounding Berkshire itself.

BERKSHIRE HATHAWAY (*www.berkshirehathaway.com*)

Berkshire's holdings are listed in the quarterly and annual reports posted on their site, going back to 1995. Between quarterly reports you can keep up to date on Berkshire Hathaway's transactions by reviewing news releases, also posted on their site.

Buffett makes no secret of his stock selection approach. His "Chairman's Letter" accompanies each Berkshire annual report. Taken together, these letters describe his stock-picking philosophy.

It's possible to download the letters going back to 1977 from the site. Don't miss Buffett's Berkshire Hathaway "Owner's Manual" posted in place of the 1999 chairman's letter.

Buffett's stock-picking style combines elements of both value and growth investing. Berkshire's largest holdings include Coca-Cola, Gillette, Wells Fargo Bank, and Walt Disney. Some critics say these stocks have had their day and will likely underperform the market in the future, and because Buffett rarely sells, he'll be stuck with these companies. Others fret that since Buffett avoids medical and technology companies, he is missing the best future investment opportunities.

These skeptical investors figure it's better to do what Buffett would do if he were just starting out today, rather than copy his existing portfolio, and there are Web sites to do it for them.

GREEN ASSET MANAGEMENT
(*www.stockresearch.com* > Click Here to Explore)

Green Mountain Asset Management Corporation's Web site uses an investment philosophy "quite similar to that of Warren Buffett," according to information on the site. Robert A. Bose, a registered investment advisor with more than 20 years of experience does the analysis and recommendations.

Bose maintains a portfolio of current buy recommendations containing around 15 stocks. Like Buffett, Bose doesn't do much trading. He added only four stocks to his portfolio in 1999. A list of the stocks with their original recommendation date and price, and current price and percentage gain or loss, can be seen by selecting Historical Results from the menu on the left side of the main page. The portfolio contains an eclectic mix of stocks that Bose considers undervalued—everything from Campbell Soup to Hewlett-Packard and Pfizer.

Bose doesn't recommend buying all of the stocks on the list at current prices. He has a list he calls "Fresh Money Buys," which are the three stocks he thinks are currently the most attractively priced. View this list by selecting Weekly Economic Update, a review and analysis of current economic news. You can even sign up for a free subscription and Bose will e-mail the report to you once a week.

Select "Buy Recommendations" to see Bose's "Executive Summary" for each stock on his buy list. The summaries assume you're already familiar with the company and provide Bose's analysis of recent events related to the stock. You can get a full report on each stock by clicking on the company name. The reports include Bose's analysis and a description of the company's operations.

A summary of fundamental data on all of Bose's recommendations can be accessed by clicking on Data, then Quotes and Graphs.

Bose follows Warren Buffett's "Look Through Earnings" approach to analyze the value of a stock. He provides a good explanation of the strategy in the Archives section of the site. The Archives also contain all of his previous postings on companies on his buy list.

Quicken's Intrinsic Value Calculator

(*www.quicken.com* > Investing > Quote > Evaluator > Intrinsic Value)

A key aspect of Buffett's analysis is calculating a company's *intrinsic value,* which is the current value of expected future earnings. Quicken has an easy to use intrinsic value calculator. From their Investing page, get a quote, then select Evaluator from the menu on the left, and finally, click Intrinsic Value. Quicken shows you the calculated intrinsic value, compares the calculated value to the current stock price, and gives you an opinion as to whether the stock is overvalued or undervalued. Even more valuable than the calculated intrinsic value are the accompanying comments, especially the "Insights" paragraph describing the future earnings growth required to justify the current stock price. The "Walk Through" section explains the intrinsic calculation in detail for your selected stock.

Value Stock's Buffettology Stock Evaluator

(*www.valuestock.net* > Stock Valuation Tools)

The silly name doesn't really do it justice, because this site provides an excellent way to learn about how Warren Buffett evaluates stocks. The Buffettology Stock Evaluator is based on information in Mary Buffett and David Clark's book *Buffettology.* The evaluator looks like a spreadsheet, but it enables you to use Buffett's methodology to estimate the future rate of return on a stock investment. When you place your cursor over an entry box, an explanation of how Buffett views each factor pops up. This feature is extremely helpful in understanding Buffett's analysis. The Buffettology Evaluator uses the program Microsoft Excel. It won't work if it isn't installed on your computer.

Find Buffett Stocks Yourself

(*www.marketplayer.com* > Sample Screens)

You can search out your own Warren Buffett stocks using Market Player's "Warren Buffett Stable Growth Screen" Sample Report. (See Chapter 6 for more information on Market Player.)

AIC Funds Business Principles

(*www.aicfunds.com* > Who We Are > Our Business Principles)

AIC Funds, a Canadian mutual fund family, has a concise but thorough summary of Buffett's selection strategies posted on its site. It's not clear from the site which, if any, of their own funds follows his strategy.

S&P's Stock Screens

(*www.personalwealth.com* > Stocks > S&P's Stock Screens)

S&P uses their stock-screening program (see Chapter 6 on stock screening) to run a search twice-yearly based on Robert Hagstrom's book, *The Warren Buffett Way*. They run the program the first week of February and the first week of August. The February 2000 screen came up with 26 stocks. The Buffett screen is featured on the S&P Stock Screens page the week of release. At other times, click on Archive near the top of the S&P Stock Screens page and then scroll to the most recent date (early February or early August).

Buffett Mutual Funds (*www.morningstar.com*)

Two mutual funds follow Buffett's selection strategy. The Sequoia Fund (SEQUX) follows it religiously. The Legg Mason Focus Fund takes some liberties with it; for instance, in early 2000 they held tech stocks America Online and Gateway computer. (Who knows, if Warren Buffett were starting out today, he might own them too.) You can get Buffett stock ideas from looking at the top holdings of these funds. On Morningstar you do that by entering the fund ticker symbol, then clicking on "Top Holdings" from the menu on the left when you get to the Snapshot page.

Warren Buffett Links (*www.townserver.com/buffett/*)

This site's only purpose—and it's a good one—is providing links to other sites with information about Warren Buffett.

Mining the Fund Managers

Let's face it—the managers of mutual funds have a big advantage over investors like us. Although we get plenty of information on the Internet, they get more. They're trading hundreds of thousands of shares each month, and generating big commissions, so naturally if analysts have new information, the analysts will tell the fund manager before they tell us.

Wouldn't it be great if you could find out which stocks top fund managers are buying or selling? It turns out you can. There are fund managers on the Web who are willing to let you look over their shoulders—in one case literally—while they trade. Here's where you'll find them:

IPS MILLENNIUM FUND

(*www.ipsfunds.com* > IPS Millennium Fund >Portfolio Manager Diary)

The Millennium Fund is rated five stars (highest rating) by Morningstar. It's easy to see why—the fund's shareholders earned 117 percent on their money for 1999. You can find out what the fund's manager, Robert Loest, is buying and selling, and why he's doing it, by viewing his Portfolio Manager Diary.

Loest's diary is a stream-of-consciousness log of his thinking as he makes buy and sell decisions throughout the trading day. It's an outstanding resource. The diary is updated irregularly, sometimes daily, sometimes only once a week. It is archived for several months and appears to include Loest's thoughts about every trade he makes for the two funds he manages (Millennium and the newer New Frontier Fund).

He is candid and brutally frank.

For instance, talking about two REITs (Real Estate Investment Trusts) he sold: "*I decided it was a mistake ever getting back into them.*" Commenting on the market that same day he said, "*I kept hearing from everyone on CNBC that Fridays are not the day to get into the market on severe declines. . . . It seems like everyone including your cab driver already knows this, so I figured I'd better buy on Friday.*"

Many of his comments are enlightening, for instance, when writing about buying RFMD (RF Micro Devices) he explains what they make (chips for digital cell phones), and why their stock is down that day (they couldn't keep up with demand). You can't get this kind of insight in newsletters or reports you pay for, and here it's free.

The site lists the top 10 holdings for the Millennium Fund and the top five New Frontier holdings as of the end of the previous

Diary of a Fund Portfolio Manager

Robert Loest, Ph.D., CFA
Portfolio Manager

Earlier Diary Entries

April 10, 2000: Splat! No, I didn't buy anything today. It looks like I was right about the Nasdaq retesting its lows, although I didn't expect it so soon. It looks like everything is speeding up due to the Internet. Remember, though, this is most likely just a retest. I think the bull market is still intact. The volume has been quite low on the downside, which is normal for a correction vs. a bear market. Furthermore, the Put/Call ratio is low, about .33 according to some figures on CNBC today. This indicates that people are not bearish - they're just staying away from buying for the time being. That also squares with the low volume numbers. In addition, there is no indication of economic weakness, and every sign of strength in a broad group of tech and Internet companies. Once again, the volatility in most of these new companies is due to the small float.

Finally, the Internet and the WWW are *not* going away. They are growing at a phenomenal pace, and so are virtually all of the dominant companies in those sectors. Any time you have money seeking growth, where would you expect it to go, mostly toward companies growing sales at 50% - 100% annually with returns on invested capital of 50% - 100%, or to companies growing sales at 6% annually, with RIOC returns of 15%? At the risk of repeating myself - duh. Clearly, no matter what temporary corrections occur, investment capital over the long term will shift overwhelmingly to those highest-growth sectors with the greatest probability of achieving their promise. Those are the large, market share-leading companies like JDSU, YHOO and others.

Robert Loest's Diary is a must-read!

month (click Top 10 Stocks on each fund's main page). It's not just a list, it includes a short description and an insightful analysis of each stock, and a link to each company's Web site, in case you want to research the company further. It's worth spending time reading these descriptions and analyses.

Loest trades fairly often, so check here about once a week for new ideas on market trends as well as his insights.

FIRSTHAND FUNDS

(*www.firsthandfunds.com* > The Funds > Technology Value Fund > Complete List of Portfolio Holdings)

The Firsthand Technology Value Fund reaped an average annual return of 62.8 percent over five years, as of January 31, 2000. That's the best return of any mutual fund, anywhere, of any type, foreign or domestic. Naturally, the fund rates five stars from Morningstar.

You can see a list of the fund's top 10 holdings on the Technology Value Fund page. What's more interesting, however, is to see what stocks fund manager Kevin Landis has been buying and selling recently. You'll find that information by scrolling down to the Portfolio Holdings section and clicking on the "complete list of portfolio holdings" link.

Firsthand's information isn't as current as IPS's Millennium Fund data. They don't want the competition to know what they're doing, so they keep their trades secret for at least a month. If you look in October, you'll see the portfolio as of August 31. In November you'll see the holdings as of September 30, and so forth.

What Firsthand lacks in timeliness, they make up for in detail. For each holding, Firsthand shows you the number of shares owned, the price they paid, the total market value of the holding, and the percent of the fund's assets represented by the holding. They also include a link to each holding's Web site. Firsthand also shows you the amount of the fund's assets held in cash.

But I haven't told you the best part yet: Firsthand lets you compare their funds' portfolios between any two report dates you select. For instance, if you enter July 2000 for the start date and August 2000 for the end date, you'll see the July and August holdings, and the difference between the two portfolios in a separate "Change" section on the right. Pay most attention to the "Shares" column in the Change section. Numbers in brackets mean the fund sold those shares between the two report dates. Numbers without brackets are buys.

By using this comparison method you can see what the fund is loading up on, and what they're dumping. Also, pay attention to their cash position at the bottom. Increasing cash as a percentage of assets means Landis is bearish on the market; if they decrease it, they're bullish.

You can find the same information on the site for Firsthand's Medical Specialists, Technology Leaders, and Technology Innovators funds. Check back once a month for new ideas.

MUNDER NETNET FUND (*www.mundernetnet.com*)

The Munder NetNet Fund, also rated five stars by Morningstar, specializes in Internet-related companies and returned a sizzling 175 percent to investors in 1999.

Munder's portfolio information (click on Holdings) on the site is current as of the end of the previous month. They list every holding, not just the top 10. What's extraordinary is their description and analysis of every stock in their portfolio. That's a lot of information, considering they hold more than 90 companies. It's similar in quality to Robert Loest's analyses on the IPS site, except Loest only describes his top holdings. Munder doesn't say how many shares they own, or what percentage of their portfolio each company represents.

Munder also displays their buys and sells for the latest reported month (click on Buys & Sells on the top menu). They not only tell you what they did—they tell you why they did it. As with IPS, you're getting information free here that is better than any you could buy. Check the site every month.

OPENFUND (*www.openfund.com*)

OpenFund is a relatively new fund specializing in high-tech stocks. The fund started operations on August 31, 1999, so they don't have much of a track record. They got off to a good start though, returning 133 percent in their first five months of operation.

OpenFund goes the other funds a step further. They show you their portfolio holdings in real-time (click Inside OpenFund, on the left of the main page). The display is updated every time they

---

Peter Lynch's Golden Rules #20 and #21

20. If you study 10 companies, you'll find 1 for which the story is better than expected. If you study 50, you'll find 5. There are always pleasant surprises to be found in the stock market—companies whose achievements are being overlooked by Wall Street.

21. If you don't study any companies, you have the same success buying stocks as you do in a poker game if you bet without looking at your cards.

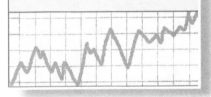

make a trade. They also give you a blow-by-blow commentary (click On the Trading Desk), again in real-time, of why they're doing what they're doing.

If you're especially bored, you can click on their Live Trader Cam and see live shots of the traders trading.

You'll get new ideas here almost every day.

KIPLINGER'S MAGAZINE INSIDER INTERVIEW ARCHIVES (*www.kiplinger.com* > Archies > Insider Interviews > Investments > Funds)

Kiplinger's doesn't do many interviews with fund managers—only four in 1999 and two in 1998. The articles are worthwhile, however, because they go into considerable detail about each manager's selection strategies. The archives go back to 1997 and include interviews with William Miller, James O'Shaughnessy, Jim Craig, Ken Heebner, and eight others.

MUTUAL FUNDS MAGAZINE (*mfmag.com* > Online Q&A)

Mutual Funds magazine interviews one fund manager each month. Although not as in-depth as *Kiplinger's* interviews, they're worthwhile. There is no archive, so you only have access to the current interview.

BRILL'S MUTUAL FUNDS INTERACTIVE (*www.brill.com*)

Brill's profiles one or two fund managers each month. The articles are relatively short, but usually describe the manager's stock-selection strategies in enough detail to be worth reading. The most current article can be accessed from their main page, and you can access an archive of all published articles by selecting Profiles from the menu on the left.

WORTH ONLINE (*www.worth.com* > The Complete Peter Lynch Archives)

Peter Lynch, former manager of the Fidelity Magellan Fund, writes occasional articles for Worth Online, the online version of *Worth* magazine. Some of them are about stocks, and some are about people, or other topics. You can access an archive of Lynch's articles back to 1993 by selecting "The Complete Peter Lynch Archives" main page in the "Worth Classics Online" section.

VALUE STOCKS.NET (*www.valuestocks.net* > Screening Lab)

Value Stocks features stocks selected according to different value gurus' selection strategies via stock screening programs (see Chapter 6). In their Screening Lab they come up with new screens on an infrequent and irregular schedule. They ran only three in 1999 David Dreman in March, Warren Buffett in July, and Benjamin Graham in October. Each screen describes the featured guru's selection strategy and the list of stocks found by searching for companies meeting their interpretation of the guru's requirements. They don't have their own search tool; rather, they use search tools available on other sites. They give you a good rundown on how they pick the stocks, so you could go to the same sites and run a current screen.

GURU STRATEGIES OUTLINED
(*www.ndir.com* > Stock Strategies > Stock Picking)

If you want to get the details of a guru's stock-picking strategies without reading their book, *Directions,* the name of this site focused on Canadian stocks, can help. They read the books and outline the selection strategies, in a style something like the Cliff Notes we bought in school. So far, they've outlined:

- Benjamin Graham's approach for the defensive investor
- Benjamin Graham's approach for the enterprising investor
- Philip A. Fisher's 15 points to look for in a common stock
- The Beardstown Ladies' 10 ingredients to choosing profitable stocks
- Dogs of the Dow approach
- Modified Dogs of the Dow
- Peter Lynch's 25 golden rules

CHAPTER FIVE

Picks and Tips from Market Experts

The Web is a bountiful resource for timely, top-quality investment ideas. Many of these come from renowned and respected market experts who publish columns on various financial sites. Here are the tops available.

Stock Pickers on the Web
CBS MARKETWATCH
(cbs.marketwatch.com > Regular Features > Commentary*)*

CBS MarketWatch is the best place to find current stock picks from well-known and highly regarded pundits you see on TV. It's a difficult site to navigate. The most reliable way of finding the columns is to select "Regular Features" just below the main headlines on the main page. Then click on "Commentary" for a list of the most recent columns. CBS MarketWatch archives three or four recent columns by each analyst. You'll find them by clicking "Commentary Library" on the Commentary page.

Here's a rundown of the CBS analysts:

- Elaine Garzarelli, an independent money manager, first came to investors' attention when she predicted the October 1987 market crash. She lost some of her allure when she forecast a crash that didn't happen in 1997. Despite the gaffe, she is still very good at what she does best: forecasting the overall market and telling us which industry sectors to avoid and which to pursue.
- Frank Cappiello, long-time regular panelist on *Wall Street Week* is a mutual fund and money manager. He favors blue-chip growth stocks. His columns mix overall market comments with specific stock recommendations.
- Courtney Smith, chief investment strategist for Orbitex Funds, uses fundamental analysis to select stocks, but also looks at the charts before buying a company. Smith's columns generally feature a single company, usually mid-cap growth, describing its business and prospects in detail. You could pay a lot of money for worse advice, Smith's columns are a must read for growth investors.

- Joe Battipaglia, chairman of investment policy at Gruntel & Company, focuses on the technology portion of the market. He sometimes recommends individual stocks, but his emphasis is on the outlook for the tech market in general. Battipaglia is good at what he does. Run for cover when he gets bearish.

MSN MoneyCentral (*moneycentral.msn.com*)

MoneyCentral's columnists aren't nearly as well known as their counterparts on CBS MarketWatch, but their advice is always specific. They name stocks, and tell you when to buy, and when to sell. What's more, MoneyCentral is fastidious about tracking the results, for better or for worse. Even better, most of their picks are moneymakers.

Jubak's Journal (Insight > Jubak's Journal)

Jim Jubak, senior markets editor for MoneyCentral, and author of the *Worth Guide to Electronic Investing*, approaches stock analysis the old-fashioned way. He analyzes their business and evaluates their long-term potential. Jim doesn't walk on the wild side; most of his picks are well-established industry leaders. He maintains at least three portfolios:

Jubak's Journal is a good source of investment ideas.

- **Jubak's Picks** include 25 stocks to hold a year or so. Jubak doesn't fall in love with his picks, he constantly monitors the portfolio and replaces four or five stocks with new picks every month. In January 2000 roughly 20 of the stocks had been in the portfolio less than a year, but four were added in 1998, and one, Cisco Systems, was added in September 1997. The portfolio is mostly tech stocks, but Jubak isn't necessarily a tech investor, he'll gladly add health care, financial, retail, or any sector he feels has strong potential. The portfolio listing compares the current and original picked price, and the gain or loss. He includes a rundown of his reasons for picking the stock, and his current view, along with sell price target for each stock.

- **Jubak's 50 Best Stocks in the World** is a portfolio designed to be held at least five years. With picks like Caterpillar and Coca-Cola, this isn't a tech portfolio. It includes his view of the strongest companies in a variety of industry sectors. Not all stocks in the portfolio are considered a buy at any given time. He labels current buys, and only 10 stocks had buy recommendations in January 2000. The remaining stocks are considered holds, meaning he wants to wait for a dip before recommending purchase. He drops stocks considered sells from the portfolio. He lists the percentage change of each pick since the portfolio's inception in September 1998. As of January 2000, the portfolio of 50 stocks was up 50.1 percent compared to 40.3 percent for the S&P 500 in the same period.
- **Jubak's Future Fantastic 50** is a more aggressive, mostly high-tech version of Jubak's 50 Best Stocks portfolio. As of January 28, 2000, it was up 62.9 percent since its inception on July 30, 1999, compared to the S&P 500's 2.4 percent rise.

Strategy Lab (Insight > Strategy Lab)

This page on MoneyCentral gives six market analysts a hypothetical $100,000 to invest using their own predefined strategy. MoneyCentral strives to find analysts who represent a cross section of strategies from value to growth to momentum. The analysts can make as many trades as they wish as long as they stick to their original strategy. They can trade anytime, and their trades are recorded in their journal along with their comments on their moves. MoneyCentral reports on their progress and account balance weekly. The competition lasts about six months. Six of the seven analysts made money in the round ending January 28, 2000. All six winners were up more than 50 percent in six months. Find the Strategy Lab by clicking on Strategy Lab under the Insight section of the MoneyCentral Investor main page. Click on an analyst's picture to read an explanation of their stock picking strategy, current portfolio, and a record of past transactions.

PACESETTERS DATABASE
(*www.prars.com* > PaceSetters Database)

The Public Register Annual Report Service (PRARS) is in the business of mailing annual reports to interested investors. You can receive an annual report from any or all of the 3,000 participating companies by filling out an order form on the site. They will mail the requested reports to you at no charge. They've been doing this since 1982, long before companies began filing reports electronically. Founder Henry Grinde began entering financial data from these reports into a database then because he felt it was a waste not to make use of the information. Grinde devised a method of evaluating companies' future prospects using the data he collected, and eventually his work evolved into what is now called the PaceSetters Database. PaceSetters are defined as companies with the best prospects out of 5,000 or so that they track.

Stocks become PaceSetters by passing screening criteria including, among others, high cash flow, high return on equity, high return on capital, and low debt. The qualifying PaceSetters companies are ranked by comparing their stock price to working capital, cash flow, sales, shareholders equity, cash on hand, and so forth.

The highest ranked companies are featured in the PaceSetters Database. The number of companies in the database varies. I've seen as few as 15, and as many 29. The database is updated once a month, on the fifteenth.

Why is this important? Because according to information on the site as of January 15, 2000, the PaceSetters Database stocks returned 830 percent since the feature's inception in March 1998, compared to the NASDAQ's 867 percent, and 447 percent for the S&P 500. That's sensational—PaceSetters' return bested the S&P 500 by 86 percent, and came close to matching NASDAQ returns. In fact, PaceSetters was ahead of the NASDAQ until the NASDAQ's spectacular spurt at the end of 1999. PaceSetters did it with a mix of value and growth stocks—all real businesses with solid earnings and solid balance sheets.

What's in the database? As of January 15, 2000, it has 19 stocks, including 11 added in 1999, six of those in December. There was no particular pattern or industry concentration. The portfolio had value stocks such as La-Z-Boy Furniture and high-tech highfliers like EMC. There were nine NASDAQ-listed stocks, one from the American Stock Exchange,

PaceSetters Database as of 03/15/2000

Rank	Company Name	Symbol	Exchange	Date Of Inception	Initial Price	Current Price	% Change
1	WASHINGTON HOMES INC	WHI	NYSE	12/99	5.06	5.56	11.26
2	D R HORTON INC	DHI	NYSE	3/99	16.25	12.06	-25.78
3	MONACO COACH CORP	MNC	NYSE	6/99	24.40*	16.13	-33.89
4	THOR INDUSTRIES INC	THO	NYSE	2/00	26.75	24.19	-9.57
5	COMTECH TELECOM CORP	CMTL	NASDAQ	12/98	5.58*	17.50	213.62
6	LA-Z-BOY INC	LZB	NYSE	12/99	16.88	16.00	-5.21
7	MANATRON INC	MANA	NASDAQ	12/99	5.38	10.88	102.23
8	TIMBERLINE SOFTWARE	TMBS	NASDAQ	4/98	9.67*	11.44	18.30
9	ROBERT HALF INTL INC	RHI	NYSE	5/95	7.66*	41.00	435.25
10	DYCOM INDUSTRIES INC	DY	NYSE	11/97	9.09*	44.50	389.55
11	MICROS SYSTEMS INC	MCRS	NASDAQ	12/99	59.75	53.25	-10.88
12	FACTSET RESEARCH	FDS	NYSE	3/98	10.08*	31.00	207.54
13	JAKKS PACIFIC INC	JAKK	NASDAQ	8/99	17.40*	18.00	3.45
14	BIOGEN INC	BGEN	NASDAQ	10/98	35.25*	78.25	121.99
15	PAYCHEX INC	PAYX	NASDAQ	10/97	17.69*	49.50	179.82
16	SERENA SOFTWARE	SRNA	NASDAQ	2/00	29.00	54.38	87.52
17	QLOGIC CORP	QLGC	NASDAQ	12/99	63.19*	126.00	99.40
18	EMC CORP	EMC	NYSE	6/99	49.13	115.25	134.58
19	COGNIZANT TECH	CTSH	NASDAQ	12/99	72.75	100.88	38.67

PaceSetters Database portfolio is a diverse mix of tech, value, and growth.

and the balance were NYSE listed companies. Of the 13 stocks added prior to December, only two were down in value from their initial listing; the biggest loser was off 22 percent. Compare that to seven stocks up more than 100 percent—and three of those were up more than 200 percent.

How much trading would you have to do to achieve these results? "We add and delete about 12 stocks each year," says Henry Grinde's son, Erik, who maintains the database.

Select PaceSetters Database from the PRARS site to see the current selections, including the date they were added, and their performance since then.

VALUESTOCKS.NET
(*www.valuestocks.net* > VSN Portfolio)

ValueStocks.net is run by Dr. Michael J. Burry, CEO and chief investment strategist at hedge fund Scion Capital, Inc. Burry developed his site as "a resource and idea pool for the individual investor who thinks independently." Burry looks for beaten-down stocks trading far below their real or intrinsic value.

Burry tracks his picks in the VSN Portfolio, a list of 20 or so stocks. You can see the current portfolio by selecting VSN Portfolio on the main page. For a disciple of value investor Benjamin Graham, Burry does a lot of trading. As of April 5, 2000, nine of the 15 stocks in his portfolio had been there less than three months.

Scroll past the current portfolio to see Burry's results compared to major indexes such as the S&P 500, NASDAQ, etc., for the current and previous years. It's impressive. The VSN Portfolio returned 68.1 percent in 1999, probably a record for a value strategy. The portfolio was up 16.9 percent year-to-date, as of April 5, 2000, handily beating all the major indexes. For instance, the S&P 500 and NASDAQ were up 1.2 percent, and 2.5 percent, respectively, for the same period.

Burry includes a commentary below the portfolio results recapping recent trades and giving his take on current market conditions.

MONEY.COM (*www.money.com* > Sivy on Stocks)

Michael Sivy is a fundamentally based, feet-on-the-ground, Warren Buffett-style stock picker. He favors companies with strong balance sheets, and a solid record of consistent earnings and sales growth. His list of hot growth stocks includes companies like Walgreens, Safeway, and Schering-Plough. Oh sure, he gets carried away and includes highly-priced tech picks like Cisco Systems, Sun Microsystems, and Lucent Technologies. But you won't find any Internet wonders, such as eBay or Amazon, on his pick lists.

Sivy maintains a list he calls his 100 Top Stocks comprising:

- **Star Growers** are companies Sivy considers reasonably priced growth companies, yet growing earnings at least 16 percent annually.
- **Solid Citizens** are companies with slower growing earnings (13 percent to 15 percent), but lower priced stocks.
- **Overlooked Talent** are value-priced stocks with annual earnings growth at 12 percent or less. Sivy says, "They're attractive because they can outpace growth stocks in periods when investors become value-conscious."

He features a detailed analysis of three stocks pulled from these portfolios each week. You can read these articles on the site, or sign up to receive them via e-mail.

SMART MONEY (*www.smartmoney.com* > Stocks > Our Latest Picks or Magazine Portfolios)

Smart Money's editors feature portfolios selected according to a theme, for instance "10 Best Stocks to Hold for the Next Millennium." OK, that's not an accurate title, but you get the picture—it's always the "10 Best" something. Actually, they're good stock pickers. You can review their archive (Magazine Portfolios) and see their previous picks, and how they've done from the original publication date up to the date you look.

New portfolios are added on an irregular schedule, usually once a month.

What's a Hedge Fund?

Hedge funds are usually partnerships limited to wealthy investors. Hedge funds typically do more and riskier trading than conventional mutual funds. They often short stocks, and invest in options, futures, and other speculative investments. James Cramer of TheStreet.com is a well-known hedge fund manager.

INDIVIDUAL INVESTOR (*www.individualinvestor.com*)

I've been a follower of *Individual Investor* magazine's "Magic 25" since before there was a Web. They would introduce 25 stocks—in those days mostly high-growth, momentum-style small caps. They told readers to buy all 25 and hold for a year, or until the editors said sell, whichever came first. That's what I always liked about the magazine—they didn't simply give you a list, shake your hand, and wish you good luck. They followed the portfolio continuously, updating readers monthly on recent events, good and bad. Some years it reminded me of the "agony and the ecstasy," but the editors were always there, sharing the good times, commiserating when things went wrong. They weren't wed to all 25 stocks for the year: if fundamentals went bad, they'd recommend selling. Of course, in those days it took a month before you got the word.

Individual Investor is still doing what they do best. Over the years they've learned from their mistakes; now they're a lot smarter in their research, and they understand the advantages of diversification. The 2000 portfolio is a mix of large- and small-highfliers, and the forgotten turnaround candidates, and the still unloved.

They still follow the portfolio through the year, but now on the Web they can give you updates as needed, instead of having to wait until the next publication date. You don't even have to visit the site to see the updates, sign up and they'll e-mail them to you as soon as they're posted online.

MOTLEY FOOL (*www.fool.com* > Stock Strategies)

If you've never visited the Motley Fool's site you probably think the Fools are a bunch of wild-eyed day traders spending their days trading insults on message boards and chasing the latest hot IPO.

In fact, they're quite the opposite of this. It's true that when they started on America Online the Fools favored small, high-growth, momentum stocks. They've also had their fling with selecting stocks using backtested screening formulas, selection strategies based on discovering what has worked in the past, the most famous being the Foolish Four, their take on the "Dogs of the Dow" (see Chapter 7). They still feature a variety of portfolios derived from the Foolish Four and other screens, but these days most of their emphasis is placed on two portfolios, the Rule Maker and the Rule Breaker.

The Rule Maker Portfolio

If you didn't know better, you'd think the Rule Maker strategy was devised by the likes of a Warren Buffett or a Peter Lynch. It's built around a long-term, buy-and-hold strategy involving buying very large companies that dominate their industry sector. They're not looking for fast growth—profit margins, efficient use of cash, and low debt are more important.

The Rule Maker portfolio consists of 15 stocks. The variety is amazing. Where else would you find Eastman Kodak and Yahoo! in the same portfolio? The idea is to hold Rule Maker companies for five years or longer.

The Rule Breaker Portfolio

The Motley Fool calls this portfolio the Rule Breaker because it violates one of their dearest tenets: fair value. The Motley Fool popularized the concept of comparing a stock's price-to-earnings ratio to its forecast annual earnings growth, which says a stock is fairly valued when its P/E ratio equals the growth rate and overvalued if its P/E ratio exceeds the forecast growth rate. For instance, a stock would be considered undervalued if analysts were forecasting 30 percent annual earnings growth for the next five years and the P/E was only 25.

That rule, however, would keep the Motley Fool out of most hot-moving stocks, including of course, Internet stocks. So the Fools threw the rule out the window, replacing it with mostly subjective criteria. Rule breaker stocks must be "the top dog and first-mover in an important, emerging industry." The company must have good management and, get this, the stock must be viewed as overvalued by "a significant constituent of the financial media." The only measurable criterion is relative strength—a measure of the stock's price appreciation over the past 12 months compared to the overall market. Rule breakers must have a relative strength of at least 90, meaning the stock outperformed 90 percent of the market during the past year.

Best Investment Sites for Models

Dogs of the Dow
(*www.dogsofthedow.com*):
Dogs of the Dow is a conservative value strategy for selecting members of the Dow Jones Industrial Average. You don't have to calculate anything. They do it all for you.

SuperModels
(*moneycentral.msn.com*): Jon Markman's SuperModels turned in market-beating returns in recent years. You can run them anytime with a click of your mouse.

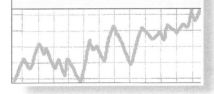

The Motley Fool adds a curious wrinkle by tacking on their Foolish Four portfolio—to balance the risks, they say. The Foolish Four are the cheapest stocks, based on dividend yield, in the Dow Jones Industrial index. These are down-and-out, out-of-favor stocks.

Consequently, the Rule Breaker portfolio (*www.fool.com/ portfolios/rulebreaker/information.com*) ends up being a mix of highfliers such as Amazon.com and unloved stocks like Caterpillar. The portfolio contained 11 stocks in January 2000. If the logic of including the Foolish Four escapes you, you can simply ignore them and still have seven good ideas.

The Fools don't have hard and fast rules for selling rule breakers. You're supposed to sell when you need to make room for a better idea. The Foolish Four formula requires annual rebalancing. If you ignore the Foolish Four component, they did four or five trades in 1999.

The Fools' buy and sell reports include a detailed explanation of their thinking behind every trade. Reading them is a good way to learn their selection process. Buy and sell reports for all Rule Breaker trades are still available. Find them by selecting "Transaction History" on the portfolio page and then clicking on a particular transaction. It's worthwhile reading.

How has the Motley Fool done? The portfolio earned in excess of 65 percent annually from its inception August 5, 1994 to February 2, 2000. A lot of that performance can be credited to America Online, up 13,145 percent since acquired as one of the Fool's initial purchases in 1994.

Motley Fool's Rising Margins (*www.fool.com* > Rising Margins)

Stock prices tend to follow earnings, particularly earnings growth. Earnings grow because of increases in sales and/or increased profit margins (earnings = sales × profit margins). Rising profit margins are apt to be accompanied by positive earnings surprises, usually a good thing to happen if you own the stock. Profit margins often move in trends. If the margin increased last quarter, chances are it will rise again in the current quarter.

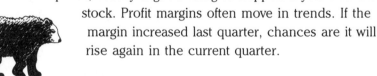

Every Monday, the Motley Fool lists companies recently reporting increased profit margins compared to the year-ago quarter. An increase in profit margins by itself doesn't mean you're going to get rich on the stock. It's possible the margins were artificially depressed the year before, or there could be other extenuating circumstances, but it's a good place to start your research.

The Motley crew tries to fool people by constantly moving features around on their site, so you may have to hunt for Rising Margins. Look for it in the Stock Screens section.

AMERICA-iNVEST.COM MODEL PORTFOLIO
(*www.america-invest.com* > Portfolios)

The site MicroCap1000.com was renamed America-iNvest.com in November 1999. It has expanded its focus beyond micro-cap stocks to encompass companies of all sizes. The site provides two good sources of tips. The Model Portfolio is a basket of about 15 stocks taken from their MicroCap 1000 index. The index consists of 1,000 companies with a maximum market cap of $500 million. These are not fly-by-night stocks, they're all listed on either the NASDAQ, New York, or American stock exchanges, and they're all followed by at least one analyst.

America-iNvest.com returned 143 percent in 1999. Select "MicroCap Model Portfolio" on the Portfolios page. All stocks listed are current buys. Click on the link at the bottom of the list to see deleted listings. You can see forecast earnings growth rates and valuation ratios by selecting the "Trailing & Projected P/E, EPS and Growth Ratios" link at the bottom of the page. I think you'll be pleasantly surprised when you see that the bulk of the selections are reasonably priced.

America-iNvest.com Editor's Choice
(*www.america-invest.com* > Editor's Choice)

Richard Heftner, America-iNvest.com's editor, highlights individual stocks in his Editor's Choice column. The updates appear on an irregular schedule, but at least once a week Heftner gives a detailed rundown on each company's business and its competitors.

BLOOMBERG TV MONEY FLOW (*www.bloomberg.com* > TV > Money Flow under Something You Saw)

Measuring a stock's *money flow,* or accumulation, is a popular method of gauging the stock's appreciation potential. Money flow is measured by tracking the volume of shares changing hands on price upticks compared to the number traded on downticks. A trade is deemed an uptick when the stock changes hands at a higher price than it did on the previous trade. Money flow advocates say an uptick occurs because there was more buying pressure than selling pressure, and the shares traded during an uptick count as positive money flow.

Conversely, a stock moves down in price—downtick—because more people want to sell than buy, and the volume on downticks is deemed negative money flow. Money flow is measured by keeping a running total of the shares traded on upticks minus shares traded on downticks. In its purest sense, the totals should be tabulated for each trade. That's hard to do, so most money flow calculations are based on the entire trading day. If the stock closed higher than it opened, the trading volume for the day is counted as positive money flow. Shares traded on a down day count as negative money flow. The Accumulation indicator listed in the newspaper *Investor's Business Daily* is based on this premise.

Bloomberg TV (features from Bloomberg's cable TV programs) takes money flow a step further. Bloomberg looks for stocks with stock prices moving in the opposite direction of money flow. For instance, suppose on Monday a stock moved from $50 to $52 on a volume of 10,000 shares. Then on Tuesday the stock moved from $52 down to $51, and this time the volume expanded to 20,000 shares. The stock moved up $1 during those two days, but 20,000 shares traded on the down day compared to only 10,000 on the up day. The money flow was negative, although the price moved up. Bloomberg says this divergence between price movement and the money flow "can only last a short time," and "it could mean the stock price is about to reverse direction."

A divergence could show up in the opposite direction as well. For instance, the stock price drops, but the money flow is positive.

Bloomberg features one stock each day representing each of the above two conditions. "Buying on Weakness," for example, highlights a stock with a falling share price and positive money flow. "Selling on Strength" highlights a stock with money flowing out although the share price is moving higher. Bloomberg shows you a price chart and a money flow chart for each featured stock so you can judge whether the divergence looks significant, or if they had to stretch to come up with a stock to feature that day.

Does the strategy work? Bloomberg keeps track of the results going back to May 6, 1999, apparently when the feature started. When I checked on January 16, 2000, their Buying on Weakness stocks averaged a 13.6 percent return compared to a 0.9 percent return for their Selling on Strength selections. That's an impressive difference.

I don't recommend relying solely on money flow to select stocks. The Buying on Weakness selections would be a good source of candidates for further research. The Selling on Weakness picks could be a source of short candidates, but don't try shorting in a strong market.

VALUE & GROWTH STOCK REVIEW (*www.vgsr.com*)

The Value & Growth Stock Review employs a proprietary stock picking strategy that combines value and growth selection styles.

Greg Wurzburger, a research analyst with an investment management firm, employs fundamental valuation ratios such as price to earnings, price to sales, etc., but in a novel manner. Instead of measuring these values against absolute or fixed criteria, he compares them to other companies with similar operating characteristics. So, a company that might be overvalued using traditional measures, could be undervalued compared to the same-size companies with comparable earnings and sales growth rates.

Wurzburger also looks for stocks, with high relative strength, that is, they have outperformed the overall market in recent months.

Wurzburger's results were lackluster until he switched from searching for small-caps to concentrating on large, blue-chip companies in January 2000. The change was for the best. His portfolios, consisting of only five stocks, have handily outperformed the market since then.

Bulletin Board Stocks

Most U.S. based stocks are traded on the New York or American stock exchanges, or on the NASDAQ stock market. Companies listed on these major markets must meet certain qualifying requirements. These requirements pertain to the size of a company's assets, sales, and so forth. Listed companies must also file the quarterly and annual reports required by the U.S. Securities and Exchange Commission.

Companies not meeting minimum size requirements can still be traded on the Bulletin Board system. Bulletin Board stocks are often penny stocks, that is, stocks selling for less than $5, and often have small trading volumes (low liquidity).

While many good companies are listed there, Bulletin Board listed stocks are the playground for stock manipulators of all stripes. Investors are cautioned to take extra care when considering these companies.

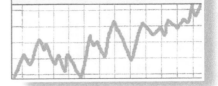

Best Investment Sites for Economic Analysis

Robert W. Baird (*www.rwbaird.com*): This long-established financial advisory firm gives you their take on the economic and market outlook.

Department of Commerce, Bureau of Economic Analysis (*www.bea.doc.gov*): A good source for detailed economic data.

The Dismal Scientist (*www.dismal.com*): Filled with the latest economic trends and reports. A must if you're interested in doing your own financial forecasting.

Raymond James Financial (*www.raymondjames.com*): Dr. Scott Brown's weekly commentary on the state of the economy.

(continued on next page)

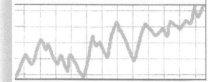

Wurzburger's picks are posted on the site, but you can also subscribe to a free, twice-monthly e-mail newsletter containing his latest picks.

The site carries no advertising, except for America's Second Harvest, a nonprofit organization dedicated to curing hunger, and offers nothing for sale.

DECISION POINT
(*www.decisionpoint.com* > Top Advisors' Corner)

Decision Point is mainly a subscription site. Their Top Advisors' Corner features snippets from a variety of newsletters. The purpose of the feature is to sell newsletter subscriptions and most of the snippets give market overviews rather than buy or sell advice on specific stocks. However, these newsletters do give you timely stock tips:

- *Pristine Day Trader* by Velez and Capra
- *Todd Market Forecast* by Steve Todd
- *The Dines Letter* by James Dines
- *Apollo Small-Cap Stock Report* by Burgess Hallums
- *SectorVue* by David Schultz

ADVICE FROM PEOPLE LIKE YOU (*www.iexchange.com*)

You don't have to rely on tips from your gardener or your barber anymore. You can get them online from tipsters with handles like Maddog, Puffy, Wild Thang, and Zen Warrior.

Anybody who registers on iexchange.com can enter a stock pick. All you have to do is fill out a form listing the ticker symbol, projected price, and when you expect your projected price to be achieved (target date). Then add your "report"—a headline and a paragraph or two explaining your reasoning, which readers pay for. You set the price you want to charge for your report. If anybody buys it, you split the proceeds 50/50 with iexchange.

Anyone submitting a pick is dubbed an analyst. Most analysts make several picks. The iexchange site tabulates the average return of each analyst's picks and his or her predictive accuracy.

The *average return* is the overall return of the analysts' picks during their "hold periods." The hold period starts on the day the pick is made and ends when the projected price or the target date is reached, whichever comes first. If a pick is still active—that is, neither the projected price nor target date has been reached—the average return is calculated from the pick date through the current date.

Predictive accuracy is a measure of how close the stock came to reaching the analysts' projected price on or before the target date. The predictive accuracy is 100 percent if the stock hits the projected price on or before the target date, even if the price drops again by the target date. A stock can be a loser by the target date, but the analyst still gets 100 percent predicted accuracy as long as the stock hit the projected price somewhere along the line.

The main page of iexchange.com shows the current 10 best pickers/analysts based on average return. Besides average return, you see each top picker's predictive accuracy, number of picks, and the ticker symbols of two or three of their picks.

To make the list, an analyst must have made at least 10 picks, with at least one pick still open. One time that I looked, an analyst named "ggecko" topped the list with an average return of 99 percent and 100 percent accuracy on 12 picks. That was impressive, especially since the next analyst's average return was 72 percent, and number three dropped down to 43 percent average return. I looked up ggecko when I returned about a month later. Things had not gone well. Poor ggecko's average return had plunged to 17 percent, but his predictive accuracy was still a respectable 84 percent.

You can click on an analyst's name to see more statistics on his or her picking prowess and current picks. Each current pick includes the company name, stock ticker, open and target date, and the headline. You have to buy the report to see the paragraph explaining the analysts' rationale for recommending the stock. Prices range from free to $5. Most are $1 or $2.

It beats me why, after you've seen all the free information on each pick, you would pay to see a paragraph more or less repeating the same information you can find in Market Guide's or Morningstar's free profiles. Maybe it's because what you read here might affect your decision to buy the stock, based on your assessment of the analyst's ability to pick moneymaking stocks. I suppose people pay the analyst as a way of thanking him or her for the tip. It's like giving a tip for a tip.

Best Investment Sites for Economic Analysis

(continued from previous page)

Martin Capital Financial Newsletters (*www.martincapital.com*): Monthly and quarterly market newsletters covering market and overall economic conditions.

Stock Research (*www.stockresearch.com*): Robert Bose of Green Mountain Research gives you his analysis of recent market and economic events.

White House Economic Briefing Room (*www.whitehouse.gov*): The latest statistics released by the U.S. government covering all economic sectors. Excellent, well-displayed information.

Edward Yardeni (*www.yardeni.com*): All kinds of information available here from the economist's economist.

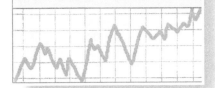

Evaluating the Tips and the Tipsters

By now you must realize there's no shortage of Web pundits out there in cyberspace making tips. The problem is, not all tippers agree. You'll often see two pundits offering conflicting advice on the same stock.

How do you know whose advice to follow, and whose to ignore? Here are some site tips to help you evaluate tips.

FINANCIAL MAGAZINES AND WEB SITES

Validea (*www.validea.com*) tracks stock picks made in printed financial magazines such as *Forbes, Bloomberg Personal, Kiplinger's, Worth,* etc., as well as on major financial Web sites such as MSN Investor, CBS MarketWatch, The Street.com, and Personal Wealth. In all, Validea tracks hundreds of Web pundits and dozens of publications.

This is not done by computer; a Validea researcher reads each commentary on a stock offering, evaluates the overall tone, and decides if the article is a pick or a pan. Picks are articles with more positive than negative statements, and vice versa. Implied picks or pans are articles primarily about the company itself, rather than the stock.

Validea rates the pundits by tracking the performance of their recommended stocks for periods ranging from one week to one year after the pick. In their lightbulb rating system, top-ranked pundits get five lightbulbs, and the lowest rated get one lightbulb. Pundits with no lightbulbs haven't been ranked. Validea says five-bulb pundits' stocks have, on average, beat the S&P 500 by at least 20 percent in the three months following the recommendation.

Validea divides the sources for their ratings into categories: personalities, magazines, and online sources. In their community category they track picks and pans made by individuals on their own message boards.

From the site's main page, click on media, personalities, magazines, online sources, or community to see the "Top-Ranked Stock Pickers," based on three-month returns. Click on a pundit's (Recommendor) name to see their "Quick Stats" page. Quick Stats shows the pundit's returns for the past week, month, three months, and year. The page also lists their recent picks, and the five best and five worst picks in Validea's database.

There's a lot more you can do from the Top-Ranked Stock Pickers page. If you're interested in a specific industry—health care, for instance, you can select Health Care from the

Sector dropdown menu, and you'll see pundits with the best health care picks.

You can use the Time Frame dropdown menu to see who has the best picks based for one-week, one-month, six-month, or one-year time spans in addition to the three-month default value.

In addition to individual pundits, you can see ratings for stocks picked in magazines or Web site columns such as *Fortune's* "Street Life" or *Barron's* "Plugged In" columns, *Smart Money's* cover stories, *Individual Investor's* "Scene & Heard," etc.

TV FINANCIAL NEWS

The Big Tipper (*www.bigtipper.com*). I'd like to be able to watch TV all day long so I could hear the advice of all the market pundits. That isn't practical for me. First, I don't have the time, and second, my cable system carries CNBC but not CNNfn or Bloomberg. Even if these factors didn't mitigate against it, I still couldn't watch all three channels at the same time.

The Big Tipper neatly solves my problem. They watch TV every day for me. They monitor the major financial channels and popular programs like *Wall Street Week, Moneyline, Nightly Business Report,* and more. They take notes on each expert's interview including the stocks they recommended and why. Even better, they keep track of the pundits' tips, so we can see how much money we would have made following their past tips.

Everything is accessible from their main page. What you'll notice first are the listings of 20 recent appearances by pundits on CNBC, CNNfn, and Bloomberg. Below those, you'll see listings of recent appearances on individual TV programs and even on some Web sites. On the bottom left you'll find recent tips from the print financial media including *Barron's, Smart Money, Forbes, Investor's Business Daily,* and more. Apparently, the Big Tipper enjoys watching TV more than reading because they include only one pundit's tips from each edition.

The "Suit Rack" feature summarizes a smattering of the CEO interviews recently aired on CNBC and CNNfn.

Click on an expert's name to see the summary of their recommendations including a list of recommended stocks and a synopsis of what the expert said about each. For instance, Jordan Kimmel with First Montauk appeared on CNBC on January 6, 2000, and recommended Hooper

Superstar Pundits

Smart Money Pundit Watch
(*www.smartmoney.com* >
Stocks > Pundit Watch) tracks
the batting averages of 12 of
the best-known stock market
gurus. These are the cream of
the crop: Abbey Cohen, Ralph
Acampora, Byron Wein, Barton
Biggs, Joseph Battipaglia, etc.

Smart Money compiles the
pundit's picks as they are featured in newspapers, magazines, and newswires and in
the publications these experts
send out to their own clients.
They compile data going back
to the beginning of 1995, evaluating each pick on a scale of
0—totally wrong—to 10, "on
the money in terms of accuracy,
timing, and confidence." Smart
Money says a 10 rarely happens. They divide a pundit's
total score by the number of
predictions to come up with a
batting average, as in baseball.

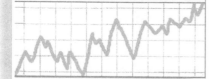

Holmes, Cymer, and Loronix Information Systems. Big Tipper showed
the ticker symbol, industry, and recent price for each, and then summarized Kimmel's rationale for his selections.

LORX has gone up 100 percent from when Mr. Kimmel
first picked the stock. He states, "I'm sticking with the
stock." He explains that their "digital surveillance system is
a brand-new product" that can generate revenues for the
company. "They have great margin increases. Only trading
10 times next year's earnings." He notes that the stock is
"one of the top picks we have."

Mr. Kimmel explains that Cymer is in the play of
broadband, silicon chips, and communications. He likes the
company's "strong charts" and "great year-to-year comparisons." He states that the "revenues are just starting to
drive in" for CYMI.

"HH dominates their market right now," Mr. Kimmel
states. The company provides health information services. He
advises early play in this company, because "this is one of
those stocks that the institutions are just finding right now."

Reading these comments is better than if I'd watched him on TV.
Usually I see these interviews while I'm doing something else and
scribble the ticker symbols on a piece of paper. By the time I look at
them, I've forgotten the pundit's reasons for recommending the stock.

Jordan Kimmel's reasons made sense, but many talking heads tell
a good story on TV. How much credence should I give to his tips?

This is where the Big Tipper really shines. I clicked on Kimmel's
name to display his track record going back to February 1999. Big
Tipper listed an even dozen of his previous tips, showing the tip date
and price, as well as the current price and the gain or loss shown
in dollars, and in percentage return. Kimmel had two losers, one
down a heartbreaking 32 percent; the other fell only 3 percent. The
remaining 10 were up, the best was 4 Kids Entertainment, up 727
percent since recommended on February 16, 1999. Of the 10 profitable tips, seven made double digit gains. The latest three—Argosy,
Global Crossing, and Zomax—made less than two months ago were
up 7.1 percent, 19.1 percent, and 31.4 percent respectively.

After seeing that, I could hardly wait to log on to my Web broker.

Thanks to Big Tipper, you don't have to spend all day in front of the tube. Just bring up Big Tipper in the evening and find out what the pundits touted that day. Don't worry if you miss a day or two. Click on "Past 5 Day's Tips" to see an abbreviated archive. You'll see the tips, though not the reasoning behind the selections.

To look up the track record of any pundit select Track Records from the Tip menu. Type in the pundit's first or last name, and then click on one of the listed names to see all of their picks logged by Big Tipper.

If after seeing these results you decide you need a new pundit, Big Tipper takes care of that too. Click on Top Tippers to bring up a list of the 10 best tippers based on the average return of all their recommendations in the database. To qualify for this list, a guru had to recommend at least five different stocks. If you think five good tips aren't enough to make a trustworthy stock picker, click on Maximum Tippers to see the best gurus with at least 15 picks.

You can see Big Tipper's entire pundit database listed with the average return of their picks either in alphabetical order (Tippers A–Z), or with the best returns at the top (Tippers by %),

Jot down the names of pundits of interest, because, inexplicably, you can't click on their names on these lists to see their tips—you have to go back to Track Records to do that.

You can request an e-mail notification when a pundit of interest makes a new recommendation by selecting "Free E-mail Service" and then clicking on the expert's name, which sends an e-mail to Big Tipper. (I haven't done that, because I couldn't find instructions for stopping the e-mails if I decided I was getting too many notices.)

Big Tipper is the brainchild of Bryan Berg. He and his team videotape the financial networks all day long and summarize the interviews, updating the Web site periodically during the day. To my knowledge, this kind of compilation of stock market advice has never been available before at any price. It's free on Big Tipper, and it's a remarkable service for investors.

CHAPTER SIX

Selection Strategies: Stock Screening

Screening Tools

Stock-screening or stock search tools are software programs accessible from certain Web pages. What's the difference between a screening and a search tool? Nothing. Both terms mean the same thing, and we'll use them interchangeably. The items you search for when screening—for instance, market capitalization or P/E—are termed variables, parameters, or indicators. They all mean the same thing. A screening tool could provide 26 search variables, or will have 26 screening parameters, or you'll plug in a value of 10 for this indicator, etc.

Screening programs come in two basic types: prebuilt and custom. Prebuilt screens are easier to use because the designers made all of the decisions. All you have to do is push the Start button. Custom screens give you the flexibility of designing screens to meet your specific requirements.

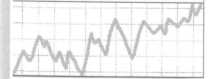

Web pundits and gurus don't have to be your only source for investment ideas. You can come up with your own hot tips by using stock-screening programs. Do you want sizzling semiconductor equipment stocks with soaring sales and earnings? No problem. Key your specs into a Web screening program, and within seconds you'll have your list.

Compare that technique to the old days when investors spent hours wading through thousands of lines of tiny print in books begged from brokers to find similar, usually stale information.

A note of caution: Stock screening is only a step in the process of finding investment candidates. Don't run out and buy stocks just because they were listed in your search results. You still have to do the research to find out if a stock is right for your portfolio.

Prebuilt Screens
QUICKEN POPULAR SEARCHES
(*www.quicken.com* > Investing > Screen Stocks > Popular Searches)

Quicken's searches are quick and easy to use. They're divided into two major categories: value and growth stocks. All searches require a minimum $5 share price; that is, penny stocks will not be eligible for a search.

Value

Quicken's value screens look for companies considered underpriced using traditional measures such as price to earnings, price to book, and price to sales ratios. Value-priced stocks underperformed the overall market in recent years as tech and other growth stocks caught investor's attention. However, fashions change, and value stocks could soon regain the limelight.

- *Small-Cap Value:* Searches for small companies with market capitalization between $200 million and $2 billion, low valuations, and strong balance sheets.
- *Large-Cap Value:* Similar to the small-cap search, except of course they search for larger companies (minimum $2 billion market-cap). They also loosen the balance sheet requirements somewhat compared to the Small-Cap screen.

- *High Yield:* Looks for stocks with positive earnings and a 7.5 percent minimum dividend yield (annual dividend/stock price). You'll find mostly real estate investment trusts (REITs) when you run this screen.

Growth

These screens search out companies with a history of strong sales and earnings growth.

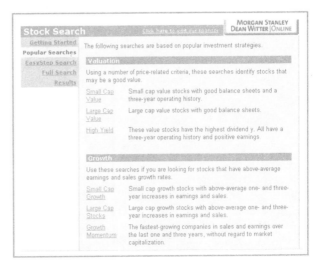

Quicken's Popular Searches help you find investment candidates with the push of a button.

- *Small-Cap Growth:* Looks for small companies with high, accelerating historical sales and earnings growth rates. High growth is where it's at these days, but high risk goes with the territory—research these companies thoroughly before buying.
- *Large-Cap Growth:* Similar to the small-cap growth screen except the required growth rates are less steep.
- *Growth Momentum:* Looks for companies with three-year average annual sales growth of at least 50 percent per year, and three-year earnings growth of at least 25 percent per year. Here's the kicker, sales and earnings must both have at least doubled within the past year. You'll find hot prospects here, but be sure to do your homework.

MARKETPLAYER
(*www.marketplayer.com* > Stock Screening > Sample Reports)

MarketPlayer's screening program is among the most sophisticated available, with more than 100 screening variables (indicators). The range is surprising—everything from basic fundamental factors such as book value to stock price performance characteristics such as relative strength. Many indicators are composed of multiple variables. For instance, the High Growth Indicator combines earnings estimates and estimated price/earnings ratio.

Learning to design custom MarketPlayer screens takes some time. You would probably spend the better part of a day just getting familiar with the indicators. Fortunately, you don't have to design

your own custom screens. MarketPlayer has a set of 15 prebuilt sample screens. Start with these, and if you're interested, ease into designing your own screens later by modifying the samples after you've become familiar with their operation.

Here's an overview of some of the more interesting search screens.

MarketPlayer's Improved PEG Screen

This screen searches for value-price companies. PEG is shorthand for comparing a company's price-to-earnings ratio (P/E) to its earnings growth rate. MarketPlayer computes P/E with a different twist. They believe analysts' future earnings forecasts are a better predictor of stock prices than historical earnings, so they use the forecast of the next four quarters' earnings to calculate P/E.

MarketPlayer adds a refinement to the usual fair value search by filtering out companies with declining earnings growth rate forecasts and limiting the search to the 1,000 largest companies in the stock market (the Russell 1000 Index).

I usually come up with too many companies to analyze when I run this screen. I use P/E to cut the list down, specifying a range of 18 to 36. That's adjusted from the 20 to 40 range I typically prefer, because MarketPlayer calculates P/E using forecast instead of historical earnings. I don't fiddle with the screening program to do this. I print the list and cross off the out-of-range companies with a pencil.

IBD New 52-Week High on Big Volume

Investor's Business Daily (IBD) is a daily stock market newspaper that caters to momentum investors who look for stocks with strong relative strength and powerful earnings growth. It's no wonder, since IBD's publisher, William J. O'Neil, authored *How to Make Money in Stocks,* a best-selling book describing momentum strategies. One of IBD's most popular features is its list of stocks breaking out to new 52-week highs on higher than normal trading volume (number of shares traded daily). Technical analysts, or chartists, are investors who believe everything they need to know about a company is imbedded in its stock price chart. Many of them consider a stock breaking out on higher than normal volume sufficient reason to buy a stock. This screen saves them the price of a subscription.

IBD New 52-Week High Plus Strong Earnings Growth Screen

O'Neil's strategy puts a lot of emphasis on long-term consistent earnings growth, and recent increases in analysts' earnings forecasts. This screen looks for stocks meeting these requirements while making new 52-week highs, but it doesn't look for high volume.

Warren Buffett Stable Growth Screen

Warren Buffett became famous by picking undervalued companies capable of long-term growth, and then holding the stocks for many years. MarketPlayer's Warren Buffett Stable Growth Screen attempts to mimic Buffett's thinking when he purchased Coca-Cola back in 1988, using indicators reflecting stable earnings growth, return-on-equity, debt, and price-to-book ratios.

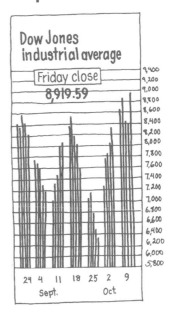

Gary Smith's Short Selling Screen

You sell stocks short when you think the stock is going to drop in price. This screen finds stocks to ride down with for a week or two, and then get out. It looks for stocks in the top half of their two-year price range that dropped at least $1 yesterday on high volume, and are below their 50-day moving average. Caution—don't try this in a rising market.

Ken Heebner High Growth Screen

Ken Heebner is an aggressive growth–style mutual fund manager with a reputation for spotting stocks poised for major price increases. The screen looks for stocks with rapid earnings growth, rising analysts' earning forecasts, and rising P/E ratios. MarketPlayer has done a lot of backtesting on this screen and they say stocks selected using the screen considerably outperform the market, especially during the first year after selection.

Low Price/Normalized Earnings Screen

Looks for beaten-down stocks with low expectations from market analysts. The stock price must be in the bottom half of a

two-year trading range, and earnings beginning to increase. This formula should turn up stocks with low downside risks.

Low P/Book, Div Yld, P/Sales Screen

This screen searches for companies with stock price-to-book value ratios less then 1.0. You could use this screen to find undervalued or out-of-favor companies.

Ridiculously High Valuation Screen

Looks for companies with P/E above 50 based on forecasted earnings, price-to-estimated cash flow ratio greater than 10, and price-to-book ratio exceeding 6.0. It's fun to run, but I'm not sure what to do with the results.

Note: MarketPlayer updates some of their databases in the evenings. You're greeted with a "Server Unavailable, Please Try Again Later" message when you access the site during these updates.

WALL STREET CITY

(*www.wallstreetcity.com* > (ProSearch > Custom Searches Complete Search List (under Stocks))

Telescan, operator of Wall Street City, has been in the business of developing screening tools using both fundamental and technical data for many years. Over time they've accumulated an impressive arsenal of search indicators. They've combined many of these indicators into a library of prebuilt searches.

Each prebuilt search gives you a list of the 25 stocks best meeting the search requirements. In addition to the 25 top matches, the program displays historical results going back one year. The historical display shows you how you would have done if you had bought all 25 listed companies at the beginning of each month and sold them the day you ran the current search. You can run searches for the 25 micro-cap, small-cap, mid-cap, or large-cap stocks or stocks of any size best meeting the screen requirements.

This is important information if you use it correctly. Since the search only comes up with 25 stocks, one outperformer can skew the results. For instance, the historical results would show

40 percent return if 24 stocks returned zero, and the 25th stock went up 1,000 percent. Look for screens showing steadily increasing historical returns over the 12 months, and consistent results between the different market capitalizations.

Some of the searches are worthwhile, and others, though sounding good in theory, don't work in the real world. All of the prebuilt searches require a minimum $5 share price.

The searches are organized into categories: stocks with reversal potential; strong stocks, undervalued stocks, insider, institutions and short interest, searching using earnings criteria, weak stocks, over-valued stocks, and cash flow. Here's my take on the categories and the searches I've found to be of most value.

Stocks with Reversal Potential Searches

These searches look for historically strong stocks that are currently underperforming, meaning their stocks prices are below their long-term trend line.

Some analysts believe a stock price tends to hover around its long-term trend line. If it's above the line, it's likely to drop down to the line, and if it's below, move up to the line. The concept works best if the stock has a long history—at least five years, and ideally, 10. Of course, there's no reason to believe all stocks perform this way. Some stocks, such as the proverbial buggy whip maker, will never return to their former growth pattern.

Projected Growth Stocks is the best screen in the category. It looks for beaten down stocks with high earnings growth forecasts. Don't expect to find dot.com companies here, though, the search requires 10 years' history.

High Earnings Growth 1 is a similar search. It looks for beaten-down stocks with superior price growth over 10 years combined with high five-year earnings growth forecasts.

The difference between the two screens is that Projected Growth Stocks puts the most emphasis on high earnings forecasts, while High Earnings Growth 1 puts as much weight on long-term stock price appreciation as it does forecast earnings growth.

Backtesting

Backtesting can save you big bucks. Say you've come up with a stock selection strategy you're convinced will yield all winning stocks. Backtesting allows someone to go back in time and see how the stocks selected by a particular strategy have performed over time.

DEFINITION PLEASE

Insider Ownership: Number of shares owned or controlled by insiders.

Insider Trading: Shares bought and sold by company insiders. It's legal as long as they follow the SEC's reporting requirements.

Short Interest: Number of shares borrowed by short sellers.

Short-Interest Ratio: Number of days it would take to cover short interest at average daily volume (short interest divided by average daily volume).

Rank Searches

Wall Street City combines indicators from the same category into super-indicators called "ranks." For instance, fundamental rank combines balance sheet indicators current ratio, debt-to-equity ratio, interest coverage, cash flow growth, and cash-to-price ratio.

Strong Long-Term Growth screen looks for high values of Long-Term Growth rank and high volume. Long-Term Growth rank combines strong historical sales, earnings, and cash flow growth, with strong earnings growth forecasts.

Rank with Short-Term Strength puts most emphasis on recent increases in earnings forecasts and recent positive earnings surprises.

Strong Stock Searches

These are stocks with high Relative Performance, Wall Street City's version of relative strength, a measure of a stock's price appreciation compared to the entire market. High relative strength is an important component of momentum strategies, including William J. O'Neil's CANSLIM system.

High Volume with Earnings Upgrades looks for stocks with high and increasing trading volume, increasing current fiscal year earnings forecasts, and high short-term relative strength. By short-term, I mean really short—this screen looks at stock price moves within the past six weeks, with emphasis on the most recent week.

Undervalued Stock Searches

A mixture of searches looking for beaten down stocks, similar to Potential Reversals, and for stocks with low valuation ratios such as price/earnings, price/sales, and price/book. None of these value selection strategies have worked in recent years.

Insider, Institutions, and Short Interest Searches

This section includes searches based on indicators of investor interest in a stock including insider buying, high short interest ratio, and low institutional ownership. None of these factors by themselves produce worthwhile candidates.

Searching Using Earnings Criteria

In the long run, earnings, or more specifically, future earnings expectations, are the engine that moves stock prices. Three of Wall Street City's best searches are in this group.

Positive Revision in Projected Earnings screen looks for companies with the highest increases in current fiscal year earnings forecasts within the past month. Increasing earnings forecasts often lead to rising stock prices.

Attractive Gross Margin screens for companies with rapidly increasing sales, earnings, gross profit margins, and analysts' earnings forecasts. All of these are important indicators of price appreciation potential.

Great Earnings, Sales, C.F. Growth looks for strong historical earnings, sales, and cash flow growth, earnings growth consistency, and strong forecast earnings growth. These are all important factors, and this screen is as good as screens get for searching out growth stock candidates. However, it will only find companies with at least a five-year track record.

Weak Stocks and Overvalued Stocks Searches

Screens for finding stock shorting candidates. None of them appear to work.

Cash Flow Searches

Cash flow is a measure of a company's cash earnings before deductions for depreciation and similar factors.

Exc. Free C.F./Share, Good Growth looks for companies with high cash flow, high historical earnings growth, and high projected earnings growth, all desirable qualities. This screen produces excellent investment candidates

MSN MONEYCENTRAL STOCK FINDER

(*moneycentral.msn.com* > Investor > Investment Finder > Stock Finder)

Microsoft offers two general categories of prebuilt screens: Stock Finder and Supermodels. The difference is subtle but important. Stock Finder searches use prebuilt screens, some simple, some

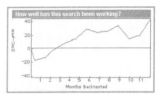

Wall Street City shows you how much money you would have made or lost buying the top 25 stocks turned up by their searches.

based on universally accepted investment principals, and some styled after a particular guru's stock-picking strategy. Stock Finder searches result in a list of candidates for further research. Supermodels are portfolios resulting from backtested and highly refined screens. They're intended to be purchased as a group and held for a predetermined period. See Chapter 7 for details.

Stock Finder searches are divided into two categories: Basic Searches and Advanced Stock Searches.

Basic Searches

As the name says, these are simple searches intended to provide quick idea lists.

- **Large-, Mid-, and Small-Cap Stocks with High Momentum.** These screens list the stocks in each market cap category that have gone up the most in the past three months.
- **Cheapest Stocks of Large, Growing Companies** looks for large-cap companies with low P/E and price/sales ratios with earnings growth of at least 20 percent per year.
- **Highest-Yielding Stocks in the S&P 500** applies the Dogs of the Dow approach to stocks making up the S&P 500 index. Contrarian, or value investors, often use high-dividend yield to find candidates for further research. Don't even think of buying stocks on this list before finding out why their dividend yields are so high.
- **Dogs of the Dow, Investor-Style** modifies the classic Dogs of the Dow (Chapter 7) stock selection strategy by looking for low P/E ratios in addition to highest dividend yields. Microsoft doesn't offer a comparison of the results obtained by this approach to the standard Dogs.

Advanced Stock Searches

Advanced Searches emulate widely used investment strategies or particular guru stock-picking styles. Here are the most promising of the bunch.

- **Distressed Stock Plays** looks for companies with growing sales and earnings, and with stock prices currently moving up but near their 52-week lows. This screen sounds like a good way to find value candidates for further research.
- **Estimated Earnings Up** is an earnings momentum screen looking for companies with already high but increasing earnings growth. Sounds like a good source for finding winners to me.
- **GARP Go-Getters** looks for value-priced small-caps with good financial ratios. Small-cap value stocks have been in the doghouse recently.
- **Great Expectations** is another small-cap value screen looking for companies with solid financials and high return on equity.
- **O'Shaughnessy Growth Stocks** creates a portfolio of 10 stocks to hold for one year. The screen looks for value-priced companies with high projected earnings growth.
- **Righteous Rockets** looks for value-priced companies with strong recent stock price appreciation during the past year. A good strategy for finding promising value candidates.
- **SAPI Slugs** applies the Dogs of the Dow dividend yield approach to the S&P 500 index.

Custom Screens

The other kind of stock-screening program is the type you customize to suit your needs.

Here's an example of how to design a custom screen. Say you want a list of value-priced, mid-size companies with consistent earnings growth.

- **To define value-priced:** Price/Earnings (P/E), Price/Sales (P/S), and Price/Book (P/B) ratios are commonly used to quantify a stock's current valuation. Definitions vary, but typical measures to define value-priced stocks would be: P/E less than 20, P/S less than 2, and P/B less than 2.

DEFINITION PLEASE

Dogs of the Dow: A contrarian stock selection strategy based upon buying the cheapest stocks of the Dow Jones Industrial Average.

Yield: Interest and dividends paid to mutual fund shareholders as a percentage of share price (Net Asset Value). Also, the effective interest rate on a bond. For instance, if a bond pays $1.00 interest annually and is selling for $10.00, the yield is (1.00/10.00) 10 percent.

- **To define mid-size:** Market capitalization (shares outstanding multiplied by stock price) is a gauge of company size. Specifying market cap greater than $2 billion and less than $8 billion would fit most analysts' definition of a midsize company.
- **To define consistent earnings growth:** Five-year average annual earnings growth is a good tool for eliminating stocks with inconsistent or nonexistent earnings growth. Requiring 15 percent, five-year growth would do the trick.

You'll plug these variables into your custom screen and then you're ready to search. Later you can fine-tune your search by adding further requirements.

Most custom screening programs operate in similar ways, and most provide similar sets of search parameters. Hoover's Stock Screener is typical of many screening programs.

Hoover's StockScreener is a quick and easy search program.

HOOVER'S STOCKSCREENER *(www.stockscreen.com)*

StockScreener, part of Hoover's online site, is a versatile and easy to use screening program. Hoover's Online is in the business of collecting and distributing detailed information on individual companies and on industry sectors. Much of the information on Hoover's site requires a subscription, but use of their StockScreener is free.

StockScreener offers 22 different screening variables, but you don't have to use all of them, just leave the ones you don't care about blank and the program will ignore them.

Let's take an example. Say you want to find fast-growing companies in the business of making equipment for companies in the red-hot telecommunications field. Here's how you do it:

Exchange

You can limit your search to stocks listed on the New York (NYSE), American (AMEX), NASDAQ (NASD National Market), or NASDAQ Small Cap (NASD Small Cap) stock exchanges. Click on an exchange name if you want to limit your search to stocks listed there, or look for companies listed on any of them (All Exchanges). The selected exchange will appear in the window. There is no advantage to selecting a particular exchange, so you're better off leaving the selection set to the All Exchanges default value for this search.

Industry Group

Skip this selection if you're not looking for companies in a specific industry. Since you have a specific telecommunications industry in mind, open the dropdown menu and scroll down until you see Telecommunications (All). That would be a good choice, but for this example, further hone your search selections by selecting the Communications Equipment subcategory.

Ratios

This category contains valuation measures such as price-to-earnings and price-to-sales ratios and financial health metrics such as debt-to-equity and current ratios.

- **Current P/E** is the most recent closing price divided by the earnings/share for the last four quarters. The average P/E of all stocks making up the S&P 500 index is about 32. I usually look for companies in the 20–40 P/E range. I figure companies with P/Es below 20 most likely have problems, and above 40 implies high risk.

- **Price/Growth Rate** is a misleading label. This is where you enter values for the PEG (P/E divided by the earnings growth). Unfortunately, Hoover's StockScreener uses historical growth instead of forecast future earnings growth, which is typically used. That's a problem, especially in this case, because many high-tech companies make frequent acquisitions resulting in charges that distort their reported earnings. I suggest leaving this section blank. If you weren't looking for high-tech stocks, you could use Hoover's PEG (see sidebar). If you use PEG, I suggest a range of 1.2 to 2.0.

- **Price/Revenue** is the ratio of the current stock price to the company's sales per share for the most recently reported four quarters. Notice that the words sales and revenues are interchanged; they mean exactly the same thing. Price/sales ratio is a better measure of value than P/E. Stocks with P/S less than 2.0 are considered value stocks, companies with P/S over 10 are momentum stocks, and ratios between 2 and 10 indicate growth stocks. Since you're looking for growth, specify a P/S range of 2.0 to 10.0. (These

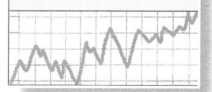

price/sales ranges for value, growth, and momentum are my estimates, you might specify different values)

- **Debt/Equity Ratio** compares a company's long-term debt to the shareholder's equity, a bookkeeping term meaning the difference between a corporation's assets and liabilities. Shareholder's equity when expressed on a per-share basis (equity/number of shares) is called book value. Some investors prefer companies with low debt to equity ratios because that signifies they are not burdened by high debt that could hurt future performance, especially in periods of rising interest rates. In reality, acceptable debt levels vary from industry to industry, and they're typically not a factor in high-tech stocks. I suggest leaving the debt/equity ratios blank.

- **Price/Book Value** compares the stock price to the book value. P/B is often used to distinguish between value and growth stocks. Stocks with lower P/B are value, and those with higher P/B are considered growth stocks. Some value investors are attracted to companies with a P/B less than 1.0, figuring they're getting the company below its asset value. In practice, except for banks and the like, book value may be unrelated to the real asset value. I suggest leaving P/B selections blank.

- **Current Ratio** compares a company's current assets (cash, receivables and inventories) to its short-term (due within one year) debt. This is an important measure of a company's financial health. If it owes more cash than it has, it's going to have to get more, and real soon. That can be bad for shareholders. Specify a minimum current ratio of 1.5 and leave the maximum box blank.

Company Size

- **Latest 12 Months' Revenue** is the total company sales over the last four quarters in millions of dollars. I never know what to enter here, so I usually leave the space blank. If you decide to use it, don't use commas. For instance, enter $1 billion as 1000 (as in millions).

- **Market Value** is more commonly labeled market capitalization. It's calculated by multiplying the latest stock price by the number of shares outstanding. For instance, a company with 20 million shares out and a $10 stock price has a market capitalization of $200 million. Companies with market caps of less than $2 billion are considered small caps, those with market caps over $8 billion are large caps, and in between are mid-caps. Small cap stocks are more volatile than larger companies. Specify a minimum $2 billion market cap if you want to avoid small-cap risk. Type that in as 2000 because the size is expressed in millions and StockScreener doesn't like commas.

Margins

- **Profit Margin** is the bottom-line, after-tax net income divided by total sales. You want profitable companies, but net income can be influenced by onetime charges related to acquisitions, inventory write-offs, or what have you. You don't want to eliminate companies with losses related to onetime events at this stage, so I suggest leaving this section blank.
- **Operating Margin** is the income from the company's basic business, such as building and marketing Internet servers, baking bread, manufacturing shoes, etc. Making money is important, but typical operating margins vary by industry. Normally, I'd specify a low number, say 5 percent as a minimum. However, telecommunication equipment manufacturers ought to do better. Specify 20 percent minimum.

Growth Rates

- **One-Year Revenue** is a company's sales growth for the last four quarters compared to the same year-ago quarters. This is the *most important factor* when searching for growth companies. It's not a growth company if sales aren't growing. More is better. Specify 20 percent minimum and leave the maximum value blank.
- **Five-Year Compounded Average Earnings** is the five-year compounded earnings growth rate. This gets tricky, since you'll eliminate all companies that haven't been around at least five years if you enter a value for five-year growth. Consistent earnings growth is a desirable characteristic in

PEG

PEG is shorthand for price-to-earnings ratio (P/E) compared to a company's earnings growth rate. A common definition of "fair value" is when the P/E and growth rate are equal. A stock is said to be overvalued when the P/E exceeds the growth rate, and undervalued when the growth rate is greater than the P/E. In this context, earnings growth typically means analysts' predicted annual earnings growth over the next three to five years. The P/E is usually calculated by dividing the current stock price by the last four quarters' per-share earnings.

A PEG of 1 is considered fair value, but in the 2000 market, any decent growth company is overvalued by that measure. In my experience, growth companies with low PEGs are likely to have festering problems that will become evident the day after I buy the stock. I've found PEGs of 1.2 to 2.0 work best.

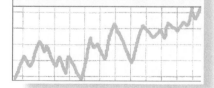

DEFINITION PLEASE

Beta: Compares a mutual fund or stock's volatility to a benchmark (usually the S&P 500 Index). A beta greater than 1 is more volatile than the index. For instance, a beta of 1.5 means the fund or stock is historically 50 percent more volatile than the index.

Dividend Yield: The annual dividend paid divided by the latest share price.

many instances, but you may not want to exclude younger companies. If you don't, leave the space blank. Enter 15 percent minimum if you are looking for established growth companies.

- **One-Year Earnings** is the percent earnings growth in the latest four quarters compared to the year-ago four quarters. Earnings growth is what drives stock prices up. Specify a minimum of 20 percent.
- **Five-Year Compounded Average Operating Margin** is the five-year average annual growth in a company's operating margin. Operating margin is calculated by dividing a company's operating profit by its sales. You'd like to see operating margins increase while you own the stock. However, what happened during the past five years doesn't predict the future. Leave it blank.
- **Five-Year Compounded Average Revenue** is the company's average annual sales growth over the past five years. As with five-year earnings growth, you'll exclude younger companies if you specify anything here. Leave it blank if you don't want to exclude younger companies, otherwise, require 15 percent minimum.
- **Five-Year Compounded Stock Price** is the average annual appreciation of the stock price over the past five years. History may repeat itself, but not for the same stock. Leave this section blank.

Rates of Return

- **ROE** is return on equity, a company's bottom line profits divided by stockholders equity (per-share earnings/book value). ROE is considered by many to be a measure of management performance. Specifying a positive ROE means you'll eliminate companies with recent earnings losses. Acquisition-minded companies often show acquisition related losses. If you want to specify ROE, use 15 percent minimum.
- **Five-Year Total Compound Return** measures the average annual appreciation of the stock price over the past five years, plus dividends paid during that time. It's better to own

stocks that appreciate while you own them, not before. Leave this section blank.

- **Dividend Yield** is the current annual dividend divided by the current stock price. Dividends aren't a factor when you're looking for technology stocks, because most don't pay dividends. Dividend yield would be important if you are looking for real estate investment trusts (REITs) or utilities.

Volatility

- **Beta (vs. SPX)** measures a company's *historical* stock price movement compared to the S&P 500 index. A stock with a beta of 2.0 is twice as volatile as the index, while a beta of 1.0 means it's exactly as volatile as the S&P 500. A beta of 0.5 means the stock was less volatile than the index. The idea is, high beta stocks will go up more in a strong market, and down faster in a weak market. Low beta stocks are supposedly less risky, but you don't make as much money. This is all true if you could go back in time to do your investing. Otherwise it's all for naught. Leave this blank.

Search

Push the "Go" button next to "Reset" when you're satisfied with your selections. StockScreener will search its database for companies meeting your criteria. You'll probably get too many—or too few—results. For the sake of learning the various variables, this time you entered all of the screening parameters before running the screen. Actually, it's better to enter only one or two at a time and then run the program to see how many companies meet your requirements. Then you can adjust your criteria if you're getting too few or too many companies.

Also, you probably won't like the selection of companies resulting from your first screen. If so, figure out how to modify your screening rules to get better results. There's a lot of trial and error involved in customizing a screening search.

**Best Investment
Sites for Industry
Sector Analysis**

Big Charts

(*www.bigcharts.com*): Lists the 10 best- and 10 worst-performing industries for time spans ranging from one week to five years.

Briefing.com via E*Trade

(*www.etrade.com*): Analysis of selected industry sectors. You have to pay to see this information on Briefing.com's own site, but it's free on E*Trade. Go to Markets, then Analysis & Commentary, and finally Sector Ratings. A must-read!

Equity Trader

(*www.equitytrader.com*): John Bollinger's Group Power formula is used to rank industry groups.

**Money Central's
Top 10 Industries**

(*moneycentral.msn.com*): List

(continued on next page)

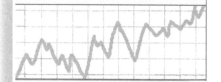

QUICKEN'S FULL SEARCH

(*www.quicken.com* > Investing > Screen Stocks > Full Search)

Quicken, the popular personal finance program, has a Web site in which a full search is nicely laid out and easy to use. Quicken gives you the choice of selecting parameter values from dropdown menus or typing in your own values. Special features include:

- **Multiple Industry Classes:** With this option you can search as many industry categories as you like. For instance, you might want to search in both the Communications Equipment and Computers—Networking classifications. Hold down the Control key (Ctrl) on your keyboard when you click on industry names to select multiple categories.

- **Three-Year EPS Growth/Revenue Growth:** With this menu choice, you can search on three-year sales and earnings growth—as opposed to the one- and five-year parameters available in StockScreener. Using the five-year parameters in StockScreener eliminates younger companies. Requiring consistent three-year sales and earnings growth of at least 20 percent, especially for technology companies, makes sense to me.

- **Revenue/Employee & Income/Employee:** These are the company's total sales, or total earnings, divided by the number of employees. Companies with higher ratios are said to be more efficient.

- **Quick Ratio:** Ratio of total of cash and cash equivalents, divided by current liabilities. This is a more stringent test than Current Ratio in StockScreener, which adds inventories and accounts receivable to cash before dividing by current liabilities.

- **Long-Term Debt/Assets (LTD/Assets):** Compares a company's debt to assets instead of shareholders' equity used in the debt/equity ratio. It's said to be a better gauge, because of the inaccuracies inherent in the shareholder's equity figure.

- **Must Be Within __% of 52-Week High/Low:** If you're a bottom fisher, that is, someone who looks for beaten-down stocks, you'll be searching for stocks close to their lows, say within 20 percent of its 52-week low. Momentum players want stocks near their highs, so they might specify within 10 percent of 52-week high.

- **% Held by Institutions:** This is the percentage of shares available for trading owned by mutual funds and other institutional buyers. See Chapter 8 to learn how to use institutional ownership.

Click on "Show Results" to run your search. You can change the information displayed, and the order of company listings, using the Display and Sort dropdown windows at the top. You don't have to rerun the search to change the display, simply click "Show."

STOCK POINT STOCKFINDER PRO

(*www.stockpoint.com* > Investing Tools > Stockfinder Pro)

The Stockfinder Pro is an easy to use screening program offering 30 screening variables. As with Quicken's stock screener, you can select more than one industry for each screen. You can program the screen yourself, or select from eight prebuilt screens, including blue chip stocks, strong growth, and insider ownership.

Stock Point provides some interesting additional parameters beyond those listed above.

Price Data

- **Price 12-Month Low/High:** With this variable, you can search for specific ranges of 12-month high or 12-month low stock prices. The search looks for intraday highs or lows, not closing prices.

- **Price 4-Week, 13-Week, 26-Week, and 52-Week Change %:** Shows percentage change in price over the designated period. You could use these to pinpoint stocks in strong long-term uptrends (for example, Price 52-Week Change minimum 100 percent), but short-term consolidation (for example, Price 4-Week Change minimum 15 percent), and close to its 52-week high (percent below 12-Month High minimum 5 percent, maximum 10 percent). This is similar to the pattern detected by Microsoft's very successful Flare-Out Growth screen (discussed in Chapter 7).

Best Investment Sites for Industry Sector Analysis

(*continued from previous page*)

of 10 best- and worst-performing industry groups over the past month.

Smart Money Sector Tracker (*www.smartmoney.com*): Visually compelling display of industry sector performance.

Stovall's Sector Watch (*www.personalwealth.com*): Weekly commentaries on sectors coming into, or passing out of, favor.

Wall Street City's Best & Worst Industry Groups (*www.wallstreetcity.com*): An excellent display of industry sectors ranked by relative strength over a variety of user-selectable time frames. A powerful tool for finding the hottest stocks in the hottest industries.

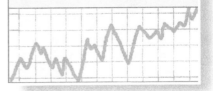

Risk Data

- **Insider Shares Purchased:** Number of shares purchased by insiders within the past six months.
- **% Insider Ownership & % Institutional Ownership:** This is the easiest-to-use screen I've seen with an insider ownership parameter. Insider ownership is the percentage of a company's outstanding shares owned by officers, directors, and certain other large shareholders.
- **Short Interest Ratio:** Short interest expressed as number of days outstanding (see Chapter 2 for an explanation of short interest).

Size/Capitalization

- **Number of Employees:** The number of full-time employees.
- **Average Monthly Volume:** Average number of shares traded monthly, expressed in millions, computed over the past three months. Limit your searches to stocks trading at least one million shares monthly to avoid problems with illiquid stocks.

Stockfinder Pro responds quickly to a search, but limits the output list to 100 stocks. You can sort the list or export it, but strangely, you can't print it out.

FINANCIAL WEB

(*www.financialweb.com* > Stocks > Super Screener)

Financial Web's Super Screener includes the typical assortment of screening parameters plus:

- **Daily Trading Range:** Average range between daily high and low trading price for the last 20 days.
- **One-Year, Three-Year, and Five-Year Total Return:** Stock price percentage appreciation over these periods of years.
- **Five-Year Dividend Growth:** Average annual percentage increase in dividend payouts.
- **P/E, P/B, and Profit Margin to Industry:** Comparison of valuation ratios and profit margins to the industry average.

- You can also screen stocks to be within a specified percentage of their 52-week high or low.

CNBC ADVANCED SEARCH

(*www.cnbc.com* > Stocks > Stock Screener > Advanced Search)

CNBC's Advanced Search is a condensed version of a screening tool available on Telescan's Wall Street City (*www.wallstreetcity.com*). You have to pay to use the full version on Wall Street City, but CNBC's version is free. Because it's condensed doesn't mean it's a lightweight. There are plenty of parameters to do just about anything you want. CNBC refers to screening variables as indicators.

The CNBC screener offers a mix of fundamental, technical, and momentum indicators—82 in all.

Indicators

- **Analysts' Forecasts and Recommendations:** Average (mean) of analysts' buy/hold/sell recommendations, forecast earnings percentage growth (Proj EPS), changes in earnings forecasts, and earnings surprises (EPS Surprise). Strong earnings projected growth combined with positive changes in analysts' earnings forecasts, is an important driver of stock price appreciation. Negative changes in earnings forecasts often move share prices down.

- **Sales, Earnings & Dividends:** Latest earnings (EPS Earnings/Share), historical earnings growth (EPS Growth), consistency of earnings growth (EPS Consistency), dividend consistency, yield, and growth, and historical sales growth (sales growth). The market often rewards stocks with consistent and robust historical earnings and sales growth with above-average valuations.

- **Fundamental:** Cash flow growth, debt (Debt/Equity Ratio), debt interest coverage (Interest Coverage), gross profit margin, market capitalization, profit measures (Return on Assets, Return on Equity, and Return on Sales), management effectiveness (Turnover-Assets, Turnover-Inventory, and Turnover-Receivable). A growing number of market experts consider cash flow growth and profit margins important gauges of a company's future prospects.

- **Valuation Measures:** P/E ratio, P/E based on forecast earnings (P/E Projected), price/cash flow, price/book, and price/sales ratios, and cash on hand/stock price (cash/price). All valuation measures

Microsoft's MoneyCentral

(*moneycentral.msn.com* > Investor-Stock Finder under Investment Finder > Custom Search)

MoneyCentral's Custom Search program offers a wide assortment of search criteria, probably as many as any program on the Web. What's more, you can compare criteria. For instance, whether the P/E ratio is lower now than it was six months ago or the income per employee is greater than the industry average.

Microsoft hasn't done much to make their search user-friendly. For instance, there's no list of available search criteria, you have to find them one by one, by selecting them when constructing a search. But this isn't an insurmountable problem, you just have to be willing to spend some time getting familiar with the program.

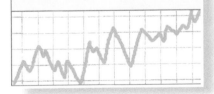

are problematical, but I consider P/E ratios based on forecast earnings, and price/sales ratios the most reliable. Value investors often rely on price/cash flow (less than 10 is considered value priced).

- **Technical Analysis:** Widely followed indicators include moving average breakouts (stocks moving above or below their moving averages) and relative performance (strong or weak recent price action) and volume ratios (stocks with higher than normal trading volume). A popular technical analysis strategy is to look for stocks breaking out above their moving average on higher than normal trading volume.
- **Miscellaneous:** Insider trading, institutional holdings, and short interest ratio (see Chapter 8). Institutional holdings include stock owned by mutual funds, pension plans, and the like. Look for a minimum of 40 percent institutional ownership.

There's not room here to describe all of the indicators on CNBC's stock screener. You can click on each indicator name to display a definition and a short explanation of how they're used.

Using the Indicators

If you don't want to use an indicator, leave all entries blank. Type in a minimum and/or maximum value, or select High as Possible, Low as Possible, or Display Only for indicators you do want to use.

High as possible means the screener will search for stocks with the highest values for the indicator. You can select High as Possible, and also specify a maximum or minimum value. For instance, say you want to search for companies with the highest earnings growth during the past year (EPS Growth One Year), but you don't want to see companies with less than 25 percent growth. You would type 25 into the Minimum column, and select High as Possible.

Display Only displays the indicator value in the results, but the indicator is not used in the search.

Viewing the Results

Push the "Search Now" button at the bottom of the screen to run the search. When the search is completed, the program displays:

- The 25 top stocks currently meeting your requirements.

- Your screening criteria
- Backtested results for the search. The backtest shows how much money you would have made or lost if you had run the screen at the beginning of each month, for the past 12 months, bought all 25 stocks listed by the screen, and sold them the day you ran the screen.

You can print out the list, and you can also expand the table to see the values of all the indicators you used in the search.

EQUITY INSIGHTS
(*www.equityinsights.com* > Market Tools > Screens > New)

The Equity Insights screening program is a fundamental investors' dream come true. Equity Insights uses sophisticated tools developed by their parent company, Applied Finance Group, to analyze a company's financial statements and other fundamental factors. Unlike Morningstar and other sites evaluating fundamentals based on historical results, Equity Insights incorporates forecasts of future cash flow and other fundamentals into their analysis. See chapter 13 for more information on Equity Insight's analysis methods.

It's tricky to find the screening program on the Equity Insight site. Select Market Tools and then click Screens, and finally, click on "New."

Economic Margin (EM)

Equity Insights says their Economic Margin (EM) indicator measures a firm's "true economic profitability." They say it corrects for distortions caused by inflation and arbitrary decisions related to accounting for depreciation, R&D expenses, depreciation charges, and the like. Negative or declining values of EM are considered a red flag signaling future problems.

Equity Insights recommends using the EM Change and Momentum variables to find companies with improving or deteriorating fundamentals.

Here's a partial description of screening variables unique to Equity Insights, along with some of their variables with obscure or misleading definitions.

- **Industry:** Equity Insights has their own unique industry definitions. Nowhere else would you be able to select Bike Manufacturers, Cosmetics, Cutlery & Tools, or Sawmills. Another

DEFINITION PLEASE

Price-to-Book Ratio (P/B): Latest share price divided by book value stated in latest report.

Price-to-Earnings Ratio (P/E): Latest share price divided by 12-month earnings per share (eps). Also a measure of the market's enthusiasm for a company.

interesting feature is you can select industries to be excluded from your search.

- **Shareholder Value:** This section includes most of Equity Insights proprietary measures.
- **Value Score:** Compares Equity Insights calculated fundamental value to the current stock price. The range is 0 to 100, where the most overpriced stocks in their database score 0 and the most underpriced score 100.
- **Accuracy:** Measures the accuracy of Equity Insights' fundamental intrinsic value indicator for predicting share prices for a stock over the past seven years. The range is 0 to 100, where 100 is the most accurate. Equity Insights recommends specifying a minimum value of 70.
- **EM +1yr:** Screening variable names couldn't get more obscure than this. The "+1yr" designates current fiscal year. EM can have positive or negative values and the maximum range is undefined. Generally higher is better for EM, but the trend is more important than the actual value. You'll probably want to set a minimum value depending on the change you specify in the next parameter (forecast change in EM). For instance, you could select a minimum value here of 5, and a minimum change of 1, or a minimum here of 40, and a minimum change of 8.
- **EM Chg +1yr:** The forecast change in EM from last year to the current fiscal year. Equity Insights says this along with EM Chg +2yr (forecasts change in EM from current to next fiscal year) are the most important factors in picking winning stocks. Experiment with minimum values of say, 20, for each.
- **EM Mon. +1yr:** Change in the current fiscal year's forecast EM compared to the value last month. Equity Insights says "it is potentially a very powerful leading indicator of sustainable future trends in EM."
- **EM +2yr:** Next fiscal year's projected value for EM.
- **EM Chg +2yr:** The forecast change in EM from the current to the next fiscal year.
- **EM Mon. + 2yr:** The change in next fiscal year's forecast EM compared to the value last month.

ANALYST INFORMATION

- **EPS +1:** This fiscal year's forecast earnings.
- **EPS +1 4 Wk Chg:** Change in this year's forecast earnings over the past four weeks.
- **EPS +1 12 Wk Chg:** Change in forecast earnings over the past 12 weeks.
- **EPS +2:** Next fiscal year's forecast earnings.

PRICE MULTIPLES

- **Price/EBIDTA:** Basically price to operating cash flow ratio.

PRICE MOMENTUM

This is one of few sites providing for relative strength screening:

- **Price Chg:** Percentage change in stock price. Periods include 1 day, 5 days, 20 days, and 60 days.
- **Rel Strength:** Change in stock price compared to change in S&P 500. Periods include 5 days, 20 days, 60 days, and 120 days.

The analysts' earnings forecasts, and particularly the change in forecasts, combined with relative strength are momentum investors' favorite search tools.

Best Investment Sites for IPOs (Initial Public Offerings)

IPO.com (*www.ipo.com*) and **Ostman's Alert IPO** (*www.ostman.com*): Both are good sources of information on recent and upcoming IPOs.

Red Herring's Street Poll (*www.redherring.com*): The Street Poll gauges which IPOs are hot, and which are not.

Technical Analysis Screens

Technical analysts (chartists) don't care about fundamental factors such as sales, earnings, cash flow, and so forth. Instead, they analyze a stock's price and volume history as shown on the price charts to make buy and sell decisions.

Most technical analysts use computer-generated technical indicators to help them make buy or sell decisions. The best place to find a complete description of practically all technical indicators in use today is the Equis site (*www.equis.com*). From their main page, select Free Stuff and then click on "Technical Analysis From A to Z."

Screening based on technical indicators is not nearly as widely available online as fundamental screening sites. Here are two good sites.

INVESTERTECH (*www.investertech.com* > Easy Select)

InvesterTech's Easy Select is anything but "easy" to use. Nevertheless, it provides more technical analysis screening variables than I've seen anywhere. You can search using moving averages, Bollinger Bands, and esoteric variables such as Stochastics, Williams %R, Commodity Channel Indicator, on-balance volume, and more.

SILICON INVESTOR
(*www.siliconinvestor.com* > Market Tools > Stock Screener from dropdown menu > Advanced Screen)

The Advanced Screener takes some looking to find. Select Market Tools on the dropdown menu on the top right, then click on Advanced Screener.

Silicon Investor's Advanced Screen includes a good assortment of fundamental screening variables including sales and earnings growth, valuation ratios, management effectiveness measures, dividends, and so forth. What's unusual is their selection of price and technical analysis criteria. You can search for stocks closing within user-selected percentages of its 40-day, 6-month, or 52-week highs or lows.

You can also screen for stocks crossing above or below their 40-day, 6-month, or 52-week highs or lows. Detecting stocks crossing above recent highs is an important element of many momentum stock selection strategies. There's more! You can limit your results based on values of: RSI, Stochastics, Momentum, CCI, MACD, OBV, DMI, Williams %R, and the Ultimate Oscillator. There's more! You can limit your screen results based on the values of a variety of technical indicators. Click on "How Stock Screener Works" for an explanation of the technical indicators and suggestions on screening values.

CHAPTER SEVEN

Selection Strategies: Models

Many people spend hours if not days researching and analyzing each stock they're considering buying. Others say it's a waste of time, even counterproductive, to analyze financial statements and company reports. They contend you'll do a lot better by looking at historical results and isolating the factors common to the best-performing stocks. Then all you have to do is find stocks in the current market with the same qualities, and you're on your way.

These selection systems are often called *models,* and the people who make them modelers.

Modelers typically use "backtesting" to develop their strategies. Backtesting involves going back in time and picking stocks according to the strategy the modeler is testing, and observing how the selected stocks performed over a selected time span, say six months or a year.

Modelers typically test a multitude of parameter values and combinations, over varying time spans and market conditions, to find the combination producing the best results. They often end up tailoring or fine-tuning their selection strategies to eliminate rough spots turned up during testing.

Once the selection strategy, or model, is finalized, screening (discussed in Chapter 6) is used to find a current list of stocks to purchase. You're not supposed to analyze the stocks found, or tinker with the results. The model has been shown to work over a variety of market conditions, and cherry picking will only reduce returns. Portfolios selected by these methods often produce a few clunkers, so diversification is necessary. Model portfolios typically contain anywhere from 10 to 50 stocks.

The Cornerstone Growth Strategy

One of my favorite stock market books is James O'Shaughnessy's *What Works on Wall Street,* a summary of results from his exhaustive study of selection strategies. O'Shaughnessy investigated a multitude of strategies based on valuation ratios such as price/earnings, price/book, etc.; fundamental factors such as profit margins, earnings growth, return on equity, dividends, etc.; combinations of different factors, and others.

O'Shaughnessy found the best results were achieved using a combination of price/sales ratio, one-year relative strength, and year-to-year earnings growth. He calls this combination the "Cornerstone Growth" strategy.

According to O'Shaughnessy, the top 50 stocks selected using the Cornerstone Growth selection strategy returned more than 18 percent per year over the 43-year test period, compared to an overall market return of less than 13 percent annually during the same time span. O'Shaughnessy eliminates utilities companies such as power or gas companies from his model.

- **Price/sales ratio** is similar to price/earnings ratio, except the stock price is divided by sales per share instead of earnings per share. Price/sales can be used when companies don't have earnings, making it a handy value gauge in this market. Cornerstone Growth looks for stocks with price/sales ratios of less than 1.5. Companies with price/sales ratios below 2.0 are generally considered value priced.
- **Relative strength** measures a stock's percentage price increase compared to the rest of the market. Stocks with the highest relative strength have the biggest percentage price gains during the previous 12 months.
- **Earnings growth,** the third Cornerstone requirement, simply requires an earnings increase of any size compared to the previous year.

WHY IT WORKS

Stocks with low valuation ratios, such as price/sales below 1.5, are considered out of favor, probably because they missed earnings expectations, botched a new product introduction, or maybe they're a member of an unpopular industry sector.

There could be good reasons why they're out of favor, and being cheap doesn't mean their stock price is necessarily headed up; the stock could stay cheap forever. That's where relative strength comes into play. High relative strength means the stock is already moving up. Probably investors with inside knowledge know the company is recovering and are accumulating the stock before word gets out.

DEFINITION PLEASE

Price-to-Sales Ratio (P/S): Latest share price divided by 12-month sales per share.

Relative Strength: Stock price performance compared to the S&P 500, or to the entire stock market. Can measure performance over any time span, but most often uses 12 months. Relative strength is different from the RSI (Relative Strength Indicator) used in technical analysis.

Best Investment Sites for Insider Trading

Bloomberg's Insider Focus
(*www.bloomberg.com*): Reports on 10 or so companies each day with significant insider trading activity.

CNET Investor
(*investor.cnet.com*):
Lists the 15 companies with the most insider sales and purchases for the previous week.

Insider Trader
(*www.insidertrader.com*): Best source for listings of insider trading activity by company.

Insider Watch
(*www.cda.com/investnet/*):
Home of Bob Gabele's Insider Alert, Daily Watch, and Insider

(continued on next page)

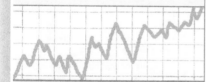

FINDING CORNERSTONE GROWTH STOCKS

The Cornerstone Growth strategy is simple to implement. First, find all stocks with price/sales ratios of 1.5 or less, and with some earnings growth compared to the previous year. From those stocks, select the 50 with the highest 12-month relative strength.

You can use Financial Web's Super Screener (*www.financialweb.com* > Stocks > Tools > Super Screener) to find Cornerstone Growth stocks. Super Screener offers around 30 screening parameters, but you need only four of them:

1. *Trading price:* Super Screener's default setting for the current trading price is $5 to $200. Stocks trading below $5 are considered penny stocks and aren't widely followed by analysts. Stocks without analysts' coverage often don't respond to good news because few investors know about them. Setting a maximum price is a good idea to reduce your capital requirements. I suggest using the default trading price settings.

2. *Price/sales:* Enter 1.5 in the Max column for Price/Revenues (sales and revenues mean the same thing) listed in the Revenues and Ratios section. I like to also require a minimum ratio of 0.01, otherwise you might end up with stocks with negative ratios.

3. *Earnings growth:* Under Growth Rates, enter a minimum 1 year EPS Growth of 1 percent (leave the maximum space blank). One percent isn't much, but O'Shaughnessy simply wants to avoid companies with falling earnings.

4. *Relative strength:* Super Screener's "1-yr total return" in the Growth Rates section can be used as a proxy for relative strength. Total return means stock price appreciation plus dividends. Most stocks' dividend yields run less than two percent. That shouldn't be a factor, since we are going to require 50 percent return. Enter 50 in the Min column for 1-year total return.

To get results: Click "Go" and Super Screener displays a list of the first 20 Cornerstone Growth stocks, listed in alphabetical order. We need the list sorted with the highest relative strength stocks on top, which is easy, just click "Desc" at the top of the Total Return column. You can see additional selections by clicking "Next Page" at the bottom of the list. O'Shaughnessy's strategy calls for buying the first 50 stocks on the sorted list, after deleting any utilities. I suggest also excluding real estate investment trusts (REITs).

You increase your risk if you arbitrarily pick a few stocks at the top of the list. Keep in mind that you don't have to buy 100 shares of a stock. For this strategy, it's better to buy fewer shares of more stocks, as long as the commissions don't get out of hand as a percentage of your total investment.

O'Shaughnessy Funds' Cornerstone Growth Fund (*www.osfunds.com* > Mutual Funds > Cornerstone Growth Fund) uses the Cornerstone Growth strategy to pick stocks. The site includes additional information on the Cornerstone strategy, the top 10 holdings, and fund return data. The fund's 37.7 percent return in 1999 was astounding in a year when value strategies in general underperformed the market.

SuperModels Strategy

The most enthusiastic proponent of the modeling approach I've encountered is Jon D. Markman, managing editor of Microsoft's MoneyCentral (*moneycentral.msn.com*). Markman's forte lies in developing market-beating selection strategies that can be implemented using MoneyCentral's stock screening program. His selection strategies, dubbed SuperModels, produced eye-popping returns in 1999. Information on the SuperModels is linked to MoneyCentral's main page in the Insight section.

Markman features several different SuperModels. Each SuperModel looks for stocks meeting certain fundamental and/or technical characteristics, and lists the stocks meeting the model's requirements sorted by relative strength. You're supposed to select the 10 stocks with the highest relative strength.

Markman combines the results of four of his SuperModels into a 20 stock year-Trader portfolio designed to be held for one year. The models used to construct the Year-Trader are:

Best Investment Sites for Insider Trading

(*continued from previous page*)

Periscope. Very informative commentary on insider trading on highlighted companies. Gabele's reports are also featured on Fox Marketwire (*www.foxmarketwire.com*).

Quicken Insider Trading (*www.quicken.com*); **Market Guide** (*www.marketguide.com*); **Smart Money** (*www.smartmoney.com*); and **Yahoo!** (*quote.yahoo.com*): Listings of insider trading activity by company.

Thomson Insider Trading Charts on Fox Marketwire (*www.invest.foxmarketwire.com*): Thomson's charts overlay insider trades on a company's price chart.

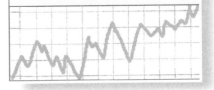

SUPERMODELS' SUPERSTAR

Flare-Out Growth is the SuperModels' superstar with a stunning 168 percent return in 1999. The strategy looks for mid- or large-cap companies with high average trading volume and strong price appreciation. It also requires companies to have some sales and earnings, but it doesn't matter if the earnings or sales are increasing or not.

Markman sorts the list of stocks meeting Flare-Out Growth's basic requirements with a twist on the conventional relative strength calculation. He looks for stocks with high relative strength that have slowed down or consolidated in the last three months. His research shows that such a breather "often sets stocks up for a new run of strong gains."

TOWERING REDWOOD

The Redwood formula takes a different tack, looking for large companies with at least 15 percent historical and forecast future earnings growth, and with a recent positive earnings surprise. Markman uses traditional relative strength for Redwood Growth, he doesn't require a recent pause, as he does for Flare-Out Growth. The Redwood Growth strategy returned 52 percent in 1999.

MVP GROWTH

MVP Growth looks for large-cap companies with annual sales of at least $200 million and high relative strength. The model uses technical parameters to eliminate very volatile stocks from consideration.

MVP VALUE

MVP Value starts with the MVP Growth criteria but require qualifying stocks to have been profitable during the past 12 months, and be value-priced using a price to sales ratio maximum of 4.0 as the value criterion.

Markman just started using the MVP models in 2000, so they don't have much in the way of a track record.

SUPERMODELS YEAR TRADER

The SuperModels Year Trader consists of 20 stocks selected using the Flare-Out Growth, Redwood Growth, MVP Growth, and MVP Value strategies.

Markman's 1999 version of the Year Trader returned 117 percent that year. Be aware, though, the three selections contributed by the Flare-Out Growth strategy returned 201.8 percent, mostly due to Internet incubator CMGI's 588 percent return.

You don't have to wait for Markman to run the screens. You can run the searches anytime by selecting Investment Finder near the top right of the page describing each model. When you do, you'll see the screening program control panel and a portion of the current stock list. The easiest way to view the entire list is to print it out, but don't use your browser's print command. Instead, click on File directly above the search title and then click print. You'll get a list of the top 25 stocks meeting the search requirements, ranked by the relative strength factor. Buy equal dollar amounts of the first 10 stocks.

Many of the SuperModels produced impressive returns in 1999. However, they all represent varying flavors of momentum strategies, based on finding stocks with high relative strength. Since 1999 was a great year for relative strength, you would have achieved a better than 70 percent return simply buying the 10 stocks with the highest relative strength on January 4, 1999. You would have lost money if you had followed the same strategy at the beginning of 1997 or 1998.

Markman is not one to stand on his laurels. He is constantly tinkering and testing new strategies. He posts updates on the site with his latest findings on Wednesdays.

Dogs of the Dow Strategy

Does spending hours at your computer selecting stocks sound like a drag? How about a conservative selection strategy that requires less than one hour per year and produces consistent returns? I'm talking about the Dow Dividend Approach, more popularly known as the Dogs of the Dow.

Dogs of the Dow is a contrarian strategy based on selecting the 10 most out-of-favor stocks in the Dow Jones Industrial Average. You hold the stocks for a year, select 10 new stocks, and repeat the process.

The strategy was first popularized by Michael O' Higgins in his 1991 book, *"Beating the Dow."* O'Higgins showed that over the

DEFINITION PLEASE

Value Investor: One who looks for out-of-favor (value-priced) stocks.

Value Stocks: Companies currently out of favor with investors. These companies usually have low valuation ratios (price/earnings < S&P 500, price/sales < 2, price/book < 2).

Volume: Number of shares traded during a specified time, usually one day.

17-year period from 1973 to 1989, his Dogs strategy averaged a return of 17.9 percent annually, compared to 11.1 percent for the Dow.

The Dogs of the Dow caught on with the investing public, and now several brokerage houses offer vehicles for following the strategy. Traditionally, many investors buy the Dogs on the first trading day of each calendar year, but you can start any time you want, even tomorrow.

You won't need a broker. You can select your own Dogs portfolio in minutes. All the information you need is on (where else?) the Dogs of the Dow (*www.dogsofthedow.com*).

From the main page, click on "Current Doggishness" to see a list of the current Dogs (based on last Friday's close). This is the list to use if you want to start investing in the Dogs today.

The list includes Friday's closing price and the dividend yield for each of the 10 Dogs. Dividend yield—the annual dividend divided by the stock price—is the metric used to determine the 10 most beaten-down stocks. These stocks usually have high dividend yields compared to other Dow stocks because the company is out of favor and their stock price is depressed.

PICK YOUR DOGS

To follow the Dogs of the Dow strategy, simply apportion 10 percent of your total investment to each stock. Don't worry about buying less than 100 shares—most stockbrokers no longer penalize you for buying "odd lots." However, the commissions could hurt your results if you buy too few shares. Since you can't buy fractions of shares, you will end up with slightly uneven dollar amounts invested in each stock. Hold these stocks for one year, sell the stocks that are not on the new list, and repeat the procedure.

SMALL DOGS

If you don't want to buy 10 stocks, O'Higgins came up with another approach called the Small Dogs of the Dow, requiring the purchase of only five stocks. You select the five companies with the lowest stock prices from the list of 10 Dogs. It's easy to pick them out because the Current Doggishness list includes a column titled "Small Dogs." The small dogs are the five stocks with a "yes" in this column.

To invest in the Small Dogs, follow the same procedure as for the 10 Dogs, except allocate 20 percent of your total investment to each stock. The performance of the Small Dogs is roughly comparable to that of the 10 Dogs.

FOOLISH FOUR DOGS

The folks at Motley Fool (*www.fool.com*) came up with a number of variations of the O'Higgins strategy. The first, developed by Robert Sheard, named the Foolish Four, calls for the purchase of only four stocks. Sheard puts the lists of 10 Dogs and the five Small Dogs side by side. The Small Dogs list is sorted according to stock price, with the lowest priced stock at the top. He compares the two lists. If the same stock is at the top of both lists, he bypasses it and selects the remaining four Small Dogs. Otherwise, he takes the top four stocks from the Small Dogs list. According to Sheard, this step reduces the chance of picking a stock that is cheap for good reason. Buy equal dollar amounts of the four stocks and hold for one year.

Sheard's research shows his selection strategy has historically outperformed the O'Higgins method. My own experience bears this out as well.

DOGS WILL HAVE THEIR DAY

The last time the Dogs outperformed the overall market was in 1996 when the S&P 500 Index returned about 23 percent compared to 29 percent for the 10 Dogs, 26 percent for the Small Dogs, and 30 percent for the Foolish Four.

In 1997 the 10 Dogs, Small Dogs, and Foolish Four with returns of 22 percent, 21 percent, and 24 percent, respectively, underperformed the S&P 500's 33 percent return. In 1998 the 10 Dogs, Small Dogs, and Foolish Four fell far short of the market with returns of 11 percent, 12 percent, and 13 percent, compared to 29 percent for the S&P 500.

The year 1999 was a mixed bag. The 10 Dogs returned 4 percent, the Small Dogs lost 5 percent, but the Foolish Four gained 20.6 percent.

The Dogs recent lackluster performance is understandable. The Dogs of the Dow is a value approach. The market's recent strong

performance is a growth stock story. Most value portfolios have been left in the dust.

History tells us the market goes through cycles—sometimes favoring growth stocks, other times favoring value strategies. Eventually, these dogs will have their day.

Graham's Net Current Asset Value Strategy

Once they become widely followed, market-beating stock selection strategies often lose their effectiveness. Here's a simple-to-understand strategy which from all reports gives great results—but hardly anyone uses it!

That's because it requires some time and effort to find the stocks—there's no ready-made screen listing them. I'll show you how to find suitable candidates but you'll have to get out your calculator to do the final analysis.

The "net current asset value approach" is the catchy name that the legendary stock analyst Benjamin Graham applied to the strategy he developed in the 1930s. Graham and David Dodd practically invented the art of fundamental analysis of common stocks. Their pioneering book, *Security Analysis*, offered investors the first logical and systematic approach to evaluate stocks. Graham introduced his net current asset value approach to the public in *The Intelligent Investor*, a book for lay investors first published in 1947.

Here's how the Graham strategy works: In accounting terms, assets are what you have, and liabilities are what you owe. Accountants divide assets and liabilities into short- and long-term categories. Short-term applies to items expected to be resolved within a year. You don't have to remember what's included in each category because the results are neatly tabulated on a company's balance sheet.

Graham's approach starts by subtracting total (long- and short-term) liabilities from current assets. The difference is the *net current asset value*. Next, you divide the net current asset value by the number of shares outstanding to get the net current asset value per share.

Graham's criteria calls for selecting stocks selling for no more than 66 percent of the net current asset value. For instance, if you calculate the net current asset value for a stock to be $10 per share, you shouldn't pay more than $6.60. It's that simple!

What kind of rewards do you get for doing the math? A study titled "A Test of Ben Graham's Stock Selection Criteria" reported in the September/October 1984 edition of the *Financial Analyst's Journal*, by Henry R. Oppenheimer, author of *Common Stock Selection: An Analysis of Benjamin Graham's Intelligent Investor*, looked at buying stocks based on this strategy on December 31 of each year from 1970 through 1983, holding the stocks for one year, and then making new selections. The mean return for the 13-year period was 29.4 percent per year versus 11.5 percent for the market in general. That certainly gets my attention.

You can use stock screening to find net asset value candidates. Hoover's StockScreener (*www.stockscreener.com*) is a good place to start. Here are some suggested values to screen for:

- **Price/Revenue: 0.01 to 0.5** Graham is looking for value-priced stocks, and price to revenue (sales) is a good starting point. Since anything below 2.0 is considered value priced, setting the maximum price/revenue to 0.5 insures candidates are in the deep value range. The 0.01 minimum precludes negative values. Note: revenue and sales mean the same thing and are often used interchangeably.
- **Debt/Equity Ratio: 0.0 Max** This ratio compares the total debt to stockholder's equity (book value). We're looking for companies with the lowest possible debt.
- **Price/Book: 1.5 Max** Price/book ratio is the classic measure of value. If the search results in too many candidates, reduce the maximum value (e.g., to 1.0) to cut down the list.
- **Current Ratio: 2.0 Min** This ratio compares current assets to current liabilities. Higher values mean high current assets, a good start for finding prime candidates. Try increasing the minimum to cut the number of companies turned up by the screen.

Best Investment Sites for Message Boards

CNET Investor (*investor.cnet.com*): Get quote then click on "Messages" to see recent messages posted on major boards. You can read the messages from there.

Company Sleuth (*www.companysleuth.com*): Alerts you to new postings on major message boards, plus recent news, changes in short interest, recent litigation, recent insider selling, and more.

Motley Fool (*www.fool.com*): Fool's boards have more of a fundamental analysis bent than the others.

Raging Bull (*www.ragingbull.com*) and **Silicon Investor** (*www.techstocks.com*): Moderated forums focusing mainly on technology companies. Silicon Investor is free to read, but charges if you want to post messages.

Yahoo! (*quote.yahoo.com*): Get a quote then click on "Msgs" to get to the message board for a specific company. The "Wild West" of message boards.

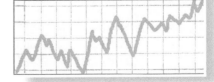

Select "Go" to run the search. Hoover's StockScreener displays only 20 results on a page, but it lists the total number of stocks found at the top of the report. You probably won't want to research more than 20 candidates, so adjust the price/book and current ratio values if the search turns up too many stocks. Once you're satisfied with the results, print out the list of candidates.

You can see balance sheet information for these stocks on several different sites, but Market Guide (*www.marketguide.com*) is easiest to use.

Enter the stock ticker symbol on Market Guide's main page to see the Snapshot report. The Snapshot displays an assortment of ratios and statistics. All you need is the most recent price and the number of shares outstanding.

A company's financial statements typically include an income statement, balance sheet, and statement of cash flows. Assets and liabilities are found on the balance sheet. You will have to calculate the net asset value because it isn't broken out separately. Click on Financials on the left to bring up an easy-to-read summary of recent financial statements. Scroll down to the balance sheet and look for a row labeled Current Assets. Use the most recent information, usually the right-hand column on Market Guide. The figures are typically shown in thousands of dollars, but check the label at the bottom of the report, because sometimes they're in millions.

Scroll down a few rows on the balance sheet until you see total liabilities. Now, get out your calculator and subtract total liabilities from the current assets. The result is the current net asset value (NAV). Divide the NAV by the number of shares outstanding to get the NAV per share.

CHAPTER EIGHT

A Quick Look at Analyzing Stocks

Analyze Not Just This!

Analyze several companies at the same time. If you research just one company, you'll find a reason to like it. You'll be more objective if you analyze 10 or 15 companies together.

If you've followed the advice in this book so far, you probably have more investment choices than you ever thought possible. You're also probably wondering how you will ever find time to analyze even a small fraction of the possibilities.

The goal of this Quick Look is to eliminate as many of these candidates as you can, A.S.A.P. Why? Well, there's no point wasting time researching stocks you're not going to buy. The sooner you eliminate unacceptable candidates, the more time you'll have to spend researching your "primo" prospects—or playing golf, going to the movies—whatever.

All publicly traded U.S. corporations are required to submit detailed quarterly and annual reports to the Securities & Exchange Commission (SEC). The reports are available the same day they are filed on the SEC's Web site (*www.sec.gov*). The reports are also made available on many other sites such as Free Edgar (*www.freeedgar.com*).

The bad news is the SEC reports are a hard read. They're lengthy, involved, and cumbersome to navigate. The good news is the Web site called Market Guide translates the SEC reports into a concise and easy-to-read format. In addition to that, Market Guide's site provides all the information we'll need for our Quick Look.

Key Ratios & Statistics			
Price & Volume		**Valuation Ratios**	
Recent Price $	74.94	Price/Earnings (TTM)	208.74
52 Week High $	82.00	Price/Sales (TTM)	35.34
52 Week Low $	24.81	Price/Book (MRQ)	31.25
Avg Daily Vol (Mil)	32.76	Price/Cash Flow (TTM)	170.70
Beta	1.34	**Per Share Data**	
Share Related Items		Earnings (TTM) $	0.36
Mkt. Cap. (Mil) $	519,892.12	Sales (TTM) $	2.12
Shares Out (Mil)	6,937.63	Book Value (MRQ) $	2.40
Float (Mil)	6,798.80	Cash Flow (TTM) $	0.44
Dividend Information		Cash (MRQ) $	0.58
Yield %	0.00	**Mgmt Effectiveness**	
Annual Dividend	0.00	Return on Equity (TTM)	20.63
Payout Ratio (TTM) %	0.00	Return on Assets (TTM)	16.33
Financial Strength		Return on Investment (TTM)	20.07
Quick Ratio (MRQ)	1.50	**Profitability**	
Current Ratio (MRQ)	2.04	Gross Margin (TTM) %	64.78
LT Debt/Equity (MRQ)	0.00	Operating Margin (TTM) %	23.40
Total Debt/Equity (MRQ)	0.00	Profit Margin (TTM) %	16.95

This section of the Market Guide Snapshot should rule out many bad apples.

Using Market Guide Stock Snapshots

Start by opening the Market Guide page (*www.marketguide.com*) and entering the ticker symbol, or the first few letters of the company name, into the "Search For" box and push "Go." If you entered the ticker symbol, or only one company corresponds to the name you typed, the Snapshot report automatically displays. Otherwise, click on the company name from the list of companies corresponding to your input.

Market Guide gives you a ton of data, more than you'll need right now. What's necessary for our Quick Look will be explained as we go along. Much of the information you'll need is in the Quick Look sidebars so read them, too. Since it's impossible to cover everything, Market Guide has excellent tutorials accessible at the top of each page (for example, "Click Here to Learn How to Use the Snapshot Report"). Each tutorial references the material displayed on that page.

The Market Guide Snapshot will tell you a lot about a company. At the top of the page is a brief description of the company, its main business, and highlights of its most recent report. For instance, Market Guide will tell you why income and revenues rose or fell during the last reporting period. You're not going to learn the whole story here since everything is compressed into a single paragraph, but you'll get some idea of the company's business and recent events. Don't rule out—or rule in—a company based on what you learn here.

PRICE CHART

The chart below the description shows the stock price action for the past 12 months. Take a close look. You don't have to be a charting whiz to draw some conclusions. If the stock is in an uptrend, the price will be higher on the right side than in the middle or left side of the chart. The price will be lower on the right side compared to the rest of the chart if the stock is in a downtrend. If the price is more or less level toward the right side, it's in a consolidation pattern (no trend). It's dangerous to buy stocks when they are in a downtrend. It doesn't matter how great the company's business prospects are, a downtrend means the price is dropping and will probably go lower.

Put the company aside if the price chart indicates a downtrend. Check back in a few weeks and consider it again when the chart has stabilized or started an uptrend.

Learning the Lingo

MARKET CAP

Just to the right of the price chart is some miscellaneous information including market capitalization. Large-cap companies have outperformed the rest of the market in recent years, and are generally considered safer investments. Small-cap companies are considered the riskiest category. Of course, you have to use some common sense—a company with a market cap of $1.9 billion is not necessarily riskier than a $2.1 billion company.

The Caps

The market capitalization of a stock is simply the number of shares outstanding (issued), multiplied by the current share price. For instance, a company's market capitalization is $200 million if it has 10 million shares outstanding, and its share price is $20. Since it's based on the share price, a company's market capitalization changes daily along with the stock price.

Companies are frequently classified according to market capitalization.

Micro-cap: less than $500 million
Small-cap: $500 million to $2 billion
Mid-cap: $2 billion to $8 billion
Large-cap: $8 billion plus

Many analysts consider small-cap companies to be the risky investments, and large-caps to be conservative investments.

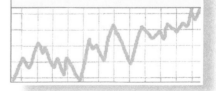

You have to decide what size companies you want to consider before you analyze individual stocks. Conservative investors may want to stick with the largest companies. For them, even $8 billion companies may be too small. After all, Cisco Systems has a market cap of around $500 billion, and Pfizer's market cap exceeds $100 billion. Conversely, you may believe that large companies have had their day in the sun, and now it's time for smaller companies to outperform the market. If you don't know what you believe, stick with companies above $2 billion market cap.

Whatever your view, look at the market cap of the company you're analyzing and decide how it fits into your investment plan.

VALUATION RATIOS

Scroll down below the price chart and look at the Valuation Ratios (Price/Earnings and Price/Sales, etc.) on the right. These ratios help you to understand the company's valuation in the eyes of the marketplace. Investors using fundamental analysis usually fall into one of three categories: value, growth, or momentum.

P/E RATIO

The market obsesses over a company's earnings—or more explicitly, its earnings per share. It's the earnings, or expectations of future earnings that drive a company's stock price up or down. The price-to-earnings ratio (P/E) is how the market compares the earnings of different companies.

The problem with using reported earnings is that a company may not have any. Sometimes it's because the company hasn't figured out how to make money yet, but often recent earnings are abnormally low due to special (nonrecurring) charges related to a onetime event such as an acquisition, closing of obsolete factories, write-off of old inventories, etc. In these instances the P/E ratio is unrealistically high, and it doesn't reflect the true value of the company.

Besides those factors, reported earnings can vary depending on accounting decisions, such as how a company decides to write off depreciation and other similar non-cash items.

Don't rule out a company with a high P/E at this point of your evaluation.

Investing Styles: Value—Growth— Momentum

Value investors look for companies that have disappointed the market, possibly by missing an earnings forecast or by experiencing slowing sales growth. The stock market reacts to disappointment by driving the offender's stock price down—often much farther down than justified by the actual events.

Growth investors look for companies with a history of consistent sales and earnings growth of at least 15 percent per year that are expected to maintain those growth rates into the foreseeable future.

Momentum investors look for companies with rapidly increasing sales and earnings, forecasting accelerating future growth. These stocks have already outperformed the market in terms of stock price appreciation and are considered overvalued by conservative investors.

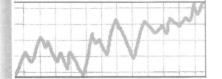

P/S RATIO

Though not perfect, P/S is a better measure of a company's valuation than P/E because reported sales are not subject to as many accounting decisions as earnings. Also, sales aren't subject to non-recurring charges due to acquisitions and the like. Because of the way the math works, companies with low profit margins such as grocery stores tend to have low P/S ratios. That can mislead you into thinking that a company is value-priced, when it really isn't, compared to other companies in the same industry. Yet at this stage of our evaluation, P/S is our best bet. It's not a fatal mistake to let companies with low P/S caused by low profit margins squeak through now, we'll catch them later.

Value investors should stick with P/S ratios below 2.0 or so, and growth investors should stay below 10. Again, use common sense. A stock doesn't switch from the growth to momentum category the day its P/S ratio moves from 9.9 to 10.1.

PER SHARE DATA

Cash Flow

Cash flow per share is the only factor you need to look at this point. Cash flow is a measure of how much a company's bank balance (and other equivalent assets) rose or fell during the past year, resulting from the company's operations—that is, from their basic business. Of course, companies can always increase their bank balance by selling more stock or borrowing money, but that's not counted in operating cash flow.

Cash flow is a more realistic measure of a company's operating results than earnings, because it's not subject to accounting decisions—such as depreciation, amortization, research and development expenses, etc., that will be deducted when calculating reported earnings.

Cash flow is arguably the most important gauge of a company's future prospects. Companies can, and often do, experience negative cash flow, though reporting positive earnings. Companies with negative cash flow eventually run out of cash and have to raise more by selling stock or by borrowing. Either of these events is bad for shareholders. Companies with surplus cash can build more factories, develop new products, make

---

TTM and MRQ

TTM is an abbreviation for **t**railing **t**welve **m**onths. What it really means is the last four reported quarters. For instance, say the current date is January 15, but the company hasn't reported earnings for its quarter (3-month accounting period) ending in December of last year. The TTM earnings are the sum of the earnings reported in the last four *reported* quarters (September, June, March, and December of the previous calendar year).

MRQ is an abbreviation for **m**ost **r**ecent **q**uarter, but it means the last day of the most recent reported quarter. For instance, assuming the same conditions as in the above example, the cash in the bank for the MRQ was as of September 30.

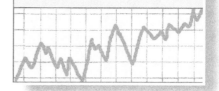

---

acquisitions, buy back stock, etc. All of which is good for share-holders.

All you have to do at this stage in our Quick Look is determine if the cash is flowing in (positive cash flow) or out (negative cash flow). Avoid companies with negative cash flow. You'll look at the actual cash flow numbers later.

PROFITABILITY MEASURES

Profit margins are calculated by dividing profit by sales. For instance, if sales are $1,000 and profits are $150, the margin is 15 percent (150 divided by 1,000).

- *Gross margin* is the profit a company makes on its products before considering overhead expenses such as marketing, research, accounting, and income taxes.
- *Operating margin* is the profit after considering all expenses except income taxes and other expenses not related to the company's basic business.
- *Profit margin* is the bottom-line profit after considering all expenses, including taxes and interest expenses. If a company's profit margin is 15 percent, that means it earned $0.15 after-tax income for every $1.00 worth of goods sold.

None of these margins mean much by themselves. Reported earnings drive stock prices, and profit margins produce earnings. However, the stock price has already reacted to earnings produced by the "historical" margins we see here. We need to know what the margins will be next quarter, but predicting their direction is an advanced task, which we'll discuss in Chapter 15.

Margins do, however, help us to compare competitive companies, especially when comparing companies in the same industry. We'll use gross margins and operating margins for this purpose.

PRICE AND VOLUME

Average Daily Volume (Avg Daily Vol) tells you how many shares, on average, trade daily. Trading volume is a measure of liquidity. Stock message boards on Yahoo!, Motley Fool, and other Web sites are full of people trying to push the price of a stock up

---

Additional Valuation Ratios

Price/Cash Flow Ratio

At this stage of our evaluation we don't need to look at the price/cash flow because we'll be looking at cash flow per share. However, some value investors pay more attention to price/cash flow than any other valuation ratio. They like to see a ratio of 10 or less.

Price/Book Ratio

Book value is the theoretical amount a company would be worth (per/share) if it went out of business and sold all of its assets. Some value investors consider stocks with a book value less than 1.0 a bargain. Academics use price/book to determine if the stock is value priced or growth priced. For instance, stocks with a price/book ratio below 5.0 would be considered value stocks. Except for certain types of industries—banks, for example—book value is not a realistic measure of a company's worth.

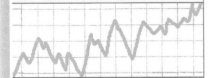

or down. They can be successful in these endeavors if only a few shares, say 10,000, are traded each day. Stick with stocks trading at least 40,000 shares (0.04 mil) daily to minimize these problems.

FINANCIAL STRENGTH

This part of the Snapshot includes ways of measuring debt measures. We'll look at two:

Current Ratio

The current ratio is attained by comparing current assets to current debt. *Current assets* include cash and cash equivalents, inventory, and accounts receivable. *Current debt* is all debts due within one year. For instance, your credit card bills are current debts, but your 30-year mortgage isn't, it's a long-term liability.

The current ratio is calculated by dividing the current assets by the current debt. The ratio is greater than 1.0 if the assets are larger than the debt. That's good! Watch out if debts exceed the assets. That means the company owes more cash than it's got, so it's going to have to borrow money or sell stock in a hurry. That is rarely good news for stockholders. Look for a current ratio of 1.5 or more. Higher is better.

Total Debt/Equity

This compares the total of long- and short-term debt to shareholders' equity.

For reasons know only to accountants, the debt/equity ratio is reversed, as opposed to the way the current ratio is expressed. In this case, debt is divided by the equity, so lower is better.

If debt and equity are equal, the ratio is 1.0. Generally values below 0.5 are ok, and zero is best. However, some industries normally carry high debt. Don't eliminate companies with high debt/equity ratios at this stage of your evaluation.

That's it for the Market Guide Snapshot page. You should have eliminated all candidates with:

- Price chart in a downtrend
- Wrong market for your investing requirements
- Price/Sales ratio out of your range
- Average Daily Volume less than 0.04 million

- Negative cash flow per share
- Current ratio less than 1.5

Let's move on to Highlights and Performance. Use the menu on the left side of the Market Guide page to select Performance.

PERFORMANCE

The Market Guide Performance page contains historical price and P/E ratio information, short interest, institutional ownership, and insider trading data. We're primarily interested in the institutional ownership, but we'll also look at insider selling and comment on the others.

Price Performance

This data shows the stock price performance for various periods for the stock compared to the S&P 500, its stock price performance rank in its industry, and its industry rank in the overall market. You've already looked at the price chart on the Snapshot page and you don't need the industry information at this stage of your evaluation.

Institutional Ownership		Insider Trading (Prev. 6 months)	
% Shares Owned	56.84	Net Insider Trades	-11
# of Institutions	2,927	# Buy Transactions	0
Total Shares Held (Mil)	3,943.384	# Sell Transactions	11
3 Mo. Net Purchases (Mil)	29.451	Net Shares Purchased (Mil)	-2.255
3 Mo. Shares Purchased (Mil)	237.352	# Shares Purchased (Mil)	0.000
3 Mo. Shares Sold (Mil)	207.901	# Shares Sold (Mil)	2.255

Watch out for stocks institutions don't want.

Institutional Ownership

Just below the price performance data is a table showing institutional ownership. Institutions are mutual funds, banks, pension plans, trust funds, etc. The table lists the number of shares owned by institutions, the number of institutions owning shares, and the percentage of the float (shares outstanding less insider ownership, see sidebar) owned by institutions. It also lists the purchases and sales of shares by institutions during the past three months.

Many market gurus will tell you the secret to making money is to find a stock before institutions discover it. They say you should look for companies with institutional ownership in the 10 percent to 20 percent range. Then just sit back and enjoy the ride when institutions discover your company and start loading up on the stock.

Unfortunately, that's a pipe dream. How could we discover a stock before a mutual fund does? Their computers are every bit as good as ours. When a stock goes public, the underwriters introduce the company to mutual funds and other institutional buyers. That's a fundamental part of the IPO (Initial Public Offering) process. If institutions don't own a stock it's because they don't want to—not because they haven't heard of it.

So this is why you should look for companies with strong institutional ownership. More is better. Avoid companies with less than 40 percent institutional ownership.

Market Guide lists the total number of shares bought and sold by institutions during the past three months. They also subtract the sales from the purchases to arrive at "Net Purchases." If the "net" is positive, institutions have been buying, if minus, they've been selling. It makes me nervous to see them unloading the stock I'm considering buying. I don't want in if they're getting out. Look for companies with net institutional buying.

Insider Trading

Market Guide shows the number of recent insider trades: buys, sells, and the net of subtracting the sells from the buys. We can also see the total number of shares bought and sold, and the net. The number of shares is more significant than the number of transactions. Look for lots of shares bought or sold; anything less has no significance. Insider trading activity is important, so note significant activity so you can investigate after you've read Chapter 11 on insider trading.

Short Interest

Displays the number of shares sold short, meaning sold by short sellers anticipating a drop in share price so they can buy them back at a lower price (Chapter 2 has more information on short selling). There's nothing that will help us make money in this section.

Price History

Some investors believe that stocks trade within a range of P/E ratios. For instance, between a low P/E of 15 and a high P/E of 30. In this example, they would conclude the stock is likely to go up if the current P/E is, say, 18, and in danger of dropping if the P/E is 30. I'd hate to tell you the opportunities I've missed because a stock was at the high end of its historical P/E range—only to see it zoom to P/Es double or triple the old high. I don't even glance at these numbers anymore.

Management Effectiveness Measures

Management quality is often gauged using these three ratios, all of which are based on reported earnings:

1. Return on Equity (ROE) is said to be a measure of how effectively the company employs the shareholders' equity. It's calculated by dividing the earnings per share by the book value. Many analysts say a company can't grow faster than its ROE, and higher is better as far as they're concerned. Often 15 percent is cited as a minimum acceptable ROE.
2. Return on Investment (ROI) is similar to ROE, except it takes debt into account. ROI is calculated by adding the long-term debt to the book value before doing the ROE calculation.
3. Return on Assets (ROA) is calculated by dividing earnings by long- and short-term assets.

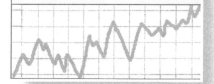

Insiders and Float

Shares outstanding (shares out) is the total number of shares issued by the company. Officers and directors of the company own some of those shares. These individuals are classified as "insiders." Insiders cannot just log on to the Web and sell their shares. They have to follow rules set down by the SEC and can only trade their shares at certain times. Insiders' shares are not considered available for trading. By the way, technically, anyone owning more than 10 percent of a company's shares is considered an insider.

"Float" is the number of shares that are available for daily trading, that is, the shares not owned by insiders. You can calculate insider ownership by subtracting the float from the number of shares outstanding.

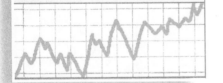

HIGHLIGHTS

That's all we need on the performance page, so let's move on to Highlights by clicking the link on the menu on the left of the page.

Growth Rates

Market Guide displays sales, earnings (EPS), and dividend growth rates for the last fiscal year, as well as the annualized average growth rates for the past three- and five-year periods.

GROWTH RATES			
	1 Year	3 Year	5 Year
Sales %	43.19	43.70	55.56
EPS %	47.37	26.54	38.70
Dividend %	NM	NM	NM

Market Guide Highlights show sales and earnings growth rates. You'll do best by choosing companies with steady or increasing sales growth rates.

The most important number is the sales growth. Companies can't grow without increasing sales. Value investors should expect at least 15 percent annual sales growth for the past three- and five-year periods, but expect less for the most recent year. The stock probably became value priced because of a recent stumble, possibly caused by a sales slump.

Growth investors should expect at least 15 percent growth for the three- and five-year periods, and more for the most recent year. Ideally you want to see accelerating growth; that is, the one-year sales growth is higher than the three-year number, and the three-year sales growth is higher than the five-year growth. The comparison of the one-year and three-year growth rates is more significant than the three- and five-year comparisons.

Earnings per share (EPS) growth rates in a well-run company should match or exceed sales growth. Erratic earnings growth signals poor management.

Dividend growth is not a factor for most companies in the current market.

Insider and Institutional Ownership

Scroll down to the Equity section near the bottom of the Highlights page. It's a collection of cryptic notations, and two are worth noting. One is the percentage of stock held by insiders, in this case meaning officers and employees. It also notes the shares held by anyone else holding 10 percent or more of the outstanding shares.

Market gurus tell us that insider ownership is important. If the people running the company own a lot of stock, their priorities will be in line with ours; making the stock price go up. If they don't own much stock, they'll be more interested in perks, such as private jets and luxury offices.

That makes sense. However, these days most high-level employees, officers or not, get a significant portion of their remuneration in the form of stock options. Just about everybody has a personal stake in getting the stock price up. In these companies, insider ownership no longer means much.

While you're looking at ownership, take note of any stock brokerage firms listed as major shareholders. Also, note the names of brokerages handling public offerings. In both cases, these firms have an interest in promoting the company's stock. Analysts employed by these firms often issue buy, hold, or sell recommendations on the company. It doesn't take a lot of imagination to see a potential conflict of interest.

Let's explore that idea further by selecting Institutional (Instit.) Ownership from the menu on the left.

Note the names of any stock brokerage firms among the top 10 institutional stockholders listed in this section. You will need this list to help you evaluate the recommendations of analysts working for these firms.

That's it! You're done with the Quick Look. Once you get the hang of it, you should be able to whiz through a list of 20 companies in less than 20 minutes.

Dividend Information

Investors these days are more interested in capital gains than collecting dividends. Dividends are taxed at regular rates in the year received, while capital gains are usually taxed at a lower rate, and the capital gains taxes don't apply until you sell the stock.

Annual dividend is the total of the expected dividends over the next four quarters.

Dividend yield is the recent stock price divided by the annual dividend, expressed in percentage. Many companies pay no dividends; of those that do, the typical yield is less than 2 percent. Real estate investment trusts (REITs) and utilities are the exception; these typically pay substantial dividends.

Payout ratio is the percentage of a company's net profits paid out in dividends. A very high payout ratio (e.g. 90 percent) means the company is paying out practically all of its earnings in dividends.

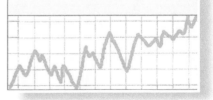

CHAPTER NINE

Profiling the Company

W ho are they? What do they do, exactly? Who does it better? To get a good sense of a stock candidate, you've got to learn about the company. On the Web there are some excellent sites on which you can explore a company's business, as well as check the current news on that company. This chapter shows how to do it.

What Do They Do?

Hoover's Online (*www.hoovers.com*) is in the business of gathering information about public and private companies. Much of Hoover's site requires a subscription, but you can get everything you need to know at no charge. A major plus for Hoover's is its Top Competitors list.

Select "ticker" on the Search dropdown menu at the top, enter the ticker symbol of your stock candidate, and click "Go." Hoover's Company Capsule will display an understandable description of the company's major products and services.

Sometimes, especially in the case of tech companies, you might want more information, or a different slant, to help you understand the company's business.

Yahoo! is a good source of company overviews. Get a quote on Yahoo!'s finance homepage (*quote.yahoo.com*), then select Profile (More Info section) and check out the Business Summary and the Financial Summary (below the Business Summary).

Morningstar (*www.morningstar.com*) is another good source for company profiles. Enter the ticker symbol on Morningstar's main page to display a quote, and then select Snapshot from the menu on the left.

SEC Reports Made Easy

A company's SEC reports are the ultimate source for information on their business. You'll find all the detail you need and much more in their latest annual report.

All publicly traded corporations in the United States must file quarterly and annual reports with the U.S. Securities and Exchange

Commission (SEC). Since May of 1996, all reporting companies have been required to file the reports in electronic format, which the SEC posts on its EDGAR (Electronic Data Gathering, Analysis, and Retrieval System) database.

Many different types of company reports are filed, and each type of report is identified by a number. Company reports of primary interest include the 10-K, the annual report; 10-Q, the quarterly report; and the 424Bx, the prospectus, which includes a detailed description of the business, risks, and competition.

Of secondary interest are the DEF-14A, the proxy statement, which includes details on management compensation; and the 8-K, which reports unscheduled material events—usually a press release announcing an acquisition, merger, etc.

SEC reports are different from the glossy reports typically mailed to shareholders. The SEC requires specific information presented in a predefined format. Quarterly and annual reports both include financial statements: income statement, balance sheet, and cash flow statement, and a management discussion of the company's financial results and future prospects. Annual reports typically include more detail on company operations, competition, risks, potential liquidity problems, and the like.

You can access the reports directly on the SEC's site (*www.sec.gov* > EDGAR Database), but it's a lot easier to get the reports through a third-party site, of which there are several sites. My favorite is Free Edgar (*www.freeedgar.com*) for two reasons: 1) access to all reports is free, and 2) these reports have a table of contents.

SEC reports are lengthy, often more than 100 pages. Finding and printing specific information such as a cash flow statement or the management discussion is time-consuming and difficult. Free Edgar provides a table of contents for each report. Clicking on a specific item—say the balance sheet—displays the item separately. That way you can print the balance sheet without printing the entire report.

Who's the Competition?

Determining a candidate's major competitors is an important part of your analysis. You usually increase your chances of success by

10-K: Annual report required by the SEC.

10-Q: Quarterly report required by the SEC.

EDGAR: Database maintained by the U.S. Securities and Exchange Commission (SEC) containing government-required reports filed by corporations.

Prospectus: A document circulated to potential investors prior to an IPO describing a company's business plan.

picking the best company in an industry. Your first step in the process is listing the major competitors. This is not nearly as easy as it sounds.

Let's take Walgreens as an example. Walgreens is the largest chain of drugstores in the United States, in terms of sales. Its two largest competitors are CVS and Rite Aid. A smaller, regional competitor is Long's Drugs. How would you find this out if you're not familiar with the drugstore industry?

Yahoo's profile report of Walgreens has a link—"Financial Links" on the left—titled "Competitors." Clicking on that link displays a list of 22 companies including Walgreens, CVS, Rite Aid, and Long's Drugs. The problem is Yahoo! also listed 18 other companies such as Accuhealth, a provider of in-home healthcare services, NCS HealthCare, a provider of pharmacy services to long-term care institutions, and Twinlab, a manufacturer of vitamins and supplements.

Morningstar lists "Industry Peers" on their Industry Snapshot page (select "Industry Snapshot" from Snapshot page). Morningstar showed me a list of 20 peers for Walgreens, including CVS, Rite Aid, and Long's. Trouble is, Morningstar also considered Staples, Office Depot, Goto.com (a Web search site), Barnes & Noble, and Stamps.com as peers.

Hoover's isn't perfect, but they do a better job of identifying competitors than other sites. Hoover's listed CVS, Rite Aid, and Eckerd as Walgreens' top competitors. Eckerd is indeed the fourth-largest drugstore chain. Eckerd didn't show up on the other lists because they're owned by J.C. Penney and not publicly traded.

The best source of competitive information is the company's own SEC filings, especially annual reports and prospectuses. These often list the names of major competitors in each of their business segments. It takes a little effort to get the information, but you'll often pick up good tips from these documents, especially if you're interested in investing specifically in that industry sector. Use Free Edgar (*www.freeedgar.com*) and look for a recent annual report or prospectus.

Read Hoover's Company Capsule for each competitor found. Often you'll find a company is not a direct competitor to another, or that only a small segment of their businesses overlap. Note significant competitors and research them later.

http://www.

How to Use Free Edgar (*www.freeedgar.com*)

Enter the ticker symbol (or company name) and click Search. Select "View Filings" when the Search Results page displays. Free Edgar displays all of the company's filings in chronological order, with the most recent on top.

If you're conducting a financial analysis, you always want to look at the most recent information, whether a 10K (annual report) or a 10Q (quarterly report). You'll probably find the annual report or prospectus more helpful if you're doing research on the company's business or looking for names of its competitors.

Select the report of interest. Free Edgar displays a table of contents on the left and the report header on the right. Use the slider bar on the left to move the table of contents until you find a section of interest. Click on the section name and Free Edgar displays the information in the frame on the right.

You'll probably have to print financial reports to see them adequately. Click your mouse in the report section before printing, otherwise you'll print the table of contents instead of the data. You may have to set your printer to landscape mode (wide) if the report is too wide to fit on a page in the regular portrait (vertical) mode.

If you're interested in a section of the management discussion, you'll save paper by copying the section onto your clipboard and pasting it into a word processor before printing.

Management discussions are lengthy. If you're looking for a specific topic, such as a list of competitors, use the "find" function of your browser to locate it. Do that by holding down the Ctrl key while pushing F. Then type "competition" into the Find window and click Find Next.

Check the News

You don't need to do an exhaustive study of business news reports now, since your purpose is to get a general feel for what's going on with a company. Is it the subject of a scandal? Is it in a battle to acquire another company, or an acquisition target itself? Are analysts turning sour, or getting excited about the company or its industry's prospects?

For stuff like that Yahoo! is the easiest place to do a quick check on the news.

YAHOO! NEWS (*finance.yahoo.com*)

Look up a quote and then click on the News link under More Info. Scan through the headlines, and click on any of interest.

If you see any analyst ratings changes, click on the story (not on the Briefing.com link), find the company on the Upgrades & Downgrades list, and then click on History to see a list of analysts' ratings changes going back a year or so. The list is far from complete, but it gives an idea of analysts' feelings about the company.

Pay most attention to headlines linking to stories from CBS MarketWatch, CNET News, Red Herring, and Upside Today. They're likely to contain an analysis of the company's competitive position or recent events.

In Chapter 21 you'll find further information on getting the news.

CHAPTER TEN

Analyzing the Analysts

Stock prices move up and down in the short term for reasons that may, or may not, have anything to do with the company. Possibly, a competitor will warn that their sales growth is slowing, and your stock will get pummeled in sympathy. Perhaps the Brazilian currency collapsed, there was a hurricane or an earthquake somewhere, or rumors of interest-rate hikes drove the entire market down. You name it—your stock's price gets knocked around on a daily basis just because it's part of the overall market.

In the end, however, share prices reflect the market's expectations of a company's future earnings growth. In stock market time, the "future" is the next quarter (three months), the next year, and possibly the year after that. Changes in market expectations can move stock prices dramatically.

What exactly are "market expectations"? They are recommendations and forecasts of the company's future earnings made by investment analysts. The analysts' recommendations for each company are tabulated into consensus buy, hold, or sell ratings, and consensus earnings forecasts (see below).

Analysts make frequent adjustments to their ratings and forecasts, and stock prices often make big moves—up or down—following these changes.

Whether you're a long-term investor or a short-term player, you have a lot to gain from studying analysts' ratings and forecasts before you buy.

Who Are These Analysts?

Stock brokerage firms are divided into two camps: full-service and discount brokers. Full-service brokers, such as Merrill Lynch or Salomon Smith Barney, offer advice on specific stocks to buy and sell. Discount brokers, such as Charles Schwab or E*Trade, studiously avoid making recommendations.

Full-service brokers employ legions of research analysts. Each analyst covers a specific industry. One might report on automobile manufacturers, while another analyst will cover telecommunications companies, and another follows retail stores.

Forecasts and Recommendations

Analysts produce detailed reports on companies they follow. The reports examine the company's business plan, their operations, and future prospects for the company and its industry. The reports always include the analysts' current buy, hold, or sell (b/h/s) recommendation for the stock and the analysts' forecasts, which project the company's earnings one or two years into the future. Analysts frequently revise their b/h/s recommendation and earnings forecasts after meeting with company executives, or when a company reports earnings, acquires another company, shuffles top executives, etc. These revisions usually move the stock price.

Analysts customarily break their b/h/s recommendations into gradations. They publish a strong buy if they're bullish about the company. If they like the company but aren't too excited about it, they'll put out a weaker buy recommendation, frequently using a euphemism such as "accumulate" or "outperform." Analysts don't like to issue sell ratings, so they'll rate a stock hold, or "market perform" if they think you should sell it.

The analysts' reports are distributed mainly to the firm's brokers and their clients. However, the earnings forecasts and buy, hold, or sell recommendations are widely circulated. In fact, some analysts issue a press release when they distribute new earnings forecasts or change their b/h/s ratings.

Consensus Forecasts: Where to Find Them

Independent third parties, such as Zacks Investment Research, First Call Corporation, and I/B/E/S International are in the business of collecting and compiling the analysts' b/h/s ratings and earnings forecasts. They average all of the forecasts for a particular company into a single number called the *consensus forecast*. When you hear a company is expected to earn so many cents a share this quarter, you're hearing the consensus, or average, of many different forecasts.

Data from each of the major compilers—Zacks, First Call, and I/B/E/S—is widely available on the Web. Timeliness is critical

Best Investment Sites for News

CBS MarketWatch
(*cbs.marketwatch.com*): Good source for breaking news, and for putting the news into context.

CNET Investor
(*investor.cnet.com*): Best source for Bloomberg news.

Infobeat
(*www.infobeat.com*): They will e-mail news on stocks you specify.

Quicken
(*www.quicken.com*): Best site to find Dow Jones news.

Yahoo! (*quote.yahoo.com*): All major news sources except Dow Jones and Bloomberg. Best overall news site.

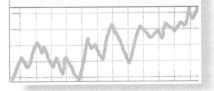

because analysts frequently change their earnings forecasts and b/h/s recommendations. It can be misleading and costly to rely on stale information.

Microsoft's MSN MoneyCentral, Quicken, and Yahoo! do the best job of getting you the earnings forecasts and b/h/s recommendations quickly, although even their information could be up to a week old. All three use data compiled by Zacks. Much of the information on the three sites is the same, but some of the data on Quicken is not available on the other sites.

We'll use **Quicken** (*www.quicken.com* > Investing) to illustrate how to use analysts' recommendations and forecasts.

Enter a ticker symbol in the Quotes and Research section. Select "Analysts" instead of the Quotes default setting, and click Go (select Analysts' Estimates from the menu on the left if your screen displays price quotes instead of analysts' estimates).

We'll look first at the Analyst Ratings summary.

Analyst Ratings	Today	1 month ago	2 months ago	3 months ago
1=Strong Buy	8	7	5	4
2=Buy	4	4	4	5
3=Hold	0	1	2	2
4=Sell	0	0	0	0
5=Strong Sell	0	0	0	0
Consensus (mean) (strong buy) 1 - 5 (strong sell)	1.33	1.50	1.73	1.82

Quicken Analyst Ratings Summary. Avoid stocks with fewer than four analysts.

ANALYST RATINGS

Quicken displays the most recent analysts' ratings in the "Today" column. The label Today is misleading since the information is updated once a week, on Sundays, using ratings as of the day before. Quicken also shows you the ratings from one, two, and three months ago.

For each date, Quicken displays the number of analysts with strong buy; buy, hold, sell; and strong sell ratings. Wall Street likes to convert everything to numeric ratings, and analysts' recommendations are no exception. Here is the formula:

> Strong Buy = 1
> Moderate or Weak Buy = 2
> Hold = 3
> Moderate or Weak Sell = 4
> Strong Sell = 5

Here's how it works. Say a stock is followed by four analysts, and two rate it a strong buy, and the other two say hold.

The consensus rating is:

Strong Buys: 2 recommendations × 1 pt = 2
Hold: 2 recommendation × 3 pts   = 6

Total   8

The average is 2.0 (8 points divided by 4 analysts). The consensus rating is interpreted as a moderate buy even though none of the analysts made a moderate buy recommendation.

Converting recommendations to numeric values makes it easy to compare ratings between different companies, or for the same company at different times. For instance, you might notice that three months ago a company was rated 3.0 (hold), and now the rating has improved to 2.0 (moderate buy).

Evaluating Forecasts and Recommendations

How should you as an investor use analysts' recommendations?

- Value investors want companies the market hates. Low analyst recommendations (2.5 to 5.0) mean the market's given up on the stock. That's good for value investors.
- Long-term growth investors should look for recommendations in the 1.0 to 2.0 range, indicating analysts in general look favorably on the company's future prospects. There's nothing to be gained by selecting stocks with strong buy (1.0) ratings compared to moderate buys (2.0).
- Momentum investors need plenty of market enthusiasm to keep the stock price moving. Look for 1.0 to 1.5 ratings.

On the Quicken screen, look at the earnings forecasts just below the analyst ratings.

Quicken summarizes the analysts' earnings estimates for the current quarter, the next quarter, and the current and next fiscal years.

How Many Analysts?

- Avoid companies with fewer than four analysts.
- Favor companies with six or seven analysts, up from two to four analysts three months ago.
- Companies with eight or more analysts are OK.

The number of analysts shown in the Quicken reports are just those reporting their ratings to Zacks. There could be many more analysts covering the company. The guidelines I've given you here are based on using the Zacks reports available on Quicken or Yahoo!

Consensus EPS Estimate	This Qtr 04/2000	Next Qtr 07/2000	This Fiscal Year 01/2001	Next Fiscal Year 01/2002
Avg Estimate (mean)	$0.04	$0.06	$1.13	$1.37
# of Estimates	9	9	11	10
Low Estimate	$0.04	$0.06	$1.13	$1.36
High Estimate	$0.06	$0.08	$1.14	$1.39
Year Ago EPS	$0.03	$0.05	$0.93	$1.13
EPS Growth	31.3%	19.5%	21.9%	20.9%

Quicken Consensus Earnings Forecasts gauge the market's expectations for the company.

(continued on next page)

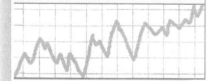

Look at the second row first (# of Estimates). That number represents the number of analysts making earnings forecasts for the period.

Now look at the third and fourth rows (Low Estimate and High Estimate). These show you the lowest and highest earnings forecast for the period.

The top row (Avg Estimate) is a simple average of each of the individual forecasts.

The fifth row shows last year's reported earnings for the same period, and the bottom row shows the percentage difference between this year's forecast and last year's actual earnings.

EVALUATING EARNINGS FORECASTS

What does all this data mean? What's important is the expected earnings growth. All things being equal (of course, they never are), earnings have to increase for the stock price to go up, especially over the long haul.

- Value investors want companies with low expectations. They're looking for beaten-down, left-for-dead stocks. High earnings growth forecasts aren't consistent with low expectations. Value investors should require growth forecasts below 20 percent, and lower is better.
- Growth investors should require strong forecast earnings growth. What's strong? In this market, 20 percent minimum and higher is better.
- Momentum investors need high earnings growth forecasts (30 percent plus) to sustain the momentum.

Using Supply and Demand to Find Happening Stocks

Stock prices reflect the forces of supply and demand. *Supply* is the number of shares available for trading (float). The supply of a particular company's shares is relatively constant. Changes in demand moves stock prices.

A stock's price goes up on days when buyers want to buy more shares than sellers want to sell, and goes down when sellers outnumber buyers. Demand is low if nobody knows about the company. Demand hinges on investor awareness—and analyst coverage is the key to investor awareness.

Major full-service brokerages employ thousands of individual stockbrokers. When an analyst issues a report, it goes to all of the company's brokers, who in turn relay the recommendations to their clients. The clients could be individual investors, or institutions such as mutual funds, retirement trusts, and banks, capable of purchasing tens of thousands of shares of a single company.

Every time a new analyst initiates coverage of a company, it opens the door to thousands of investors who may have never heard of the firm before. The goal of many investors, including me, is to discover a stock before everybody else gets on the bandwagon. The information in Quicken's Analyst Ratings section can help us apply the supply and demand principal to find stocks on the verge of discovery by increasing numbers of investors.

Quicken's Analyst Ratings show us the number of analysts following the company (making b/h/s recommendations) today, and one month, two months, and three months ago.

A company can do great things, but it's all for naught if nobody knows. Nobody will know if only two analysts are following the company. It takes coverage by five or six analysts before a stock comes to the attention of enough investors to make a big move. You can see the trend in analyst coverage by looking at the current number of analysts compared to two or three months ago.

The ideal time to own a stock is when coverage increases from three or four analysts to five or six. The company is coming to the attention of the market in general, and if things go well, coverage will continue to increase.

Surprises and Trends

Momentum investors look for stocks with a high probability of increasing consensus earnings forecasts in the weeks preceding the next earnings report, and then, they hope, a positive surprise on earnings announcement day. Rising earnings forecasts and positive surprises usually push a stock's price up.

Investors with a long-term outlook often overlook these momentum factors. They shouldn't. Falling earnings forecasts drive

Analysts' Jargon

(continued from previous page)

LONG-TERM ACCUMU-LATE: Expected total annual return in the range of 10%–20% if anticipated contingencies materialize over the next 12–18 months or longer

HOLD: Stock is fairly valued and may provide returns which approximate returns expected from its peer group in the equity markets over the next 12–18 months, or perhaps less

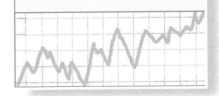

How Do Analysts Get Their Numbers?

In theory, an analyst researches a company by first analyzing broad economic and demographic trends. Is the overall business climate favorable; and is the market for the company's products growing at a healthy pace? Does the company have an advantage over its competitors, or will it have to cut prices to remain competitive?

In reality, analysts are busy people. They often don't have enough time to do as much detailed research as they'd like. So they depend on guidance from the companies they cover for much of their information. This guidance might take the form of meetings attended by groups of analysts, conference calls on the telephone, or private conversations with company officers.

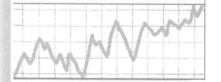

stock prices down. So do negative surprises. It's discouraging when stock prices fall shortly after you bought the stock, even if you plan to hold the shares for a long time.

SURPRISES

A surprise in the stock market is the difference between analysts' consensus earnings forecasts and the actual earnings reported by the company. If a company reports earnings higher than consensus forecasts, it's a positive surprise. Conversely, if reported earnings fall short of forecasts, it's a negative surprise.

Most companies guide analysts to forecast earnings one or two cents below what they think they'll actually do. That's no secret, so the market expects earnings to come in a penny or two above consensus forecasts.

A negative surprise of even two or three cents almost always produces an immediate sharp drop in the stock price. A positive surprise of one or two cents usually doesn't move a stock very much. Larger positive surprises often do push the stock price up. If they don't, it's usually because the earnings didn't exceed the whisper number (see below).

The surprising thing about surprises is that the percentage that earnings come in over or under consensus doesn't matter much. A $0.04 negative surprise does about the same amount of damage whether it's four cents out of $0.50, or four cents out of $4.00.

Analysts often adjust their earnings forecasts for future quarters in response to a recent surprise. Since changes in earnings forecasts move stock prices, an earnings surprise can have a double whammy. First the price reacts to the surprise, and then moves again when analysts adjust their forecasts.

USING ANALYSTS' ESTIMATES TO ANTICIPATE SURPRISES

Trends

Analysts forecasts often move in trends. That is, once consensus earnings estimates start to move, either up or down, they'll continue on the same path. This is because once one analyst makes a significant change in forecast, other analysts reexamine their estimates to see if the analyst making the change caught something they missed. They will probably end up revising their estimates in the same direction.

Some analysts won't get around to revising their estimates by the earnings report date, and reported earnings will probably surprise in the same direction.

Look at Quicken's Consensus EPS (Earnings Per Share) Trend display. It shows you the consensus forecasts going back 90 days. You can see the movement in analysts' consensus forecasts by comparing the current forecasts to older forecasts. Forecasts that are steadily moving up portend a positive surprise.

Let's take an example. Say forecasts for the current quarter were $0.75 90 days ago, $0.80 60 days ago, $0.82 30 days ago, and $0.83 last week. That's strong upward momentum, and predicts a positive surprise.

It works the same way in reverse. Falling earnings forecasts signal a possible negative surprise—disaster if you own the stock.

One or two cent changes in forecasts don't mean much. They could be due to an analyst initiating or dropping coverage. Look for an ongoing trend over 90 days.

How to Interpret Consensus EPS Trend

- All investors should avoid stocks with a negative trend in earnings forecasts. It's OK for value and growth investors to buy stocks with no trend in earnings forecasts.
- Momentum investors should only buy stocks with a positive trend in forecasts.

SURPRISE HISTORY

When in comes to earnings surprises, momentum investors believe history foretells the future. A popular saying is, "Earnings surprises are like cockroaches, you just don't see one." A company with a history of positive earnings surprises is likely to continue the trend in the next quarter. Companies with a recent history of disappointing earnings will probably continue to fall short.

Quicken's Quarterly Earnings display shows you the history of surprises going back five quarters. If you see a history of $0.01 or $0.02 surprises, you can assume the next surprise will be in the

Research for Value

If you're fundamentally inclined, your time will be well spent reviewing any research available on stocks you're considering. You should also check for new reports on the stocks already in your portfolio about once a month.

Sell Side vs. Buy Side Analysts

The earning forecasts we see on Yahoo!, Quicken, and other sites are made by analysts working for brokerage companies such as Morgan Stanley/Dean Witter, Paine Webber, and Salomon Smith Barney. They are called *sell-side analysts* because their function is to support the firm's brokers by issuing reports the brokers can relay to their clients, hoping to encourage those clients to make stock transactions.

Buy-side analysts work for institutions such as mutual funds, retirement trusts, banks, and the like. The don't publicize their findings.

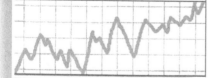

same ballpark. If you see a history of large positive surprises, say $0.08 to $0.20, you can expect a positive surprise next time too. Everybody will be on to that though, and the stock price will drop sharply if the company doesn't come through with another big surprise.

It works the other way too, a history of negative surprises raises the specter of another one.

How to Interpret Quarterly Earnings Surprises

- All investors should avoid stocks with a history of negative surprises of any size, even one or two cents. Value and growth investors can buy stocks with flat or positive surprise histories. Avoid stocks with excessive expectations, say a history of $0.20 or higher positive surprises. There's too much risk of disappointment.
- Momentum investors should only pick stocks with a history of positive surprises in the $0.04 to $0.15 range.

Whisper Numbers

Analysts like to be conservative when they forecast earnings to lessen chances of an unpleasant surprise if the company falls short. Consequently, analysts expect actual earnings to come in above their published forecasts.

Of course, nobody can keep a secret, and analysts sometimes tell their important customers what they really think. Other times, company executives might reveal their earnings expectations to outsiders.

Whatever the source, other numbers, usually higher than the published forecasts, begin to circulate. These are *whisper numbers*. The whisper numbers get around, and investors expect the company to report the whispered earnings. If earnings don't come in at or above the whisper number, the stock drops even if the reported earnings were above the published estimates.

Fortunately, we can tune into whisper numbers too. And not by listening to whispering. At least three sites specialize in compiling whisper numbers: Earnings Whispers (*www.earningswhispers.com*),

Whisper Numbers (*www.whispernumbers.com*), and streetIQ (*www.streetiq.com*).

EARNINGS WHISPERS (*www.earningswhispers.com*)

My favorite site to track down whisper numbers is Earnings Whispers. It's easy to use: enter a company name or ticker symbol and Earnings Whispers displays the published consensus forecast, the whisper number, and the date the company is expected to report earnings.

It can be even easier. Sign up and they will periodically send you an e-mail whisper number report. You can set up a portfolio and check the whisper numbers for all your stocks at once.

You may wonder how Earnings Whispers gets the numbers. According to chief eavesdropper Shannon Puls, they rely primarily on contacts either within or involved with the company. Possibly an officer, accountant, employee, customer, or vendor. Failing that, they'll check with brokers, analyze e-mail tips, or monitor online bulletin boards.

Whatever the source, Earnings Whispers doesn't take the information at face value. They look at a company's history of beating or missing forecasts, check the forecasts of analysts who've been historically most accurate, etc., before coming up with their whisper number.

Whisper numbers are posted about three or four weeks before the expected report date. You can check a calendar on the site to see companies expected to report within the next few days, or look up a company to find their anticipated report day.

As far as accuracy goes, a recent study found that published consensus reports underestimated earnings by about 6 percent, while whisper numbers overestimated them by almost 5 percent. So it looks like you could do best by averaging the published and whisper numbers.

Where to Get Analysts' Reports

Even though analysts' inherent conflict of interest can influence their buy/hold/sell ratings, there's still much to be gained by reading analysts' research reports.

Earnings Reports

Corporations are required to report their financial results four times a year (each quarter). They issue a press release announcing the sales and earnings for the recently completed quarter. The announced earnings are compared to the consensus forecast and the stock price reacts accordingly.

Every company is required to file detailed quarterly reports with the Securities and Exchange Commission (SEC) within 45 days of the end of the quarter. The SEC requires a more thorough discussion of the company's prospects in the annual report, required within 90 days of the end of the company's fiscal year. These reports are made available to the public on the SEC's Web site (*www.sec.gov*) the same day they are filed. The reports filed with the SEC are considerably more detailed and factual than the quarterly and annual reports mailed to shareholders.

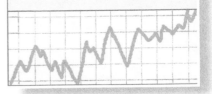

Analysts know a lot about the industries they cover and their reports often provide an overview of the entire industry sector, not necessarily just the companies they're following.

An analyst's report reveals much about a company's expansion plans, operating strengths and weaknesses, competitive advantages and disadvantages. Many analysts release updates following earnings releases, conference calls, analyst meetings, and the like. You'll learn their insights on the event and the resulting changes in their recommendations and forecasts.

Analysts' reports are supposedly available only to clients and potential clients of their brokerage houses. Some are offered for sale on Zacks (*www.zacks.com*) and other sites. Fortunately, many of these reports are available at no charge, some for limited trial periods, and some indefinitely.

MULTEX INVESTOR (*www.multexinvestor.com*)

Multex Investor is a hub for distribution of analysts' research reports. They distribute reports from major brokerage houses such as Merrill Lynch, independent research companies such as Ford Investor Services, and reports created by Multex Investor themselves.

The reports generally fall into two price categories, free and exorbitantly expensive. For instance, a report from Bear Stearns, entitled "Bear Stearns Focus List" was available for $50 when I looked. A Multex Investment Review on Microsoft was $25. But reports from several major brokerages, called "sponsors," are available at no charge. In February 2000, participating brokers included:

- Gruntal
- Merrill Lynch
- Morgan Stanley Dean Witter
- Prudential Securities
- Robertson Stephens
- Salomon Smith Barney

Most of these reports can also be obtained directly from each broker's own Web site. It's easier using Multex, however, because you can see a list of available reports from all participating brokers at once.

You have to register with Multex to access the brokers' reports, and you may also have to register with the originating broker to access their reports. You also need the Adobe Acrobat reader installed in your computer to read many of the reports. The program is free, and you can download it from most sites requiring its use to view reports.

Here are some other sources for analysts' reports:

Internet Stocks (*www.internetstocks.com*)

Robertson Stephens's Internet Stocks site publishes the *Weekly Web Report*, an extensive analysis of companies in a variety of Internet-related industry segments. These voluminous reports, authored by Robertson Stephens's analysts are exceptional in quality and detail. They are must reading for anyone interested in Internet stocks.

You can read the *Weekly Web Report* on the site, or register and they'll e-mail it to you.

Wit Capital (*www.witcapital.com*)

Wit Capital's analysts cover 80 or so Internet-related companies, in about eight industries. Their research reports are available free on the site. Their analysts also report on industry segments such as e-commerce, Web hosting, e-health, and so forth.
Wit Capital's reports are in-depth and extensive. You can register to receive e-mail notifications of changes in buy/hold/sell recommendations.

The More Analysts the Better?

CNET Investor
(*investor.cnet.com*) puts a different spin on analyst coverage. CNET's "Momentum Ratings" looks for companies with the most analysts giving the best ratings. CNET figures that "the more clients in any single stock, the more money fueling that issue's advance." CNET adds points for each buy, and subtracts points for hold and sell ratings. CNET only looks at ratings less than 90 days old, figuring older reports don't carry much weight with investors.

CNET says "any stock with a rating of 20 or higher is worth a closer look." Can you make money buying stocks with the highest momentum rankings? You tell me. Here were the top ranked stocks as of January 3, 2000: America Online, Yahoo!, Cisco Systems, Intel, Microsoft, Amgen, Altera, Applied Materials, Guidant, Lucent Technology, and Staples. Momentum ratings ranged from 76 for AOL to 48 for Lucent and Staples.

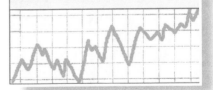

CHAPTER ELEVEN

Cashing In on Insider Info

In every company, some individuals know what's going to happen before word gets out. Maybe sales on a hot new product are taking off, or perhaps the sales force isn't meeting quota, or costs are spiraling out of control and profits are going down the drain.

This is inside information. If you knew your company had problems that hadn't become public information yet, what would you do? You would probably sell your stock. Take the opposite scenario. You know profits are taking off—they're going to beat everyone's expectations. Wouldn't you buy more stock before word got out?

That's what insiders do. They buy stock when they think it's going up—and they sell if they think it's heading down. Despite all the stories you read about arrests for insider trading, it's legal if insiders follow the rules. One of those rules says they have to report their trades to the Securities and Exchange Commission (SEC) by the tenth of the month following the trade.

Once reported, the information is public knowledge, and these days anything public is available on the Web. Insider trading information is available, in differing formats, on a variety of sites.

Assuming we want to analyze insider trading in companies we've already found through our research, let's look for ways of identifying companies with strong insider buying.

Researching Insider Trading

Market Guide (*www.marketguide.com*) gives us a handy way of taking a quick look at insider trading with its simple-to-read tabulation of insider purchases and sales over the past six months.

Type the ticker symbol into the Search For box near the top left of the main page. Select Performance on the menu on the left after Market Guide displays the Snapshot report for the stock you're researching.

When the page displays, scroll past Price Performance. You'll see Insider Trading next to the display of Institutional Ownership.

There's a lot of information in that little box. Market Guide shows us how many buy and sell transactions took place in the past six months and the number of shares traded. They even add up the numbers for us, so we can see the "net" of buys minus sells. For instance, if five insiders bought stock and two sold, we

The First Reported Investment Mania

Tulips were the center of one of the first recorded investment manias shortly after the Dutch first imported bulbs from Turkey in the late 1500s. The bulbs became popular throughout Europe and demand outpaced supply. Prices skyrocketed. One rare variety of tulip bulb reportedly sold for 4,500 Dutch gilders ($2,250). People reportedly mortgaged their homes and businesses to buy the bulbs. Eventually demand slackened, tulip prices plunged to normal levels, and investors holding tulips lost everything.

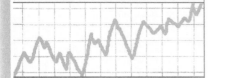

would see three net insider trades. Same thing with the number of shares traded. For instance, we would see a net of –1,500 shares traded if those five buyers each bought 100 shares, and the two sellers each sold 1,000 shares.

Insiders are buying and selling shares all the time. The number of shares traded is more significant than the number of transactions. Be on the lookout for significant trading, as in hundreds of thousands of shares. Ignore trading netting out to less than 100,000 shares. If you do spot significant trading, you'll need to investigate more to see exactly who's buying or selling.

Insider Trading Activity					
Filers Name	Title	Trade Date	Trade Type	Shares Traded	Price Range	Shares Held
Saunders, Charles H.	OFF	01/04/00	Option	6,600	$9.26	145,800
Hirschbiel, Paul O. Jr	DIR	01/04/00	Option	109,000	$0.38	0
Luft, Klaus	DIR	01/04/00	Option	345,600	$0.63 - $2.07	576,000
Hirschbiel, Paul O. Jr	DIR	01/04/00	Sell	109,000	$47.52	343,056
Saunders, Charles H.	OFF	01/04/00	Sell	6,600	$48.06	422,784
Luft, Klaus	DIR	01/04/00	Sell	345,600	$48.05	0
Topfer, Morton L.	DIR	12/23/99	Option	200,000	$52.81 - $52.88	4,290,818
Parra, Rosendo G.	OFF	12/23/99	Sell	158,938	$53.00 - $53.13	588,623
Parra, Rosendo G.	OFF	12/23/99	Option	158,938	$0.98 - $9.26	261,338
Luce, Thomas W. Iii	DIR	12/22/99	Option	26,800	$2.07	217,040
Topfer, Morton L.	DIR	12/22/99	Option	200,000	$1.11	5,200,000
Luce, Thomas W. Iii	DIR	12/22/99	Sell	26,800	$49.88	0
Dell, Michael S.	CB	12/20/99	Sell	4,000,000	$47.43 - $47.59	NA
Dell, Michael S.	CB	12/20/99	Option	5,000,000	$0.98 - $1.81	9,720,000
Saunders, Charles H.	OFF	12/17/99	Option	7,600	$9.26	152,400
Bell, Paul D.	SR VP	12/17/99	Option	74,000	$1.49	448,000
Saunders, Charles H.	OFF	12/17/99	Sell	7,600	$45.00	422,784
Bell, Paul D.	SR VP	12/17/99	Sell	74,000	$47.00	0
Lambert, Michael D.	OFF	12/07/99	Sell	100,000	$45.50	824,331
Rollins, Kevin B.	VCB	12/03/99 to 12/17/99	Sell	350,000	$45.00 - $45.50	9,800

Market Guide Insider's Trading Report. Would you buy a stock if you knew the CEO was selling?

Who's Buying, Who's Selling

By selecting Insider Trading from the menu on the left, Market Guide will display a list of insider trading activity going back about 12 months. You can see the name and title of each insider making a trade, the trade date, action (type of trade), number of shares, the trade share price, and the shares held by the insider after the transaction.

You'll probably notice many instances where two trades occur on the same date for the same number of shares. One trade type is labeled option, and the other sale. These represent insiders who are exercising options and selling them on the same day. This is normal and not a cause for alarm. Many companies compensate employees with stock options in lieu of higher salaries. Employees consider the option a part of their normal compensation, and simultaneously exercise the option to sell the shares as a matter of course.

Pay most attention to the actions of two people; the CEO and the chief financial officer (CFO). Watch for significant purchases or sales by them unrelated to the exercise of options. Significant sales of their existing holdings is a cause for alarm. What's significant? A single sale, or a series of sales resulting in a 25 percent or more reduction in their holdings. Conversely, stock purchases on the open market are a good sign. Again, look for significant numbers of shares.

You can hone in on the transactions for each insider by clicking on his or her name. That lets you put the current transaction in context. Insiders know their trading is being watched, so sometimes an insider will sell a large portion of their holdings—say 200,000 shares—and then make a couple of small purchases, say 500 shares each, a couple of months later. The insider knows that many analysts look only at the number of insider trades without regard to the number of shares traded, and to them it will look as if there have been twice as many buys as sells.

Sites That Track the Insiders

INSIDER TRADER (*www.insidertrader.com*)

Insider Trader supplies insider trading data to several major sites, including Market Guide and Quicken, but as you might expect, the trades are often posted on Insider Trader first. I've noticed as much as a week's lag between postings on Insider Trader and updates on Market Guide and Quicken. On the downside, Insider Trader's lists are harder to interpret. They use arcane codes to describe transactions or the position of the insider within the company. I prefer Market Guide because it's easier to use, but sometimes I'll look for recent trades on Insider Trader before I buy a stock, especially if Market Guide shows a lot of insider trading activity.

Insider Trader has one feature that you won't find on Market Guide. When you click on an insider's name, you'll not only see all of the insider's trades for this company but the trading for any other company where he or she holds insider status. This is especially interesting for members of boards of directors. Directors often sit on the boards of more than one company, and this is a valuable way to find out this information.

Insider Trader recently added another feature that, as of April 2000, had not been added to Market Guide or Quicken. Insider Trader displays two years of trading history, instead of the one-year history displayed on Market Guide and Quicken. The extra year's worth of data is helpful in putting a particular insider's trading into context.

YAHOO! (*quote.yahoo.com*)

Yahoo! gets insider trades online faster than Insider Trader, Market Guide, or Quicken. On the downside, where Market Guide groups individual trades made by the same insider over a two-week period into a single listing, Yahoo! shows each and every insider trade on a separate line. This may not sound like a big problem, but it is when an insider makes 20 or 30 trades of 200 shares each. Yahoo! doesn't show the insider's title or shares remaining on the main display. However, you do see that information if you click on the insider's name. Yahoo! describes each transaction type with a word such as *sold* or *exercised*. Click on the letter next to the transaction type to see a definition of the transaction type. Get a quote and then click on Insider to access Yahoo!'s insider trading data. Yahoo! lists trades going back 12 months.

THOMSON INSIDER TRADING CHARTS
(*www.invest.foxmarketwire.com*)

Thomson's insider trading charts show a company's insider trades in a useful way: overlaid on the company's stock price chart, going back one year. The chart shows each insider trade—buys with up arrows, and sells with down arrows. The most valuable part is the volume display at the bottom showing the number of shares involved in each transaction. The chart gives you a good feel for insider trading in an instant. Be sure to pay attention to the volume scale; it's different for each company. (I ignore trades involving fewer than 10,000 shares.)

The charts are part of Thomson's Research Reports. Thomson charges for them on their own site (*www.thomsoninvest.com*), but they're free on Fox Market Wire. You have to register with Market Wire before accessing the report. Get there by requesting a quote on Market Wire's home page, then select Stock Research from the dropdown menu. Scroll past the First Call Earnings Consensus report to see the insider trading chart. The other information in the Thomson reports is nothing special. The reports also list individual insider trades, but they only show you the last 20 trades, and they don't show you much detail.

WALL STREET CITY INSIDER TRADING CHARTS
(*www.wallstreetcity.com*)

To display Wall Street City's insider trading information, display a stock chart and then select Insider Trading from the menu on

---

Stock Options

A stock option is a right granted by a corporation to purchase a specified number of the corporation's shares at a predetermined exercise price. The option cannot be exercised until a specified exercise date. Stock options become valuable when the market price significantly exceeds the option's exercise price.

It has become common in recent years, especially within technology companies, to pay employees by granting valuable stock options in lieu of higher pay. There is considerable advantage for the corporation by doing this because employee salaries and other compensation is a cost deducted from corporate earnings. Conversely, the granting of stock options does not appear as an expense anywhere on the corporation's financial reports.

All goes well as long as the current market stock price exceeds the option exercise price by enough to make the employee feel justly rewarded when the exercise date comes to pass.

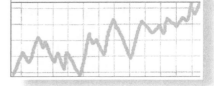

the left. Their list of insider trades comes from Insider Trader and the information is the same on both sites. What's different here is Wall Street City's stock price chart, which shows insider trading activity, and their "Dcipher" feature.

Wall Street City's insider trading price chart looks just like a regular stock chart except insider trades are shown at the bottom. Buys are shown above a zero line, and sells below. The chart displays the number of trades, not the number of shares traded. The buy/sell levels aren't labeled, so it's difficult to tell how many trades are represented. What's really interesting is the time span covered—you can set the chart to display insider trading activity back to 1974, that is, if the company has been around that long. Insider trading charts are hard to come by on the Web—the only other one I've seen is on ThomsonInvest, and that only goes back one year.

Wall Street City's Dcipher program can help you interpret the insider trading information. Press the Dcipher logo and the program displays a computer-generated analysis of the company's insider trading, including an insider trading rank ranging from –10 to 10 (best).

I've never been a believer in looking at the number of insider trades by themselves as an indicator, but these charts are convincing, especially if you look at a three-year or five-year chart.

SMART MONEY (*www.smartmoney.com* > Quote > Insiders)

Smart Money's insider trading page displays a stock price chart with insider trades designated with green circles for insider buys and red circles for insider sales. The size of the circle varies with the number of shares traded. It's very snazzy—place your mouse pointer over a trade and Smart Money displays the trade details: who's trading, their position, number of shares, etc.

Smart Money also displays the trades in conventional list form below the chart. They display each trade on a separate line, so the list can get cluttered if the insider made several trades in a short time span. The display is easy to read, and Smart Money clearly shows the position the insider holds within the company. They only display 20 trades per page, so you may have to download several pages to see an entire year's worth of trading data.

Access Smart Money's insider trading data by getting a quote on the main page, and then selecting Insiders.

Finding Companies Whose Insiders Buy

So far we've been concerned with looking up data about insider buying or selling on stocks we're researching. Now let's explore doing it the other way around, instead of looking for a specific stock, we'll look for companies with interesting insider buying patterns.

INSIDER TRADER

(*www.insidertrader.com* > *Insider Weekly Review*)

Insider Trader publishes a weekly report called the *Insider Weekly Review*. Click on "Latest Review" under *Insider Weekly Review* to display the latest report. You can display older reports by selecting Insider Review Archive and then use the dropdown menu to select report dates of interest.

Some analysts use the combined level of insider trading done at all public corporations to predict future stock market direction. Each edition of *Insider Weekly Review* starts with a commentary on the overall market outlook based on their reading of overall insider trading.

Besides giving you the big picture, *Insider Weekly Review* usually features about a dozen companies with significant insider buying activity. The report provides a one-paragraph, reasonably detailed discussion of the insider trading activity that caught their eye, along with overall comments on the company. They present quite a bit of information on each company, but their analysis is preliminary, and they don't suggest buying a stock just because it appears on their list. The report's featured stocks are candidates for their Insider Trader's Buy List, but you need a subscription to see that.

BOB GABELE

(*www.cda.com/investnet/*) or (*www.foxmarketwire.com*)

Bob Gabele is arguably the leading expert on insider trading analysis. He doesn't just look at the numbers, he analyzes the significance of every trade in detail. He is known for tracking insiders' previous trades to see how good the insiders have been at predicting future moves of their company's stock price. Gabele's

Using Insider Trading Information to Your Advantage

You can use insider trading information two ways:

1. When you're researching a company, insider trading analysis should be part of your due diligence. Wouldn't you think twice if you found out the CEO of a company you're considering buying is dumping his or her shares?

Conversely, it's heartwarming when you spy officers buying shares of their company on the open market. Most likely, they think it's headed up.

2. Another way of using insider trading is to come at it from the other direction, looking for companies with strong insider buying. Key executives may not always be right when they buy their company's stock, they could be overly optimistic, but it's a good place to start.

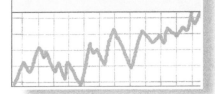

commentary is heard regularly on CNBC, and his "Insider Trading Spotlight" appears in the *Wall Street Journal* on Wednesdays.

Gabele writes at least three different reports, the daily *Insider Alerts*, *Insider Tips*, and the weekly *Insider Periscope*. Thomson Financial, operator of Thomson Investors Network (*www.thomsoninvest.net*), recently acquired Gabele's company, CDA/Investnet. As of this writing, all three reports are still available free on the CDA/Investnet site. However, it's possible Thomson will eventually close the CDA/Investnet site. Gabele's reports are also available free on Fox Market Wire. All three reports are available from the menu on the left side of the main page.

- **Insider Alerts** (*Stock of the Day* on Fox Market Wire) are published daily and highlight companies with substantial recent insider buying or selling. The Alerts chronicle recent events that may have driven the company's stock price up or down, and its future business prospects. Gabele's discussion of insider trading goes into considerable detail, describing how each insider currently trading has fared with past trades. Gabele's analysis does a good job of putting insider trades into context of other things going on with the company. They're always interesting reading, and you'll get some moneymaking ideas here.
- **Gabele's Insider Watch** (*Tip of the Day* on Fox Market Wire) is a short two- or three-sentence squib on a company highlighting recent insider buying or selling. Gabele packs a lot of information into these concise reports.
- **Gabele's Insider Periscope**, also a syndicated weekly newspaper column, usually highlights three companies, sometimes in the same industry, sometimes not. The write-up on each company is similar in content to the daily *Insider Alerts*.

In my view, Gabele's reports are quality information and among the best on the Web. I suggest you bookmark CDA/Investnet or Fox Market Wire and check the reports once a week.

BLOOMBERG

(*www.bloomberg.com* > Markets > Columns > Insider Focus)

Bloomberg's *Insider Focus* is another good resource for insider trading. The reports are almost hidden on the site: select Markets from the top menu on the main page, then click on Columns at the bottom of the News section on the menu on the left, and finally, select *Insider Focus* under People.

Insider Focus is published daily. Each report covers 10 or so companies, some domestic and some foreign, with recent substantial trading by key executives and directors. The lengthy reports go into considerable detail on each company, including its recent history and stock performance. The reports are written by reporters, not analysts, so they're heavy on interviews and quotes, but they don't examine the insiders' past trading history the way Gabele does. *Insider Focus* is published every business day, so it covers about 50 companies a week. The reports are about a week old by the time they're included in *Insider Focus*.

CNET INVESTOR (*investor.cnet.com*)

CNET lists the 15 companies with the largest insider sales and purchases for the previous week. You'll find it by scrolling down to Insider Trading on the main page. CNET shows you the company and the insider's name, along with the trade date, number of shares involved, and the insider's holdings after the trade. They don't tell you the insider's position within the company.

You can read also recent insider trading news stories here by selecting Insider Trading News just below the Insider Trading link.

Who Are Insiders?

Technically, insiders are company executives, members of the board of directors, and anyone who owns more than 10 percent of the outstanding stock.

Screening for Insider Buying Tips

Several sites offer screening programs for finding stocks with notable insider trading activity. With one exception, they all use programs and data supplied by Wall Street City. The lone exception is Zacks, which uses their own database and their own screening program.

WALL STREET CITY

(*www.wallstreetcity.com* > ProSearch > Custom Searches)

Telescan's Wall Street City offers a choice of two predefined searches: High Insider Buying and Surging Insider Trading. They are both accessed from the same page. Select ProSearch from the menu on the left on Wall Street City's main page, and then click Custom Searches. You'll see a list of prebuilt searches. The two insider searches, High Insider Buying and Surging Insider Trading, are near the bottom, on the left.

High Insider Buying looks for the 25 companies with the greatest number of insider buys. In this instance, Wall Street City defines insider buying as the net of actual insider buys and sells. For instance, if within the past three months 15 insiders bought shares and 10 sold, the net—or number of buys—is 5. The program doesn't consider the number of shares traded. So a 100,000-share purchase and a 100 share sale would net to zero.

Click on High Insider Buying to start the Wall Street City search screen. The program lists the 25 stocks in the $5 to $999 price range with the highest number of net insider buys. It also shows you Historical Results, your return if you had run the program one, two, three, . . . up to 12 months ago and bought the 25 stocks turned up by the screen. I don't recommend taking the results of any screen, much less this one, and buying the stocks without further research. However, if you're screening for high insider buying, you'd expect most of the stocks found to have that trait. Unfortunately, it just doesn't pan out, probably because looking solely at the number of insider buys without considering volume doesn't ferret out the real buyers. In my experience, the 25 stocks yielded by this screen yielded about the same number of companies with strong insider buying as a randomly selected group of 25 stocks.

Surging Insider Trading works better. This search screen looks for companies with net buys of at least four trades within the past three months, but it also looks for companies with highest net increase in insider trading within the past three months and past six months. The screen also requires stocks to trade for at least $7, to have been traded for at least a year, and to trade at least 100,000 shares a day, on average, over the past 30 days.

The search yields a good list of suspects. In my experience, about half of the 25 stocks turned up by the screen do indeed have significant insider buying. You can narrow the search by specifying company size (micro-, small-, medium-, or large-cap), searching for optionable stocks only, or looking for stocks traded on specific exchanges such as the New York Stock Exchange or NASDAQ.

ZACKS (*www.zacks.com* > my.zacks.com > Screening > Predefined Screening or Custom Screening)

Zacks is the supplier of analysts' recommendations and forecasts for Yahoo!, Quicken, and many other investment sites. Zacks also collects fundamental and insider trading data and accumulates it in their database. Zacks developed a program for screening their database a number of years ago, but until recently it was available only to subscribers. Now you can use it free.

You have a choice of using their predefined screens or creating a customized screen. The two insider trading predefined screens are: Top Insider Buying and Top Insider Selling. The screens search for companies with largest positive (insider buying) or negative (insider selling) changes in insider holdings over the past 12 weeks. Each screen lists 25 stocks, and the screens are very effective in ferreting out stocks with high insider trading.

NEWSTRADERS (*www.newstraders.com* > Insiders Daily)

Newstraders presents a list of significant insider trades reported by the SEC that day. The page is updated throughout the day. This is the fastest source I've found for reporting insider trades, but they give you the bare bones details with no background. They archive each day's report and save them for several months. You can search the archives (search New Traders on main page) for mentions of specific companies, or for particular insiders. Select Insiders Daily from their main page.

Insiders Aren't Much Different from Us

Some experts give a lot of weight to insiders buying on the open market—as opposed to buying their own company's stock. And when selling shares, insiders may have reasons unrelated to their expectations for their company's future stock price—they may simply need the money to buy a new house, send their kids to college, or pay a divorce settlement.

On the other hand, insiders usually buy stock on the open market for only one reason— they think it's going up.

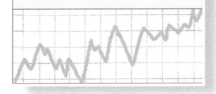

TULIPS AND BEARS (*www.tulipsandbears.com* > Daily Screens > Insider Buying and Selling)

This site displays a list of the 20 companies with the most insider buys of the 20 companies with the most insider sales over the past three months. The list is updated on Thursdays. Get there by clicking Insider Buying and Selling under Daily Screens, toward the bottom of their home page.

INSIDER SCORES (*www.insiderscores.com*)

This site keeps track of each insider's track record—or in their parlance, batting average—that is, how did the stock go up or down after the insider bought or sold. You can look up the activities and batting averages of insiders in a company of interest, or see what insiders with the best track records are up to.

CHAPTER TWELVE

Getting the Most out of Quotes and Charts

Quotes and charts are available free on virtually every financial site. We'll use Yahoo! to demonstrate how to use them.

Go to *finance.yahoo.com* and enter a ticker symbol or select "Symbol Lookup" to find the symbol. Select Basic, DayWatch, or Detailed from the dropdown menu. You can enter multiple symbols separated by a space (not a comma).

LUCENT TECH (NYSE:LU) - More Info: News , SEC , Msgs , Profile , Research , Insider					
Last Trade 4:41PM · **53.19**	Change -2.12 (-3.84%)	Prev Cls 55.31	Volume 14,462,800	Div Date Mar 1	
Day's Range 53.00 - 55.81	Bid N/A	Ask N/A	Open 55.25	Avg Vol 21,068,590	Ex-Div Jan 27
52-week Range 49.31 - 84.19	Earn/Shr 1.10	P/E 50.28	Mkt Cap 169.5B	Div/Shr 0.08	Yield 0.14

Yahoo! Detailed Quote shows just about everything in one display.

Pick Detailed, unless download time is a critical consideration. The Detailed view gives you everything you need in one display including a thumbnail price chart and recent news headlines. Stock price information is delayed 20 minutes.

CURRENT TRADING DATA

Bid/Ask: Latest bid and ask prices. The bid price is the price you'll get if you're selling. The ask is the price you'll pay if you're buying.

Open: Trade price of the day's first transaction.

Day's Range: High and low trade prices for the day.

Last Trade: Price of the last transaction (delayed 20 minutes). This is the day's closing price if you're looking after the market closed.

Change: Difference between the last trade today and yesterday's close, expressed in dollars and percentage. The spread of extended hours trading is causing confusion as to yesterday's closing price. Different services will quote different closing prices.

Volume: Number of shares traded today.

Previous Close: Previous trading day's closing price.

HISTORICAL TRADING DATA

Average Volume: Average daily trading volume over the past three months.

52-Week Range: High and low closing prices for the past year.

FUNDAMENTAL DATA

Earn/Shr: Earnings per share for the last four reported quarters.

P/E: Price-to-earnings ratio based on the previous day's closing price and earnings per share.

Mkt Cap: Market capitalization; the number of shares outstanding multiplied by the previous closing price of a share.

Div/Shr: Annual dividends, typically four times the quarterly dividend.

Div Date: Date the next dividend will be paid

Ex-Div: First trading day share buyers will not be entitled to current dividend. (Dividend was paid to shareholders of record on previous day.)

Yield: Annual dividend divided by the previous closing price, expressed in percentage.

PRICE CHARTS

The thumbnail price chart covers one year. Click on 1-day or 5-days (scroll) to see a shorter-term chart in the same location. Select any of the time spans listed in the "Big" row to see a larger chart. The larger charts include trading volume displayed at the bottom of the chart.

Click on "Moving Avg" to display 50-day and 200-day moving averages. Click on "vs S&P 500" to see the performance of the selected company compared to the performance of the S&P 500 index over the chart period.

Yahoo! one-year price chart with 50- and 200-day moving averages. The current stock price is below both moving averages, indicating the stock is in both a short-term and long-term downtrend.

Charts Made Simple

MSN MONEYCENTRAL'S CHARTS

MoneyCentral's charts are flexible, easy to use, and surprisingly fast. Get there by going to *moneycentral.msn.com* and linking to the Investor page. Enter a ticker symbol in the box on the upper left of the Investor page and select Chart from the dropdown menu. You'll have to download special software from Microsoft the first time you use the charts. It's not complicated, just select "Start Download" and follow the instructions.

The default chart for any stock is a one-year bar chart. Click on Analysis and select volume chart. You'll be amazed at how fast the volume appears. Now click on Analysis again, select Moving Averages and then 200-Day Moving Average. Use your mouse to

Quicken Quotes

Quicken (*www.quicken.com*) is another good site for quotes and charts. Quicken works much the same as Yahoo! Like Yahoo!, Quicken's data is delayed 20 minutes.

Enter the ticker symbol at the top right of the main page and you'll see essentially the same information as shown on Yahoo!'s Detailed Quote. Quicken doesn't display the price chart with the quote, however. You'll have to select the price chart separately. Quicken displays related news headlines below the quote. Click on a headline to read the full story.

"Day's Overview" displays a price chart for the current day and current price information. The "Last 5 Days" page displays open, high, low, close (last), and volume data for the previous five trading days.

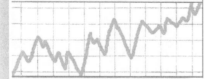

move your cursor over the price chart. Up pops the date, closing price, and price change.

Click on Analysis again and select Indexes. Your choices include the Dow Jones Industrial Average, S&P 500, NASDAQ, AMEX, or Relevant Industry—that's the industry group relevant to the stock. Pick an index and you'll see the performance of the stock compared to the index.

Select the Period dropdown menu and try different time spans. You'll notice all stock splits and dividends indicated by icons on the chart. Place your cursor on the icon to see the details. If the stock is in a portfolio you maintain on MoneyCentral's Portfolio Manager, you'll see your buys and sells on the chart. You can see the details of those too by moving your cursor over the icon.

Real-Time Quotes

The security exchanges give away their delayed quote feeds to financial Web sites and other reporting services, but they charge for real-time quotes. That's why most free financial sites display quotes delayed around 20 minutes. Several sites sell real-time quotes, but times are always changing on the Web, and free real-time quotes are available.

Most Web brokers give away a certain number of free real-time quotes. The number of free quotes available is sometimes tied to your trading volume. This usually works out fine because the people who need a lot of real-time quotes probably do enough trades to warrant a high freebie allocation.

Recently, sites not affiliated with brokers started offering free real-time quotes. Some of them put a limit on the number of free quotes, typically 50 to 100 quotes per day. That's not a particularly onerous limitation, but at least two sites offer unlimited real-time quotes.

Moving Averages

Moving averages are the simplest technical indicators. Many investors who don't believe in technical analysis still look at moving averages.

The moving average is the average closing price of the stock over a specified period. For instance, the value of the 10-day moving average is the average closing price for the past 10 days. The most widely used moving averages are 50 days and 200 days. Long-term investors tend to use the 200-day moving average, while active traders are more likely to look at the 50-day moving average. Many investors look at both.

The relationship between the stock price and its moving averages helps you determine if the stock is in an uptrend, downtrend, or no trend (consolidation). The stock is considered in an uptrend if its price is above the moving average, and it's in a downtrend if it's below its moving average. The distance between the stock price and the moving average indicates the trend strength. The trend is weak if the stock price is hovering near or crisscrossing the averages, and strong when the index is far above or below the average.

Sometimes you'll notice that the stock price is below its 50-day moving average, but above the 200-day average. That says the stock is in a short-term downtrend, but a long-term uptrend. In other words, a "dip." Unfortunately, you can't tell the difference between a dip and the start of a downtrend until much later.

There are two types of moving averages: simple (SMA) and exponential (EMA). The simple moving average is calculated as described above, by averaging the closing prices over the selected period. An exponential moving average uses a more complicated calculation that results in giving more weight to the most recent closing prices, and less weight to prices near the beginning of the selected time span.

There is no clear-cut advantage to using either type over the other.

WALL STREET CITY (*www.wallstreetcity.com*)

Access the quotes by entering a ticker symbol and selecting "Real Time" in the box near the top right of their main page.

Wall Street City not only gives you a real-time quote, but they also show you a real-time intraday (today's trades) price chart. If that's not enough, they list the time, trade price, volume (number of shares), and the exchange the last 10 trades were traded on. They also display any "breakout alerts" (buy or sell signals) triggered by a variety of technical indicators.

Wall Street City's real-time quotes give you a lot for free—it's an amazing service, even for the Web.

FREE REAL TIME (*www.freerealtime.com*)

Once you register and logon, simply enter the ticker symbol near the top right of the main page and you're off. Free Real Time gives you the time, trade price, and size of the last trade, plus the usual data on the day's trading activity: high, low, volume, and the like. They show you the average trade size and the number of trades for the day, but they don't give any details on previous trades as Wall Street City does.

Charts for Chartists: Technical Charts

Technical charts are used by technical analysts, or chartists, to make buy or sell decisions based on the stock's previous price action. Chartists often use computer-generated indicators to help them analyze the chart. Here are some sites that will help you get an idea of what chartists do. You may even decide to become one yourself!

CLEARSTATION (*www.clearstation.com*)

ClearStation is a place for technical analysts to hang out. It's all about charting and community. ClearStation strives to make charting simple.

Try it out by entering a ticker symbol in the box labeled Get Graphs near the top right of the main page. There's no "Go"

Registering for Real-Time Quotes

Registering for real-time quotes (free or pay) is an interesting experience, no matter which site you use. You have to execute a separate contract with each of the three exchanges, the NYSE, NASDAQ, and the AMEX. Each contract is lengthy and written in difficult to interpret legal terminology. Each contract includes several places where you have to indicate agreement by clicking a checkmark with your mouse. Then there are other places you have to type your name. If you miss one, you usually have to do the whole thing again.

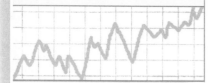

button, so push your Enter key or click on Get Graphs to display the price chart.

ClearStation displays the price chart in red, except on days the stock made a new high, those days are shown in blue. ClearStation plots two moving averages, a 13-day EMA (exponential moving average) shown in green, and a purple 50-day EMA.

Just above the price chart are green and red horizontal bars. Green indicates uptrends—you're supposed to buy when the green bar first appears. Red signifies a downtrend, and you're supposed to short the stock when the bar goes red. The absence of either color signifies no discernable trend. You should get out of the stock altogether then.

Below each price chart are four technical indicators.

1. Trading *volume* is shown in blue on the days the stock went up in price and is shown in red on days it dropped. If you're long (buying) the stock, you'll want to see tall blue lines and short red lines—indicating high buying power—and not much enthusiasm on down days.

2. Below the volume is a technical indicator called the MACD (moving average convergence divergence) and below that is the MACD Histogram. Little green circles appear on the MACD chart when they interpret the MACD as indicating an uptrend, and red circles when the MACD is pointing to a downtrend.

3. The MACD Histogram is added to clarify interpretation of the MACD, and to identify divergences, which can't be seen on the two-line MACD display. A divergence is a condition when a stock price makes a new high, but the indicator doesn't. Divergences are an important indication of a change in trend direction.

4. The fourth indicator is the Stochastic Oscillator. ClearStation recommends using the relatively short-term Stochastic to time entries when the MACD indicates an uptrend. Ideally that would be when the Stochastic crosses below the bottom reference line indicating temporary weakness and a buying opportunity.

Electronic Network Trading Order Book

The Island ECN, Inc., (*www.island.com*) operates one of the largest stock market electronic communication networks (ECN). ECNs eliminate the traditional channels of stock trading. That is, you don't go through a specialist for New York Stock Exchange traded stocks or a market maker for NASDAQ-listed stocks. ECNs are springing up like wildflowers and it's widely speculated that the major exchanges will start their own or buy existing ECNs before long.

You can view trading of NASDAQ stocks handled by Island from 8 A.M. to 8 P.M. EST using their Book Viewer. Enter a NASDAQ stock symbol and the viewer displays up to 15 buy orders and up to 15 sell orders for the stock.

Each buy order lists the price the buyer is willing to pay (bid) and the number of shares the buyer is willing to buy at that price. Sell orders show the offering price (ask) and the number of shares.

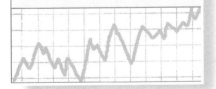

Click on Tag & Bag while you're at ClearStation. There you'll find lists of stocks exhibiting significant technical, fundamental, or community events:

- Technical events are stocks exhibiting bullish technical signals.
- Fundamental events highlight stocks with positive earnings surprises or analyst upgrades.
- Community events spotlight stocks getting the most recommendations on ClearStation's message boards.

WALL STREET CITY (*www.wallstreetcity.com*)

Access the Wall Street City technical charts by entering a ticker symbol in the Free Real-Time Quote box on the top left, but select Corporate Snapshot, then click View/Analyze large chart (default setting). The default setting selects a one-year chart with volume shown as the indicator. Use the buttons below the chart to select time spans ranging from one-day to 10 years, to maximum for the selected stock. Use the menu below the chart to select from the menu of 12 technical indicators.

Use the default values, or select your own parameters for each indicator. If you do, you can set up custom profiles so you don't have to enter your parameters when you select the indicators. You can also access a variety of fundamental reports from the drop-down menu on the left. Click on the indicator name below the chart for a detailed explanation of how the selected indicator is calculated, when to use it, and how you should interpret the indicator chart. It's an excellent tutorial.

METASTOCK ONLINE
(*www.equis.com* > Free Stuff > Online Charting)

Metastock is Equis's brand name for their charting software for personal computers. Metastock Online's Java charts give you a menu of 17 indicators. Metastock also includes an indicator they call "Compare Relative Strength." Usually called Relative Strength, it compares the stock's performance to the S&P 500 index, or any other index, or even to another stock.

Stock prices tend to move with the overall market. A stock may drop simply because the whole market took a fall. Relative strength

---

Trading in Tokyo or Caracas: International Indexes

CBS MarketWatch (*cbs.marketwatch.com* > Market Data > International Indexes under Global Markets) lists current quotes for major international indexes in the Americas, Asia/Pacific, and Europe. Click on the index symbol for more information.

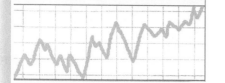

"Live" Stock Charts

Even if you never look at stock charts, you'll find the Live Charts at Quote.com (*www.quote.com*) mesmerizing. Click Live Charts on their main page and enter a ticker symbol where it says "Sym," and then push the Enter key on your keyboard. The Live Charts display shows you a price chart on the left and the last 12 trades for the stock on the right.

The price chart is a bar chart, meaning each vertical line (bar) shows you the highest, lowest, opening and closing prices for the time period. Here's what's different: You can set the bars to represent periods ranging from one minute to three months (use the Time setting), and the chart automatically updates itself after each period. It's fascinating to set the time to one minute and watch the chart move. The dropdown menu on the bottom-left displays "volume" or one of 11 different technical indicators. Try selecting "volume" and watch which way the price moves on relatively high-volume trades. I bet you'll learn something.

As interesting as the price chart is, watching the individual trades go by is even

Quote.com's Live Charts are fun to watch even if you don't trade stocks.

better. Live Charts shows you the time, price, originating exchange, and size of each transaction. Every trade is shown, regardless of the period you selected for the bar chart. The times are listed in military format, and are East Coast times. So 14:00:00 is 2:00 P.M. Eastern Time, or 11:00 A.M. Pacific Time. Live Charts shows you trades for two hours after the official closing time of the major markets, so you see much of the after-hours trading.

Live Charts data is delayed 20 minutes. Real-time displays are available on a subscription basis.

(*continued on next page*)

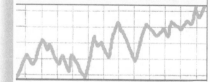

charts take the market movement factor out of the chart and show
you how the stock is performing compared to a relevant index. In
my view, relative strength charts give you a better picture of how a
stock is performing than you get by looking at conventional price
charts.

Don't confuse relative strength derived by comparing a stock
to an index with the similarly named Relative Strength Indicator
(RSI). Equis is the one site I've found providing this type of
charting capability.

The relevant index for any given stock depends on the particu-
lars of the company. Here are some suggestions:

SECTOR	INDEX	TICKER SYMBOL
Large-caps, general	S&P 500	.SPC
Mid-caps, general	S&P 400	.MID
Small-caps, general	Russell 2000	.RUT
Technology, general	NASDAQ	IXIC

Use Metastock's defaults or enter your own parameters for each
indicator. You can compare up to five stocks on one chart. You
can draw your own trendlines right on the chart by holding down
your mouse button. Placing your cursor on the chart gives you the
date, open, high, low, and closing prices for the day.

You're limited to displaying one year with daily charts and two
years with weekly charts. To see five years of data, you'll have to
go to monthly charts.

Quotes for Day Traders

Day traders move in and out of positions (stock ownership) in minutes. Long term for them is two hours. Day traders try to close out
all their positions before the close, so they own nothing overnight.

Traditional day traders rely on charting techniques, just as
longer-term chartists do.

In recent years, a new kind of day trader has emerged who
doesn't use stock charts. These day traders seek to capitalize on an
anomaly particular to the NASDAQ market system called NASDAQ
Level II quotes.

NASDAQ-listed stocks are traded through market makers. Market makers keep inventories of stocks they make a market in, and post bid (what they'll pay to sellers) and ask (what they want from buyers) prices on the NASDAQ trading system. The quotes for NASDAQ-listed stocks you see free on the Web, whether delayed or real-time, are termed NASDAQ Level I. They show only the best bid (highest) and best ask (lowest) offers currently quoted by market makers. Sometimes you'll also see the number of shares the market maker is willing to buy or sell, associated with those offers.

Since there may be a dozen or more market makers offering to buy and sell shares at various prices at any given time, NASDAQ offers another level of quotes—NASDAQ Level II—to show all active market makers' bid and ask quotes, including the number of shares each is willing to buy or sell.

Day traders watch the changes of NASDAQ Level II quotes in an attempt to predict the stock's price movement for the next few minutes—an hour at most. They're not looking to make much on a single trade, $0.50 per share is good and $1.00 would be extraordinary. Commissions and slippage (difference between bid and ask prices) eat up much of their profits. Transaction speed is critical, and they often do their trading using terminals located in the offices of brokers specializing in day trading.

PHACTOR.COM (*www.phactor.com*)

Phactor.com, run by Phil Huether, an employee of MB Trading, Inc., is an excellent source for just about everything you need to know about day trading. Whether it's basic tutorials, testing the speed of your Internet connection, or advice on how to hook up two monitors to your computer, you'll find it here.

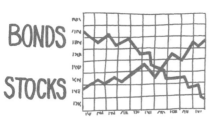

His tutorials are detailed and generously illustrated with screenshots. He lists links to day traders' message boards, chat rooms, day-trading software, etc.

Extended Hours' Quotes

(continued from previous page)

NASDAQ Trader
(*nasdaqtrader.com* > Trading Data > Extended Hours Trading)

Here you can see summaries of the top 10 stocks traded after hours for the most recent trading day and going back about one month.

Stock Winners
(*www.stockwinners.com* > After Hour Prices)

Stock Winners lists all stocks traded in after-hours and pre-market trading. They display the regular hours closing price and the last off-hours trade.

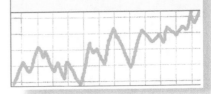

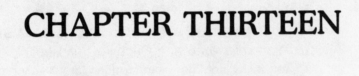

CHAPTER THIRTEEN

Decoding Financial Statements

You've done an excellent job of research so far; in fact, you've done more than 90 percent of investors ever dream of doing. From your original list of candidates, you're left with the few survivors. You know what they do, you've analyzed the competition, checked momentum factors, read research reports, and you like what you see.

So now it's time to take an in-depth look at your candidates' financial statements. Wait—don't run away! There are two Web sites that will do the heavy lifting for you.

First, let's use Morningstar to rate the company's long-term financial health. Then we'll enlist Equity Insights to help you detect clues to future disaster.

Clues to Future Earnings

MORNINGSTAR'S FINANCIAL ANALYSIS

(*www.morningstar.com* > Quotes > Snapshot)

You might not know that Morningstar's highly regarded mutual fund ratings are computer generated. That's right, there's no human intervention in the process. Now, Morningstar applies the same principle to rating individual stocks. Their computer program analyzes almost every publicly traded company's financial statements. The best news is they don't give us the results using arcane terms we can't comprehend. Morningstar talks in a language we all understand: they give a company grades. In this case, A through F.

Start by entering either the ticker symbol into the Quotes and Reports box on the Morningstar page, then select Snapshot from the menu on the left.

You may have already read the profile (Company Basics) at the top in an earlier stage of your research. Morningstar does an excellent job of describing the company's business. We'll look at some other information about the company at the top right of the page before we delve into the financials. Ignore the industry and sector designations, they're too broad to help us much.

Rating Companies by Stock Type

Analysts say companies go through definable stages as they progress from the speculative start-up phase to maturity. Morningstar tells us where they think the company fits in the cycle by assigning them to a stock type category:

- **Speculative-growth** companies (e.g., America Online) are growing sales rapidly but are producing little or no profits. Buy these companies in the hope the company will move into the aggressive growth stage.
- **Aggressive-growth** firms (Cisco Systems) are posting rapid sales and earnings growth in both sales and earnings.
- **Classic-growth** companies (Walt Disney) are showing steady and consistent sales and earnings growth, but at a slower rate than when they were aggressive growers. They're producing lots of cash flow, high returns on capital, and rising dividends.
- **Slow-growth** firms (Gillette) are growing earnings and sales slower than the overall economy. They are probably paying out most of their earnings as dividends.
- **Cyclicals** are companies (Boeing) sensitive to changes in the overall economy, such as automobile manufacturers or paper producers.
- **Hard asset** companies (Texaco) rely on assets such as real estate, oil, gold, etc.
- **Distressed** companies (Sunbeam) are experiencing serious operating problems.
- **High-yield** companies (Philip Morris) pay more than twice the average dividend yield of large-cap companies.

You can use the stock type rating to evaluate how the stock fits in with your portfolio and your investing goals. For instance, you might eliminate a speculative growth company simply because your portfolio is already overweighted with speculative stocks.

Rating Companies by Style

Another Morningstar tool for evaluating the suitability of a stock for your portfolio, is how they classify stocks into styles, based on company size and valuation:

- *Size:* Five percent of U.S. companies in the Morningstar database are categorized as large-cap; the next 15 percent mid-cap; and the rest are small-cap.
- *Valuation:* Morningstar uses Price/Earnings and Price/Book ratios to categorize a company as value, blend (valued between growth and value), or growth.

You can have any combination of size and value; for instance, large-cap value, small-cap growth, etc. Large-cap growth companies have seriously out-performed the rest of the market in recent years. Of course, fashions change, and the past doesn't necessarily predict the future.

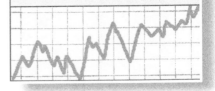

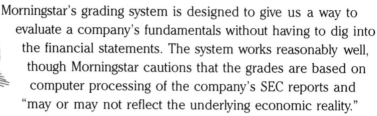

Grading Stocks

Morningstar's grading system is designed to give us a way to evaluate a company's fundamentals without having to dig into the financial statements. The system works reasonably well, though Morningstar cautions that the grades are based on computer processing of the company's SEC reports and "may or may not reflect the underlying economic reality." They say "investors should view the grades as a starting point . . . rather than a definitive judgment on the company."

- *Growth*: Morningstar looks at historical sales growth over the past five years. Growth rates are compared only to firms in the same sector, not the overall market. The highest grades go to companies with consistently high growth rates. Companies with volatile or slowing growth rates get low grades.
- *Profitability*: Morningstar uses return on assets (ROA), that is, earnings compared to total assets, to grade profitability. Morningstar says ROA measures how efficiently the company uses investors' money. As with sales growth, higher is better, and a consistent rising trend of ROA gets the best grade.
- *Financial Health*: Morningstar looks at balance sheet items such as debt levels and cash in the bank, along with cash flows to measure financial health. Low debt and high levels of cash flow and free cash flow earn high ratings. As with the other measures, companies with improving trends get the best grades.
- *Valuation*: Morningstar's valuation formula starts by calculating an intrinsic value for the company. The calculation involves adding the current value of estimated future earnings to the book value. This method of valuing companies is favored by Warren Buffett and other value-oriented investors. Of course, the result depends on the accuracy of earnings forecasts. Morningstar uses a secret formula to assess the predictability of future earnings: they adjust the calculated intrinsic value based on their predictability score. Companies with stock prices below the adjusted intrinsic value are considered undervalued and get the best grades.

You must be cautious when considering Morningstar's valuation grade. Going for stocks with high valuation grades will put you into a value portfolio. These stocks are undervalued because the market doesn't like them. Sometimes the market overreacts to bad news and goes overboard in knocking down the stock price. Conversely, the market is often correct in their assessment. Cheap stocks often get cheaper.

How to Interpret the Grades

Morningstar's grades make it easy for us to evaluate a company's fundamentals without having to put on a green eye-shade. However, you must be aware of the limitations.

Morningstar's analysis relies mostly on the company's annual reports. Since the grades are based on the company's long-term financial trends, they don't give enough weight to information from recent quarterly reports—which can be a fatal mistake. The market's assessment of these long-term results are already reflected in the stock price. Astute investors always scrutinize the most recent information, looking for changes that forecast future changes, good or bad. (You'll learn how to do that in the next section.)

Morningstar's valuation grade compares the current stock price to Morningstar's calculation of the company's intrinsic value. Intrinsic value, in turn, is based on analysts' long-term (e.g., five years) earnings growth forecasts. These forecasts are almost always wrong, usually too high. Investors pay close attention to earnings forecasts for the next few quarters; few notice the long-term growth forecasts. Consequently, analysts are slow to change them, often waiting long after they've downgraded the stock and lowered near-term projections.

Morningstar winds up giving A valuations to beaten-down companies—for instance, Tommy Hilfiger and Airborne Freight in 1999. You can't evaluate a company's recovery prospects from Morningstar's grades. Take Nike for example. Nike was a solid, well-managed company with a history of consistent growth spanning several years until sneakers went out of fashion, at least with teenagers, in 1997. Nike would have probably had all A grades if Morningstar had been grading stocks back then. There is nothing in Morningstar's grading system to evaluate fads or changes in fashion.

Here's how to make the most out of Morningstar's grades, depending on what kind of an investor you are:

- Value investors should look for high Financial Health and Valuation grades; ignore Growth and Profitability grades since it was probably a drop in sales growth, profitability, or both that sank the stock price originally.
- Growth investors should look for high grades (minimum A minus) for Growth, Profitability, and Financial Health.
- Momentum players don't analyze financial statements.

Consequently, growth investors should either ignore the valuation grade altogether, or use it as a contrary indicator—that is, look for companies considered overvalued (grades B to F). Value investors, on the other hand, should look for A-grade valuations. They signal currently out-of-favor companies with turnaround potential. Of course, they have to do their research to avoid picking another Nike.

Clues to Future Disaster

Now let's go on to evaluate the most recent information and look for clues to future disaster. A disaster is when a stock you own loses 25 to 50 percent of its value in one day, usually in the first minutes of trading. Short sellers make a science of detecting disaster candidates, and you'll learn to use their tools to help you avoid disasters in the making.

EQUITY INSIGHTS (*www.equityinsights.com*)

I'm one of a very tiny percentage of investors who enjoys delving into financial statements. But even I can't do what the real sleuths do—you know, the ones who discover a company's financial shenanigans, make headlines, and drive a company's stock price down.

Equity Insights, a service of Applied Financial Group, knows how to scrutinize financial statements in that kind of detail, and they make it so easy you'll find yourself analyzing financials just for fun. Applied Finance Group (AFG) is a Chicago-based privately held firm that works with Arthur Anderson & Company to provide stock market analysis to institutional investors such as Fidelity, State Street Research, Putnam, and many more. AFG also consults with large corporations such as Daimler Chrysler to help the company understand how their strategic decisions affect shareholder value. The fact is, AFG is a heavyweight, not some guy posting stock recommendations on his Web site while he keeps his day job.

And remarkably, AFG lets us use many of the same tools employed in their institutional work on their Equity Insights site for free.

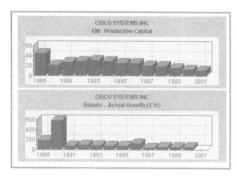

Equity Insights economic margin and asset growth charts. Equity Insights would interpret the downtrend in EM as a negative indicator.

Here's how AFG's analysis works:

The stock market is hooked on earnings. Stock prices often move dramatically in response to changes in earnings expectations. Some analysts, including AFG, believe that reported earnings are not a reliable measure of a company's future growth prospects. Why? Because reported earnings are the result of myriad arbitrary decisions concerning accounting treatment of depreciation, inventories, R&D expenditures, and on and on.

Show me the cash: AFG prefers to measure operating cash flow, the amount of money that flows into, or out of a company's bank account resulting from its basic business. Companies are required to report cash flow as part of their quarterly reports filed with the SEC.

It's not as simple as looking at reported cash flow, however, because reported cash flow doesn't tell the whole story, at least as far as AFG is concerned. To make an apples to apples comparison between different companies, cash flow has to be adjusted for R&D expenditures, leasing costs, pension plan income, etc.

The good news is AFG figures it out for us. They give us the answer with a simple gauge they call Economic Margin (EM), their measure of a company's profitability. EM can be a positive or negative number, and AFG says EMs for public corporations, measured over the past 20 years, average out to zero. In general, positive EM values signify healthier companies than negative values.

AFG doesn't predict future performance by looking at history. Instead, they project EMs for the current and next fiscal years using analysts' forecasts and their own research, and compare those to historical EMs.

STOCK ANALYZER

Let's get started by typing a ticker symbol into the entry box at the top left of the Equity Web site and select Stock Analyzer under Stock Tools. You'll see a current quote if you pushed your Enter key instead of clicking on Stock Analyzer. If that's the case, click Stock Analyzer now.

Stock Analyzer consists of 12 pages selected by clicking on a number at the top. Each page includes two or three bar charts

Best Investment Sites for Direct Investing

BuyandHold.com
(*www.buyandhold.com*): Offers Direct Stock Purchase plans for at least twelve hundred companies, whether or not the companies themselves have such a plan. Best resource in this category.

Netstock Direct
(*www.netstockdirect.com*): The place to find companies offering Direct Stock Purchase (DSPs) and Direct Reinvestment Plans (DRIPs).

ShareBuilder
(*www.sharebuilder.com*) and **Universal Stock Access**
(*www.universalstockaccess.com*): Offer Direct Stock Purchase plans similar to BuyandHold.com.

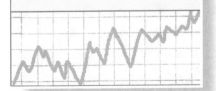

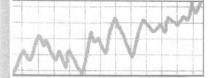

graphically illustrating trends in fundamental characteristics such as operating margins or sales trends. AFG provides a two or three sentence interpretation of the information below the charts, along with a numeric score ranking the company's characteristics compared to other companies in AFG's database. The ranking scale is 1 to 10, where 10 is best. You'll only need to look at the following pages.

Economic Margins

Page 1 of the Stock Analyzer displays past and projected future EMs on a bar chart. Each bar represents one year. The two right-hand bars show AFG's estimates for the current fiscal year and for the next fiscal year. In the AFG system, positive EMs are better than negative values, but the trend from last year to the current fiscal year is more important. Improving (up) trends are good, and downtrends are bad.

If the chart is confusing, scroll down to the second explanatory sentence below the graphics. It will say something like "AFG estimates a negative (or positive) trend in EMs next year." What could be simpler?

There are two additional charts on this page: Asset Growth and Return. You don't need them, but here's an explanation if you're interested:

- *Asset Growth* measures the annual growth of AFG's version of invested capital, total assets plus various adjustments. AFG says to look for a pattern of stable, as opposed to erratic growth, but they don't rate it nearly as important as EM.
- The *Return* chart compares the performance of the stock price compared to an index of the 2,000 largest publicly traded corporations. AFG likes to see a "history of, or a developing trend of increasing returns."

Sales Trends

The chart at the top of page 2 illustrates the quarterly sales growth compared to the same year-ago quarter. Sales growth is one of the most important factors in fundamental analysis. Companies can't grow without increasing sales. Ideally, you'd like to see steady or increasing sales growth. Falling sales growth is a danger sign. All companies' sales growth naturally fluctuates from quarter to quarter, so ignore small fluctuations. An important danger sign or red flag is when the sales growth drops in half—for instance, from 50 percent a year ago to 25 percent this year, or from 200 percent last year to 100 percent this year. A drop from 30 percent to 25 percent is not significant.

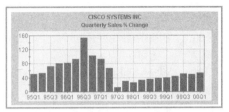

Equity Insights Sales Growth Chart

The lower chart compares the company's sales growth to its competitors. All things being equal, faster is better, so a diligent investor should investigate competitors with faster sales growth.

Operating Margins

Page 3 illustrates a form of operating margin; that is, operating income expressed as a percentage of sales. AFG uses EBITDA—reported net earnings with the interest, taxes, depreciation, and amortization deductions factored back in.

Operating margin tells you how much a company makes on each dollar of sales. A 20 percent operating margin means the company makes 20 cents for every dollar of goods sold. More is better, but again, the trend is most important. You want level or rising margins. Falling margins is an important clue to future disaster. Drops of 20 percent or more—e.g., from 20% to 16%, or from 40% to 32%—are significant.

The lower chart compares the company's operating margins to its competitors. Generally, in any given industry, the company able to maintain the highest margins usually has the best products, and is the industry leader. Check out any competitors with higher margins.

(Page 4 displays asset efficiency, or sales per dollar of assets. You can skip this page.)

Accounts Receivable

Page 5 shows the accounts receivable (apply to manufacturing companies) compared to sales. AFG expresses it as Days Sales Outstanding (DSO). This arcane term is important to your financial health. Manufacturing companies don't usually sell COD; their customers have a

Other Equity Insight Valuations

- Page 7: Compares the company's stock price to intrinsic value, determined by computing the present value of future cash flows. Most hot performers in this market are overvalued by this measurement.
- Pages 8, 9, and 10: Show the company's price/earnings, price/sales, and price/book ratios. Value investors look for low ratios. The recent market has favored growth over value, and higher-priced stocks have outperformed stocks with lower ratios.
- Pages 11 and 12: Display earnings surprise and earnings forecast histories. These are important factors, but you can get better information on Quicken or Yahoo!

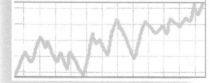

specified time to pay, typically 30 to 90 days. Accounts receivable measures the money owed by customers. Rising receivables means customers are taking longer to pay, which is never a good sign. Ideally, you like to see flat or falling receivables. Rising receivables, especially compared to the same year-ago quarter is another important signal of future problems. An increase of 25 percent, compared to same year-ago, e.g., an increase in DSO from 40 to 50, is a clue to future disaster.

Accounts receivable is not an important factor when analyzing restaurants or retail stores. Use inventory turnover to analyze retail stores.

Inventory (Apply to Retail Stores)

Page 6 displays how fast a company sells its inventory (inventory turnover). In theory, higher is better. Inventory is low when a company is selling product faster than it can build it. Merchandise piling up in warehouses is a sign of slowing sales. However, it's not that simple. Inventory is made up of raw materials, work in process (on the assembly line), and finished goods. Finished goods piling up is bad, but a company may have good reasons for stocking up on raw materials. Most manufacturing companies don't report inventory in enough detail to analyze, but retail stores are another story. Retail inventories become stale and depreciate rapidly if held too long. Increasing inventories (lower turnover) signal problems ahead for retail stores. Negative trends of 25% or more, compared to year-ago in inventory turnover, e.g., from 15 turns to 12 turns, are a clue to future disaster.

That's it! Morningstar and Equity Insights make analyzing Financial Statements easy. Check Morningstar's grades for an initial evaluation of your investment candidates, and take the survivors to Equity Insights.

CHAPTER FOURTEEN

Second Opinions

No matter how carefully we analyze a company, it's helpful to get another opinion before we buy its stock. Here are my favorite sites for second opinions.

The Gurus' Input

In Chapter 4 we used Validea to pick stocks based on famous gurus' selection strategies. Now it's time to see what Validea's gurus have to say about your stock picks.

Validea's nine gurus fall into distinct investing categories:

- Value and Contrarian: Benjamin Graham, Kenneth Fisher, David Dreman and James P. O'Shaughnessy
- Growth: Peter Lynch, Martin Zweig, and Motley Fool
- Momentum: William J. O'Neil
- Internet Momentum: Olympic Internet (Validea's homegrown formula for evaluating Net stocks)

The analyses are Validea's computer-generated interpretation of each guru's stock selection strategy based on the guru's published writings. You can get their analysis of almost any stock by opening the Validea site (*www.validea.com*) and entering the ticker symbol in the data box labeled "Quick Stock Search" and selecting "Guru Analysis."

The Guru Analysis page lists the nine gurus on the left along with lightbulb icons indicating each guru's interest in the stock.

Strong Interest	Bright yellow
Some Interest	Dim yellow/brown
No Interest	Dark brown

Validea displays Peter Lynch's analysis of your stock when you first access the page. You can see any of the other gurus' analyses by clicking on their name on the guru list. You'll usually find that only a couple of gurus are interested in any one stock. That's understandable. You wouldn't expect interest from value-oriented gurus in growth stocks or a momentum guru to care about value stocks.

It's tempting to pay most attention to gurus expressing strong interest in a stock you want to buy, but that could be an expensive mistake. Instead read and pay close attention to the analysis of a guru who should be interested but isn't. For instance, if you're analyzing a growth stock, you would like to see strong interest from Peter Lynch and Martin Zweig—and if you're lucky, William J. O'Neil. If they're not interested, you better know why.

Validea's guru analysis is the best stock analysis tutorial you'll find on the Web. Each analysis includes a straightforward and understandable explanation of the guru's selection strategy, and why the stock does or does not meet the guru's specific requirements.

For instance, the guru might say something like "This methodology looks for annual earnings growth above 20 percent, but prefers higher than 25 percent, XYZ's annual earnings growth rate of 35.6 percent, based on the three-year historical growth rate, passes this test." Or "A positive cash flow is typically used for internal expansion, acquisitions, dividend payments, etc. A company that generates rather than consumes cash is in much better shape . . . XYZ's free cash flow of -$0.65 per share fails this test." or "When inventories increase faster than sales, it is a red flag . . . inventory to sales for ABC was 14.9% last year, while for this year it is 22.92%. Since the inventory has been rising . . . it would fail this test."

Read these comments carefully. The analyses are computer-generated, so sometimes the reasons for rejection are off base, but I'm amazed at how often they point out something that I've overlooked.

The analyses are based on Validea's interpretation of each guru's selection strategy. The real gurus are not making these analyses, and may not even agree with the conclusions. Validea hasn't done any testing to show how much money you would have made—or lost—following their emulated guru strategies.

Nonetheless, Validea's guru analysis ranks among the best investment tools on the Web. But remember it's only a tool, and by no means lessens the need to thoroughly research a stock before you buy.

Best Investment Sites for Portals: Quotes, Charts, Commentary, and Research

CBS MarketWatch (*cbs.marketwatch.com*): Quotes, news, etc.; best site for analysis and commentary.

Quicken (*www.quicken.com/ investments/stocks*): Good source of market news, commentary, and fundamental data.

Yahoo! Finance (*quote.yahoo.com*): Quotes, profiles, news, earnings estimates, insider trading, Motley Fool, Street.com. You can set up a portfolio and get quotes and news on the companies in your portfolio.

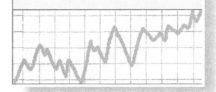

What the Pundits Say

You've heard from the gurus, now let's see what the pundits are saying about your investment candidates. We can use another Validea page to do that.

Validea's Source Buzz summarizes and tabulates investment recommendations in articles found on major Web sites and in leading financial magazines. Validea rates the pundits and the publications in terms of how you would have fared following their recommendations. Validea grades their stock-picking ability using one to five lightbulbs, where five is best. See Chapter 4 for more information on Validea and their pundit rating system.

You can see the pundits' views on your candidates by entering the ticker symbol in the data box labeled "Quick Stock Search" and selecting "Source Buzz" on the Validea page (*www.validea.com*).

The articles are listed in chronological order. Each listing shows the publication date and where Validea found the article, the pundit involved, and the pundit's lightbulb rating. A Validea researcher writes a synopsis of each article, including reasons why the pundit was bullish or bearish about the stock. The listing includes a portion of the synopsis. To see the complete synopsis, click on "See More."

Try picking a stock that tanked recently and then go back and see what pundits said about the stock before it dived. There's a good chance you'll learn something very important about stock analysis.

Validea's Source Buzz is a terrific timesaver. They do a good job of summarizing each article. You'll be able to get the gist in seconds, instead of taking time to read the entire article.

Analysts' Advice

There are many places on the Internet to view summaries of analysts' earnings forecasts and buy, sell, or hold recommendations for a stock. We discussed some of them in Chapter 10. These summaries are compilations of many different brokers' reports. You don't know which analysts made specific recommendations or what they actually said. At least three sites offer detailed lists of analysts' recommendations. CNET Investor gives the most information about each recommendation, but doesn't list reports by all analysts. So start with CNET Investor, and then check with Financial Web, and Stock Selector for additional listings.

CNET INVESTOR (*investor.cnet.com*)

CNET Investor summarizes reports from 45 brokers, including most of the majors. Enter your stock's ticker symbol and select Broker Reports from the dropdown menu near the top of the main page to see a list of broker's reports going back one year. Scroll past the current quote to see the list. Each listing includes the broker firm name, date of the report, and a short summary, or a link to a summary of the analysts' comments.

For instance, a typical summary might say, "Upgrade from accumulate to buy, raise 4th quarter estimate from $0.55 to $0.60, and raise target price to $75." They also often include additional comments such as "exceeded our estimates," or "future looks bright," etc.

The listings are in chronological order with the most recent at the top. You'll find it interesting to go back six months to a year to see who was right and who was wrong. You'll learn something by looking at comments made before a stock tanked.

FINANCIAL WEB (*www.financialweb.com* > Research > Brokerage Recommend > See Detailed Recommendations)

Financial Web shows the date, brokerage firm, recommendation type, and actual recommendation for each listing. Recommendation types include reiteration, upgrade, downgrade, and coverage (starting coverage). Access the list by selecting Brokerage Recommend on the Research page and entering the ticker symbol in the Brokerage Search entry box. You'll see a short list there, but you'll see more by clicking Go in the Review Recommendation History box.

STOCK SELECTOR (*www.stockselector.com*)

Stock Selector gets recommendations from a long list of analysts, possibly more than CNET Investor. But the site can be slow in posting the information. The information presented is skimpy—they don't include any comments, and they don't tell you if the recommendation is an upgrade, downgrade, etc. One nice feature is

DEFINITION PLEASE

Surprise: Difference between reported earnings and analysts' consensus forecasts. It's a positive surprise if reported earnings exceed forecasts and a negative surprise when reported earnings come in below forecasts.

Undervalued: A stock trading below its fair value.

Value Stocks: Companies currently out of favor with investors. These companies usually have low valuation ratios (price/earnings < S&P 500, price/sales < 2, price/book < 2).

that they list the analyst's name. You can click on the name to see all the other recommendations on file for that analyst.

Find the recommendations list by entering a ticker symbol in the box in the upper left hand corner of the main page and selecting Analysts from the dropdown menu before clicking Go.

Computer-Generated Wisdom

VECTOR VEST (*www.vectorvest.com* > Free Stock Analysis)

The analysts followed by CNET and other sites are human beings, subject to potential conflicts of interest, biases, and inconsistencies of thought known to afflict our species. Wouldn't it be nice to have a methodical stock evaluation system not subject to human quirks?

Vector Vest uses a computer program to analyze a combination of fundamental and charting factors to produce a buy, hold, or sell recommendation for most listed stocks. The Vector Vest formula relies heavily on the stability and consistency of historical earnings, earnings growth, and stock price perform-ance to establish value and safety ratings for a stock. Those factors are combined with earnings forecast trends and recent stock price performance to come up with buy, sell, or hold recommendations.

Since Vector Vest's business is selling programs using the same formula, free access is limited. Visitors can use the program at no charge to ana-lyze up to three stocks each day. Click on Free Stock Analysis, and enter the stock symbol. Vector Vest displays a lengthy computer-generated report on the stock, going into consider-able detail on how it applies all factors involved in the analysis.

Vector Vest's buy, sell, or hold recommendation is buried smack in the middle of the report. Scroll down until you see the para-graph titled "Recommendation (REC)." That's the bottom line, as far as Vector Vest is concerned. Their recommendation looks at a variety of Vector Vest's ratings including Relative Value and Relative Safety, but won't give a buy rating unless the stock is at least

| Free Stock Analysis | Vectorvest OnLine | Special Trial Offer | Contact Us |

Watch GRT trends very carefully. If the GRT trend is up, the stock's Price will likely rise. If the GRT trend is down, the stock's Price will increase more slowly, cease to increase, or subsequently fall.

Recommendation (REC): AMZN has a Sell recommendation. REC reflects the cumulative effect of all the VectorVest parameters working together. These parameters are designed to help investors buy safe, undervalued stocks which are rising in price, and to avoid or sell risky, overvalued stocks which are falling in price.

VectorVest is tuned to give an "H" or "B" signal when a stock's price is approximately 10% above a recent low, and an "S" signal when the stock's price is approximately 10% below a recent high. High RV, RS stocks are favored toward receiving "B" REC's, and sheltered from receiving "S" RECs.

STOP-PRICE: AMZN has a Stop-Price of 63.70 per share. This is 7.32 or 13.0% above its current closing Price. VectorVest analyzes over 6,000 stocks each day for Value, Safety and Timing, and calculates a Stop-Price for each stock. These Stop-Prices are based upon 13 week moving averages of closing prices, and are fine-tuned according to each stock's fundamentals.

In the VectorVest system, a stock gets a "B" or an "H" recommendation if its price is above its Stop-Price, and an "S" recommendation if its price is below its Stop-Price.

DIV (Dividend): AMZN does not pay a dividend. VectorVest focuses on annual, regular, cash

Vector Vest's buy/hold/sell recommendation is buried in the middle of the report.

10 percent (approximately) above its recent low. In effect, that means a stock has to be in an uptrend to receive a buy signal.

More important then Vector Vest's Recommendation, in my view, is "RV (Relative Value) located near the top of the report. Relative Value reflects Vector Vest's long-term view of the price appreciation potential of the stock. The rating considers earnings, earnings growth, balance sheet factors, and a host of other variables. The RV scale ranges from 0.00 to 2.00. Values above 1.00 are considered good.

Third in importance is "RS (Relative Safety)," delineating their view of the risk in the investment. The rating looks at consistency of financial performance, stock price history, and other factors. The RS scale also ranges between 0.00 and 2.00, and values above 1.00 are considered good.

Another factor of interest is "Relative Timing," a technical indicator attempting to predict the short-term future price trend of the stock. Again, the range is 0.00 to 2.00 with values above 1.00 considered positive.

Vector Vest provides a summary of fundamental factors at the bottom of the report.

WRIGHT RESEARCH CENTER

(*www.wisi.com* > Research & Analysis > Company Analysis)

Wright Research Center, located in Connecticut, employs more than two hundred people involved in the generation of research analysis reports on over eighteen thousand companies around the world. Wright advises clients ranging in size from individual investors to institutional clients, and it manages two mutual funds.

Subsets of their reports available on their site include a company profile, an extensive research report, and tons of financial data. Much of their research report is computer-generated. It goes into considerable detail, but much of the detail involves comparison of the company's results to its three major competitors. The list of competitors is also computer generated and can be off. For instance, it listed Qualcomm, Nortel, and Motorola as the three major competitors to Lucent Technology. They were on target with Nortel, but off on Qualcomm and Motorola.

What's special here is the Wright Quality Rating, a computer-generated measure of the "overall investment quality of a company's stock," according to Wright. The ratings, made up of three letters and a numeral, are listed at the top of the Company Profile report.

The letter ratings can be A (outstanding) through D (fair) plus L for limited, N for not rated, and an asterisk means they can't rate it because of a volatile history, or recent or expected developments that haven't been evaluated. Interpret the letters as follows:

- *First Letter Grade*: Investment Acceptance rates liquidity, trading volumes, and other factors related to the acceptability of a stock to institutional investors. Institutions buy hundreds of thousands of shares, and need to know if there are enough shares traded so they can easily move into and out of positions in a stock.
- *Second Letter Grade*: Financial Strength rates debt, equity, and other balance sheet factors.
- *Third Letter Grade*: Profitability & Stability evaluates return on equity, earnings stability, earnings growth, sales growth, dividend payout, etc.
- *Numeric Rating*: Corporate Growth measures the amount and consistency of historic earnings, equity capital, and dividend growth. The rating ranges from 0 to 20, and higher is better.

You can see the Wright rating by entering the company name or ticker on the Company Analysis page. Wright displays the Company Profile, and the Wright Quality Rating is below the company name at the top of the page.

Ignore the Investment Acceptance rating unless you're an institutional buyer.

The financial strength and profitability ratings are important measures of management quality, especially if you're researching growth companies. The ratings

of turnaround situations, or value-priced companies in general will look bad, because these kinds of companies probably have not had consistent profitability and sales growth in recent quarters. That is how they came to be value priced.

Strong and consistent earnings growth is what the market adores and is willing to pay high prices to get. Growth investors should look for a minimum Growth rating of 15.

Wright likes to see five or six years of history when making their ratings, so you will see a lot of N (not rated) ratings when you look up younger companies. Companies that recently awoke after a long slumber such as Nortel Networks, or most companies involved in broadband or optical communications won't get high ratings. Companies that have recently completed large acquisitions such as MCI WorldCom don't show up well either.

ASK THE EXPERT

(*www.america-invest.com* > Ask the Expert)

You could get an in-depth analysis and opinion on a stock of interest for the price of an e-mail stamp by submitting questions to America-iNvest's "Ask the Expert." America-iNvest's resident experts pick two e-mail questions to answer each market day. They get many questions, so there's no guarantee your question will be answered.

The answers are posted on the site daily, there's also an archive going back several months. The answers are interesting and informative. You might find some good investment ideas here.

The form for asking questions is at the bottom of the Ask the Expert page, just below the day's answers. You can also use the form to sign up to receive the daily "Ask the Expert" newsletter.

Gurus vs. Pundits

What is the difference between a pundit and a guru? Not much, but for our purposes here, we consider a pundit to be anyone who gives an opinion on a stock. Gurus are well known and universally recognized superstars, experts such as Peter Lynch, Warren Buffett et al.

CHAPTER FIFTEEN

Forecasting the Future

When the whole market takes a dive, even great stock pickers lose money. Of course, no one can predict the market's future course with certainty, however it's worthwhile taking time out to see what the experts do when they try to predict it.

First things first, which is to take a look at which way the market's heading now before delving into the future.

Market Indexes

To find out what the current condition of the market is, you'll consult indexes, each of which represents important market segments. Here are three important indexes:

- S&P 500 index reflects the action of 500 of the largest companies in almost every industry. (The S&P 500 is more representative of this market segment than the Dow Jones Industrial Average because the DJIA is made up of only 30 stocks, versus 500 stocks in the S&P.)
- NASDAQ composite index shows you the performance of large technology companies.
- Russell 2000 index shows the action of smaller companies.

You can view charts of these and other indexes at many sites—we'll use Yahoo! (*finance.yahoo.com*) for illustration. Select "Major U.S. Indexes" listed after U.S. Markets on Yahoo!'s Finance page. Scroll down to the index of interest and click "chart" on the right to view a one-year chart of the index. One year is a good time frame for observing current market direction.

Yahoo! plots the 50-day and 200-day moving averages for the index on the chart. The relationship between the index and the moving averages gives you information about the state of the current market. The 50-day moving average reflects short-term conditions, and the 200-day moving average gives you a longer view.

The index is considered in an uptrend if the index price is above the moving average, and it's in a downtrend if the index is below its moving average.

The distance between the index and the moving average indicates trend strength. The trend is weak if the index is hovering near, or crisscrossing the averages, and strong when the index is far above or below the average.

Sometimes you'll notice that the index is below its 50-day moving average, but above the 200-day average. That says the index is in a short-term downtrend, but a long-term uptrend—in other words, a "dip."

In recent years investors have gotten in the habit of buying on the dips because the market always recovers and moves to new highs. Of course, this happy trend will end some day, and a short-term dip will turn into a long-term downtrend, or bear market.

Try viewing different time span charts by clicking on the links in the row labeled "Big" below the chart. Two-year charts give you a long view, and a 3-month chart shows the current picture in better detail.

To look at indexes representing different market segments use your browser's Back button to return to Yahoo!'s list of major indexes. You'll learn something interesting by viewing the Value Line index (Other U.S. Indexes), especially on 3-year and 5-year time frames. Here's why.

The S&P 500 and NASDAQ indexes are capitalization-weighted, meaning price changes of larger companies move the index more than smaller companies. For instance, Cisco Systems (CSCO) and Milacron (MZ) are both members of the S&P 500. In February 2000, Cisco's market capitalization was $438,000 million ($438 billion), and Milacron's market-cap was $493 million. That means a $1.00 movement in Cisco's share price will move the S&P 500 index 888 times as far (438,000 ÷ 493) as a $1.00 movement in Milacron's share price.

Thus, the movement of the S&P 500 would be representative of your own market experiences only if you invested 888 times as much money in companies like Cisco Systems as you did in companies the size of Milacron.

The Value Line, an index of about 1,700 companies, is not capitalization-weighted. A $1.00 change in Milacron's price moves the index just as much as a $1.00 change in Cisco. Consequently, the Value Line index is a better representation of a typical

Other Troves of Data

Smart Money
(*www.smartmoney.com* > Tools-Economy Watch). Shows bar charts of eight major economic indicators for the latest period compared to year-ago data. Smart Money displays an overview of the meaning of each indicator and a short analysis of recent trends.

U.S. Department of Commerce Bureau of Economic Analysis
(*www.bea.doc.gov*). A good source for balance of payments, export and import data, and breakdown of U.S. economic data by region of the country.

White House Economic Statistics Briefing Room
(*www.whitehouse.gov* > The Briefing Room > Economic Statistics Briefing Room). Yes, it's that White House! Here you'll find the latest statistics released by the U.S. government covering all economic sectors. This is the place to go if you need to know the amount of airline domestic revenue passenger miles sold, or the value of single-family housing starts compared to apartment units.

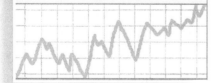
investor's experience than capitalization-weighted indexes like the S&P 500 or the NASDAQ.

Unless you're a short-seller, you'll do best by investing in strong uptrending markets. One market segment can be strong while others are weak. For instance, the NASDAQ index soared 39 percent during the last six months of 1999, while the Russell 2000 rose 6.5 percent and the S&P 500 was up less than 3 percent.

WHAT ABOUT THE FUTURE?

There are two ways to approach forecasting the market's future direction. If you majored in economics, or you just like getting under the hood, as it were, you can use the economic data to construct your own forecasts.

Speaking for myself, that's not for me. Economists spend their lives studying and perfecting forecasting methods. Even then, they often disagree with each other. I don't know anything about the subject and have no desire to figure it all out now. Fortunately for people who feel this way, economists and market professionals post their forecasts on the Web for all to see.

We'll start with ready-made market predictions, and then go on to overall economic reviews, and finally, sources for raw data so you can make your own forecasts.

Ready-to-Wear Market Forecasts
ALSTON BOYD'S COMPOSITE INDICATOR

(*www.martincapital.com* > Economic/Financial Data > Stock Market Analysis)

Alston Boyd is economic director for Martin Capital Advisors of Austin, Texas. His Composite Indicator is intended to forecast major market turns, not short-term squiggles. Martin employs market performance indicators such new highs vs. new lows, and market breadth, plus broader measures such as interest rates, commodity prices, earnings, and other data reflecting the overall economy. The indicator moves slowly, typically giving a signal no more than once a year.

Get there by selecting Economic/Financial Data on the Martin Capital page, then click Stock Market Analysis, and finally, Composite Indicator.

Boyd has been developing the Composite Indicator since 1991 and has backtested it on data going back to 1961. His tests show that the indicator catches most market moves, though it didn't give sell signals prior to market declines in 1962 and 1977. Recently, it gave a wrong sell signal in September 1999. The false sell was triggered by the same thing that tripped up so many market forecasts in 1999—the narrowness of the market. That is, although the major indexes hit new highs, more stocks went down than up in 1999.

FUND ADVICE (*www.fundadvice.com*)

Fund Advice displays timing signals for three major markets: stocks, gold, and U.S. bonds. The stock indicator includes four gradations: 100 percent, 75 percent, 50 percent, or zero percent invested. The bond and gold indicators show only two choices: in the market or in cash. You can see the timing signals on the site by clicking Timing Hotline from the main page, or receive e-mail every time a signal changes by signing up for their free newsletter on the site.

HOWARD PHILLIPS, PH.D.

(*www.coe.uncc.edu/~hphillip/* > Click Here for More Info/Business-Sector Mutual Fund)

Phillips teaches digital electronics and computer hardware design at the University of North Carolina at Charlotte, and has developed a method of forecasting the future direction of stocks, mutual funds, and market indexes based on computerized artificial intelligence principals. He says the accuracy of his predictions typically runs in the 70 percent to 80 percent range. Phillips modestly claims his predictions are the most accurate available anywhere. He says he predicted market downturns in October 1997 and October 1998, lesser sell-offs of the NASDAQ in February 1999, and of the Dow in January 1999.

Phillips sells customized portfolio investment consulting to institutional clients, but he also posts forecasts every market day on his Web site. Once you're there, select "Click here for more info" and then click the second link (Business-Sector Mutual Fund) to see Phillips's current forecasts for the Dow Industrial and S&P 500 indexes, along with forecasts for 38 Fidelity Select mutual funds

---

Best Investment Sites for Screening
(*continued from previous page*)

MSN Investor (*moneycentral.msn.com*): A variety of prebuilt searches plus a sophisticated custom screening program.

Quicken (*www.quicken.com*): Simple mutual fund and stock selections. Their mutual fund screens are especially good.

S&P's Personal Wealth (*www.personalwealth.com*): Results of a different predefined screen displayed here every week.

Silicon Investor (*www.siliconinvestor.com*): Screen on fundamental and technical analysis variables.

Stock Point Stockfinder Pro (*www.stockpoint.com*): Another easy-to-use screening program.

Wall Street City (*www.wallstreetcity.com*): A variety of backtested prebuilt screens.

Zacks (*www.zacks.com*): Their custom and pre-made screening programs are strong in seeking out all sorts of nuances relating to changes in consensus ratings and forecasts.

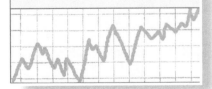

representing a variety of industry sectors. If you go back and click the top link (Dow Jones 30) on the previous page, you'll get forecasts for the 30 stocks that constitute the Dow Jones Industrial Average.

Phillips lists each stock, fund, or index on a separate line starting with the ticker symbol and name followed by a column labeled "Current TRPRI," the price when the current recommendation was first posted. The next two columns list the latest and previous day's closing prices along with position recommendations. The recommendation can be "L" meaning long or buy, or "S" for sell or short. The Trend column shows the expected price change expected during the forecast uptrend or downtrend. The Wins column indicates if the current trade is profitable based on the latest price compared to the original price, and the Paper Profit shows the percentage profit based on that difference without regard to trading costs.

NEURAL NETWORK DOW PREDICTIONS
(*www.markettrak.com*)

Market Trak uses a neural networking approach to predict the direction of movement of the Dow Industrial Average for the next 15 trading days. Neural networking is a complex software concept where the program is supposed to learn from its mistakes and grow smarter as time goes on.

Forecasts are published on Mondays before the market opens. Market Trak only forecasts the direction the Dow will move, not the amount. However, each forecast includes a strength indicator ranging in value from 50 to −50. Values above zero result in up forecasts and negative values give negative predictions. Higher strength forecasts are more believable than small strength forecasts. For instance, a negative direction forecast with a strength indicator of −50 would be more believable than a negative forecast with a −5 strength. Registration is required.

JEFF WALKER'S MARKET TIMING SIGNALS
(*www.lowrisk.com*)

Jeff Walker says he's been developing signals for timing the stock market on a full-time basis since 1990.

He has come up with four different timing strategies. They could be used as general market timing signals—that is, you could use them to determine when your asset allocation should be weighted toward stocks or cash—but Walker intends the signals to be used for timing trades of the S&P 500 index. He suggests using S&P index mutual funds, but some fund families try to discourage the frequent trading called for by some of Walker's models. You can accomplish somewhat similar results using Spiders, a trading instrument that represents the S&P 500 index.

Walker's timing signals are based on an indicator he calls "signal strength," with values varying between 0 and 20. The "higher the number, the more bullish" the signal, according to Walker. The details of the signal strength calculation are secret, but they're based on the usual suspects: comparison of number and volume of shares advancing and declining, recent price action of the Dow Industrial and S&P 500, current interest rates, and dividend yield and inflation measures.

Walker offers four strategies designed for different investment approaches, but the same signal strength indicator is used for each. The only difference is the signal strength level required to trigger buy or sell signals.

1. **Disaster Avoidance** is intended to keep you in the market most of the time. You hang in through the minor bumps and only get out when Walker's indicator thinks a real bear market is coming. The strategy would have kept you in the market from April 1994 until October 1999 when the strategy whipsawed—that is, it gave a sell signal quickly followed by another buy. Since 1983, the strategy averaged about one move every two years. According to Walker's backtests, the strategy's returns slightly underperformed the S&P 500 on a calendar-year basis going back to 1983. It outperformed the S&P 500 substantially in 1987 and 1990. With this strategy, you're either in the market or in money market funds. Walker includes the money market interest in figuring the returns when you're out of the market.

2. **Graduated Strategy** is Walker's most aggressive. Sometimes you're in stocks, sometimes in money markets,

Spiders

Spiders are a nickname for Standard & Poor's Depositary Receipts, an investment vehicle designed to track the price and performance of the S&P 500 Index. You can use Spiders to represent the overall market, buying them when you think the market is headed up, and selling them short if you think the market is going lower

Spiders trade just like stocks, using the ticker symbol (SPY). One Spider share trades for 10 percent of the current value of the S&P 500 index. You pay the same commission for buying or selling Spiders as you would for buying or selling any listed stock. One disadvantage of Spiders is the dividend payout method. Dividends paid by companies making up the index are credited to Spiders at the end of each quarter. You don't collect them if you sell before then. The current dividend yield for the S&P 500 is about 1.25 percent.

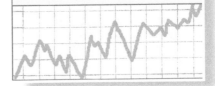

and sometimes you're shorting the market (you can do that with Spiders). On average, you end up making about 10 moves each year. It's hardly worth the effort in good years when it barely outperforms the index, but the Graduated Strategy shines in weak or down years. For instance, it returned 60.3 percent in 1987 when the S&P 500 was up only 5.7 percent. The most recent weak market was 1994, when the Graduated Strategy returned 7.5 percent compared to the S&P 500's 1.3 percent.

3. **Timing Strategy** is a less hyperactive version of Walker's Graduated Strategy. You'll still find yourself sometimes short, sometimes in money markets, and sometimes in stocks. But you end up doing less trading, averaging around four trades per year. Apparently, less is better: Walker's backtesting shows the Timing Strategy outperforming the Graduated Strategy in most years.

4. **SuperBear Strategy** might be better named the Super Bull. You're only in the market when it's hot, otherwise you're in money market funds. You end up making about four moves a year.

You won't find the timing signals on Walker's site. He includes them in his free *Walker Market Letter*. Sign up for the e-mail letter on the site. If comes out every two weeks, sometimes more often.

You won't be impressed with Walker's strategies if you've only been in the market during the last three or four years. "Why bother?" you might ask. "The market goes up every year, and those short downdrafts are merely buying opportunities."

But I am impressed with Walker's strategies because, according to his backtests, none of them have lost money in any calendar year. Not losing money is the first secret to successful investing. Keep in mind, though, backtesting is not real life. Walker has only been running his current strategy live since 1998. It remains to be seen how they perform in the future.

CHARLES BIDERMAN'S LIQUIDITY ANALYSIS
(*www.trimtabs.com*)

We've seen a variety of approaches to forecasting future market direction. Most of these rely on internal market indicators such as the ratio of new highs to new lows, or advancing stocks vs. declining stocks, or on economic measures such as inflation rates, interest rates, investor sentiment, and the like.

As far as Charles Biderman is concerned, none of those matters. Biderman, a former *Barron's Financial Weekly* editor, established Trim Tabs Financial Services in 1990 to provide professionals with unusual investment ideas. He says forecasting the market isn't that complicated. The market simply follows the laws of supply and demand. Supply is simply the shares available to be bought, and demand is the amount of money available to buy them. Here is how he defines them:

- **Supply:** The amount of stock available for sale is constantly changing. For example, say a company uses cash to buy another company. The acquired company's stock is removed from the market, reducing the supply. The supply also drops when companies buy back their own stock, or insiders buy stock in their own company. The supply increases when new companies go public, existing companies issue more stock, or company insiders sell their stock.
- **Demand:** Demand increases when investors add cash to the market through buying mutual fund shares, or by putting additional cash directly into stocks.
- **Supply vs. Demand:** The unbalance of supply vs. demand determines the direction of the stock market. If demand exceeds supply, prices move up, and the market falters when supply exceeds demand. Biderman calls the amount of stock available for sale at any given time the "float," and he calls the demand "available cash." The difference between supply, or float, and demand, or available cash, is called "liquidity."

According to Biderman, liquidity analysis explains the "January effect," which says stock prices, especially small company stocks, tend to boom in January. Biderman says the number of new companies bringing their stock to market via Initial Public Offerings (IPOs) goes to zero in the period starting from Christmas through the first three or four weeks of January. That's the time when investors pour new money into mutual funds. So you have a double

DEFINITION PLEASE

Charting: Making buy and sell decisions based entirely on stock price and volume history (same as technical analysis).

Downtrend: Stock price is heading down.

January Effect: Refers to the belief that small stocks make a big move up in January.

Spider: A security representing one-tenth the value of the S&P 500 index. Spiders trade like a stock. Spiders are a means of owning the index without buying mutual fund shares.

Uptrend: Stock price is trending higher.

whammy: a shortage of supply because of a lack of new stock issues and increased demand from new money going into funds.

You often hear the amount of mutual fund inflows or outflows quoted in the media. Commentators often attach predictive significance to the fund flow data. For instance, if investors pulled money out of funds during a particular week, they'll interpret the data as a sign of market weakness.

Biderman's research shows mutual fund flows by themselves don't mean much. For instance, the sudden drop in October 1987 spooked investors for over a year. They took $11 billion out of equity mutual funds in 1988. Did the market fall in 1988? No, it went up more than 12 percent. Why? Because in 1988, over $130 billion of cash takeovers were completed—considerably reducing the supply of stock. Demand went down a little, but the supply went down much more, forcing prices up.

Biderman's Trim Tabs Financial Services sells liquidity data to portfolio managers and other market professionals. Trim Tab tracks just about everything affecting liquidity, including fund flows, stock buybacks, IPOs, etc. Trim Tabs' Web site gives you free access to the same reports they send to paying customers, including *Daily Liquidity Trim Tabs*, *Liquidity Trim Tabs* (weekly), and *Mutual Fund Trim Tabs* (weekly). The daily and mutual fund reports are posted on the site more than a week after their release. The weekly *Liquidity Trim Tabs* report is posted late also, but a summary is posted on Wednesday, only two days after its release to paying customers.

The weekly report is the most interesting. It provides more detail than you need, but includes Biderman's interpretation of the information. You can see the summary on your browser, but you'll need Acrobat Reader to download the full report.

Click on "An Interview with Charles Biderman" for more background on liquidity analysis. Liquidity is a long-term indicator; it doesn't reflect short-term influences, and it only works for the

market as a whole—it doesn't tell you whether Amazon.com is worth more than General Motors.

Hanging Out with the Economists

The Dismal Scientist (*www.dismal.com*)

The Dismal Scientist is an economic analysis and consulting organization. Their site focuses on the economy, the latest economic trends and reports, and their analysis of the news. Check this page often if your interests include economic forecasting.

Robert W. Baird & Company

(*www.rwbaird.com* > Current News > Monthly Economic Perspective)

Baird, established in 1919, is an investment bank and financial advisory service owned by Northwestern Mutual Life Insurance. It's unusual to find advice of this quality available to the general public, but here Baird gives you their take on the economic and market outlook. The monthly report includes recommended asset allocations between stocks, bonds, and cash for four different portfolios ranging from "stable principal" to "aggressive growth."

The Economist's Economist (*www.yardeni.com*)

Dr. Ed Yardeni is chief economist and a managing director of Deutsche Bank Securities (North America). He's been hailed as one of the best economic forecasters by *Barron's, Investor's Business Daily*, the *Wall Street Journal*, and others.

Yardeni's site includes economic indicators from the U.S. and around the world, in the form of charts or tables. But the real value lies in the studies and analysis done by Yardeni and other economists. You'll find a constant stream of new reports on the U.S. and global economy, stock and bond markets, you name it. Yardeni doesn't boil down his information to buy or sell signals. You have to read the reports and apply your own interpretation.

Don't overlook the U.S. Forecast Table listed under Global Economy. The table lists forecasts for the overall U.S. economy as well as important segments including automobile production, housing starts, unemployment rate, and the like. The forecasts cover

Best Investment Sites for Portfolio Trackers

CNBC (*www.cnbc.com*): Best tracker for keeping up with changes in fundamentals on your stocks.

CNET Investor (*investor.cnet.com*): Easiest-to-use portfolio tracker that automatically adjusts for splits.

MSN MoneyCentral (*moneycentral.msn.com*): The best portfolio tracker on the Web.

Morningstar (*www.morningstar.com*): Good for tracking mutual funds because it lists year-to-date returns.

Yahoo! (*quote.yahoo.com*): Good for keeping up with the news on stocks of interest.

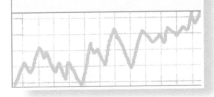

the next four quarters. Many of the reports must be read using an Acrobat Reader.

Martin Capital Financial Newsletters

(*www.martincapital.com* > Market Viewpoint > Monthly *Financial Market Newsletter* or Quarterly Economic Review)

Alston Boyd writes the monthly *Financial Market Newsletter* that includes, and comments on, the current value of his Composite Indicator. The newsletter discusses broader economic issues as well. If that isn't enough, Martin Capital produces a quarterly economic newsletter called *The Compass*. It discusses the economic outlook from a broader and longer-term perspective than Boyd's monthly publication (*www.martincapital.com* > Market Viewpoint > *The Compass*).

Stock Research

(*www.stockresearch.com* > Weekly Economic Update)

Here Robert A. Bose, president of Green Mountain Asset Management Corporation, gives you his analysis of recent economic and stock market events.

Raymond James Financial (*www.raymondjames.com* > Financial News & Research > Economic Monitor Commentary)

Raymond James's stock analysts are usually ranked among the top five of all brokers. Dr. Scott Brown, chief economist, writes a weekly commentary on the state of the economy available to everyone.

Data Central

MARTIN CAPITAL'S MARKET AND ECONOMIC INDICATORS

(*www.martincapital.com* > Economic/Financial Data)

Martin Capital Advisors maintains the most complete and easy-to-access collection of economic data I've seen on the Web, or in the library, or anywhere, for that matter. You'll find everything you need, and more, to make your own economic forecasts.

- **Monthly Cycle of Economic Data:** Thirty-three indicators, including industrial production, building permits, factory orders, leading indicators, payroll data, just about any measure of the U.S. economy is here. Martin shows you the last reported value, scheduled release date, and the expected new value for each indicator. What's more, they show you a 10-year graph for each one.

- **Table of Recent Data:** the monthly value of each U.S. economic indicator going back six months, plus values for 12 and 13 months ago.

- **Stock Indexes:** Major U.S. indexes, including Dow Industrials, S&P 500, NASDAQ, Dow Utilities, and Russell 2000 going back 30 years. Also includes all major foreign indexes going back five years, and U.S. Hi-Tech indexes going back one year. They have an interesting chart comparing the S&P 100 (large-cap) to the Russell 2000 (small-cap) indexes.

- **Stock Market Analysis:** Includes charts of Alston Boyd's Composite Indicator plus charts of S&P dividends and earnings, comparisons of dividends and earnings yields to T-bill rates, market sentiment and breadth indicators, and more. Many of the charts go back 30 years.

- **Interest Rates & Yields:** Charts of short and long-term interest rates, dividend yields, and earnings compared to interest rates, money supply changes, commercial, industrial, and consumer loan data and more. Many of the charts go back 30 years.

- **Commodity Prices & Inflation:** Commodity cash prices and indexes, changes in inflation measures, John Murphy's Inflation Index, and a fascinating 30-year chart comparing the S&P 500 to the U.S. inflation rate.

- **Major Currencies:** Five-year charts of major currencies around the world.

Handle Forecasts with Care

Interpreting economic information and forecasts is not a cut-and-dried procedure. You'll frequently find different economists making opposite forecasts from the same information. Even if you have a lot of confidence in a particular economist, treat a stock market prediction like a weather forecast—it's based on constantly changing information, so keep checking back for updates.

What you do with the forecasts depends on your investment plan. Some investors with a long-term view say it's useless to try to time the market, so they remain fully invested and ride out short-term downdrafts. Others move their money out of stocks into safer areas such as money market funds, bonds, or T-bills if they think the market is heading down.

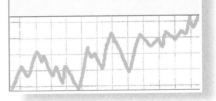

CHAPTER SIXTEEN

What the Sectors Say

Sectors Defined

"Stocks, like sheep, move in herds. If you want your sheep to move north, you'd better pick a sheep in a herd moving north." That pithy advice from technical analyst John Bollinger explains why many experienced investors believe your success depends more on picking the right industry group than the right stock.

The definition of the terms industry, group, and sector often differ depending on who is talking.

For our purposes we'll define industry as a major business category, such as retail, and a sector, or an industry sector, as a narrow subset of an industry, such as office supply stores, disk drive manufacturers, airlines, etc. Stocks within industries and sectors tend to move together because companies within the same industry are affected in similar ways by market and economic conditions.

Mutual fund and other institutional managers track industries and sectors closely to determine which are cooling down and which ones are coming into favor. Once a trend is identified, the industry or sector "rotates into favor" as one institution after another begins accumulating shares in the best companies in an industry or in a specific sector.

Once an industry or sector group is "in favor," it usually remains so for a year or two—sometimes a lot longer. Eventually it becomes overpriced, or economic conditions for the sector or group turn unfavorable, and money rotates into the next hot sector.

You can improve your investment success if you identify the strongest industries and sectors before you select individual stocks. Even though the market as a whole may be going nowhere, there is usually a bull market in some sector. A popular stock selection strategy is to find a strong sector, and then pick the strongest stock in that group.

Finding Hot Industries and Sectors

SMART MONEY

(*www.smartmoney.com* > Stocks > Stock Tools > Sector Tracker)

Smart Money magazine presents the most visually compelling display of industry sector performance I've seen anywhere. Even if you're not interested in sectors, you ought to look just to see what's possible on the Web.

On their site select Stocks and look for Stock Tools on the bottom left, and click Sector Tracker to see a bar chart showing the five best and five worst sectors based on price action for the day. One day's action doesn't tell you much, but you can change the time span to the last five days, the last month, year to date, or the last 52 weeks. The display changes instantaneously when you select each period.

Besides the best and worst sectors, you can select other categories, including Smart Money Sectors, Basic Materials, Capital Goods, Communications, Consumer Staples, Consumer Cyclicals, or Energy. (In this instance Smart Money itemizes the terms industries and sectors.)

Click on a sector to display a list of companies making up the group, including the current stock price and stock price performance over the time span you selected.

Click on an individual company to see Smart Money's snapshot for the stock. From there, you can access all of Smart Money's research data on the company.

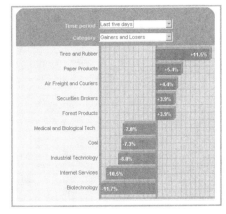

Smart Money Sector Tracker

STOVALL'S SECTOR WATCH
(*www.personalwealth.com*)

Sam Stovall wrote the book on sector investing—literally. His *Standard & Poor's Guide to Sector Investing* was the first in-depth guide on the subject. Stovall still works for Standard & Poor's and you can read his free weekly commentary called *Stovall's Sector Watch* on S&P's Personal Wealth site. From the home page, click Industries to get there.

Each week he reviews an industry sector in depth or gives his take on up-and-coming, or down-and-going, sectors. It makes for interesting reading and you'll find moneymaking ideas here.

BRIEFING.COM VIA E*TRADE (*www.etrade.com* >
Markets > Analysis & Commentary > Sector Ratings)

Briefing.com takes a different approach to industry analysis. Instead of relying on stock performance statistics, Briefing.com employs real people to analyze the future prospects of each industry.

Briefing.com charges $6.95 per month to see the ratings on their site, but E*Trade gives it to you free. You have to register, but you don't have to be an E*Trade customer to see the reports.

Briefing.com covers 26 industries (sectors), from aerospace/defense to tobacco. Briefing.com gives each sector a rating from 1 (outperform) to 5 (underperform). Obviously, 1 is best. The ratings are summarized in a chart at the top. Some sectors are given both short-term and long-term ratings, e.g., 3/2, in this case meaning the short-term rating is 3 (market performer) and the long-term rating is 2 (slightly outperform).

Briefing.com writes a detailed analysis of each industry sector. In it they summarize current events in the industry and explain how they came up with the rating. For instance, in talking about the Internet group, they pointed to the "still undersupplied business-to-business segment," holiday and pre-Y2K buying in the commerce/portal groups, and "many investors want in—no matter what the price," as reasons for giving it their highest ranking.

They minced no words when talking about the tobacco industry, saying they "expect Philip Morris to end up declaring bankruptcy," and they expect others in the field to "face a similar threat."

Briefing.com lists all the major companies in each group. They only occasionally comment on individual companies, and then only in passing. For instance, they named 17 companies in the top-rated telecommunications equipment sector without differentiating between the investment quality of any of them.

The ratings for each sector are usually updated about once every three months.

Finding Hot Stocks in Hot Sectors

WALL STREET CITY

(*www.wallstreetcity.com* > Stocks > Industry Groups)

Telescan's Wall Street City maintains their own extensive database of stock, mutual fund, and industry data. They provide the data and screening programs found on CNBC and *Fortune's* Web sites.

Wall Street City in general, and the Industry Group section in particular, makes extensive use of the Java programming language. Older-version browsers often experience problems with Java sites.

There is a lot of moneymaking information here, so let's get started by selecting ProSearch on Wall Street City's main page, and then clicking on Industry Groups (really industry sectors) on the menu on the left.

Select Best & Worst Industries from the menu to see the entire list of industry sectors sorted with the best-performing sector on top, based on one day's returns. Unless you're a short-term trader, one day doesn't mean much, but you can select other periods ranging from one week to five years by clicking on the corresponding links. Six weeks is a good place to start.

It's pretty fascinating to scroll down the list and see how the different industry sectors are faring. By browsing like this the list gives you a good feel for what's hot and what's not.

Now scroll back to the top to find the strongest stocks in the strongest industries.

Click on the industry name to see the stocks making up the group and—here's the cool part—they're sorted with the best six-week performers on top.

That's all there is to it. You are looking at a list of the strongest stocks in a hot industry.

You can start researching these hot stocks right from this screen. Click on the company name and up pops a one-year price chart. Notice the "Select Company Reports" dropdown menu above the price chart. The menu lists 17 reports, and all but four of them (*Company Profile*, *Macro World Price Forecast*, *ProSearch Criteria*, and *S&P Company Report*) are free. It's possible to do considerable research with these reports. Here are my favorites.

Quick Facts compiles most of the Market Guide data we used as the first step in our stock analysis. Refer to Chapter 8 for information on using the Market Guide data.

Telescan Rankings crams a variety of related data into single composite indicators in 11 different categories.

- Growth Rank (short and long term). Combines historical (one- to three-year) earnings, sales and cash flow growth

Best Investment Sites for Second Opinions

Validea Guru Opinions (*www.validea.com*): Find out how famous gurus would rate your stocks. Very good.

Vector Vest (*www.vectorvest.com*): Get up to three free computer-generated analyses of your stocks based on fundamental and technical factors each day. Worthwhile.

Wright Research Center (*www.wisi.com*): Computer-generated measure of the overall investment quality of a stock.

data with forecast earnings growth. The short-term indicator emphasizes recent performance, while the long-term rank looks back five years. Top ranked stocks have high growth expectations, and consequently are high risk investments.

- Value Rank (short and long term). Uses price/earnings ratio, price/book ratio, forecast earnings growth, and current stock price compared to long-term price history. Top-ranked stocks are trading below their long-term trends based on these measures. Watch out, playing the value card has been a losing strategy in recent years.

- Technical Rank (short and long term). Employs a variety of indicators to evaluate overall technical strength. Useful for short-term trading only.

- Analyst Rank. Combines analysts' ratings, recent changes in earnings forecasts, earnings surprise history, and the number of analysts following a stock into a super earnings momentum indicator. Pay close attention to this important indicator.

- Insider Rank. Uses recent insider trading along with changes in insider trading patterns. Good for alerting you to companies warranting further research.

- Fundamental Rank. Combines debt ratios, cash flow growth, debt interest coverage (compared to earnings), and cash on hand compared to stock price. Avoid companies with low fundamental rankings.

- Momentum Rank. Combines recent changes in accumulation/distribution, price acceleration, industry group rank acceleration, and earnings growth into another super momentum indicator. Value, growth, and momentum investors should all keep a close eye on Momentum rank.

- Volume Rank. Measures increases in trading volume, thought by many technical analysts to be a precursor to rapid price growth. Use it together with Momentum rank.

Click on the "Decipher this Stock" logo to view a computer-generated analysis of the ranks. It's an amazing bit of computer programming. Wall Street City does a lot of the heavy lifting for you in calculating these rankings, but don't take the list and run. Use it to identify stocks worth further investigation.

Return to Wall Street City's Industry Group Center by selecting Pro Search and Industry Groups to continue your industry group research. You can use the Industry Group Center menu on the left to navigate to major sections.

Analysts' Ratings

A listing of all industry groups sorted by average analysts' buy/hold/sell recommendations on companies in each group is powerful information, because analysts' recommendations are a major influence on stock prices. Few analysts recommend selling a stock, even if they think you should, so you have to look closely at the gradations from buy to strong buy. The strongest sell signal you'll see here is a rating halfway between buy and sell.

Graph – Industry

It's helpful to view a price chart of an industry index. Click on the industry index symbol to display the chart. The default time span is one year, but once you're there you can set it to display up to 15 years, or even longer if the industry index has been charted that long. Wall Street City plots two special indicators on each industry graph.

- The advance-decline line, plotted on top, is calculated by subtracting the percentage of stocks in the industry declining from the percentage advancing, and adding the result to a running total. The line moves up when more stocks in the group are advancing than declining, and vice versa. Wall Street City says the A/D line is useful in forecasting tops in the index.

- The high-low index (H/L) is constructed by comparing the number of stocks making new 52-week highs to stocks hitting 52-week lows. The H/L line is said to be helpful in determining when an industry index is approaching a top or a bottom.

Insider Trading

Lists all industry groups sorted by Wall Street City's Insider Rank indicator, a measure of insider buying and selling averaged for all companies making up the group. Many analysts look for trends in industry sector insider trading because insiders know

---

Best Investment Sites for Tip Analysis

Big Tipper (*www.bigtipper.com*): They watch TV all day long, so you don't have to. They list just about every financial adviser, money manager, or stock analyst who has been interviewed on television each business day. Big Tipper covers all major financial cable networks: CNBC, CNNfn, Bloomberg, etc.

Smart Money Pundit Watch (*www.smartmoney.com*): Tracks the batting averages of 12 of the best-known pundits.

Validea (*www.validea.com*): Tracks stock picks made on financial magazines and on Web sites, and grades the tippers based on the performance of their tips.

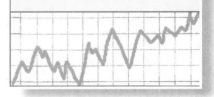

when business is picking up or slowing. Taken as a group, insiders tend to buy months before stock prices begin their move up. Click on the industry symbol to see the industry group name and a price chart.

News

Gives you a way of finding news pertaining to specific industries and/or companies within the industries. You'll find more than press releases here. Many of the stories originated from newspaper articles or columns. A surprisingly good source of news. Unfortunately, there is no way of searching for news by individual companies in this section.

One final note: you'll need patience when using Wall Street City; some of the pages seem to take forever to load.

EQUITY TRADER (*www.equitytrader.com* > Groups)

John Bollinger, a respected technical analysis guru, developed a technique he calls Group Power to forecast whether a particular industry sector is likely to over or underperform the overall market in the near future. Clicking on Groups takes you to Group Power Industry Structure page, where you'll see a list of 13 major industries, such as Utilities, Technology, Financial, etc. Each industry has an accompanying set of six red, yellow, or green signals—they look like traffic lights. Two green lights on the right, two red lights on the left, and two yellow lights in the middle. Interpretation is intuitive. If both green lights are on it means Bollinger is very positive on the sector, and red lights mean stay away. You can see a price chart of the group index going back three months by clicking on a link in the second column.

Usually companies are assigned to industry groups based entirely on their main lines of business. However, Bollinger takes the process a step further by requiring all stocks in a group to show similar trading characteristics; that is, their price movements tend to correlate with the movements of the group as a whole. Stocks that don't correlate with their industry group are listed separately as non-correlated.

Click on an industry name to see a list of sectors within the industry. For instance, if you select Technology, you'll see 16 sectors, such as computers, software, networking, etc. The sectors use the same red, green, and yellow lights to indicate group strength. You can click on a sector name to display a list of companies making up the group. For instance, clicking on "Computers PC" lists Apple Computer, Micron Electronics, Gateway 2000, Dell, Compaq Computer, CDW Computer Centers, and Intevac.

Click a company's ticker symbol to see a four-month price chart for the company. Equity Trader's price charts look strange and intimidating at first, but there's some good information to be had here. At the top of each chart are performance and potential ratings for the company, both using the red, green, and yellow light indicators. The performance rating looks at past performance, while the potential rating reflects Bollinger's assessment of the stock's future potential. Both are based on a combination of fundamental and technical factors. Performance and potential ratings for the sector are shown near the bottom of the screen.

You can view charts of stocks in the same group with stronger or weaker ratings by clicking on Stronger Sibling or Weaker Sibling above the chart. Click on Parent to see a chart for the next higher-level industry group. If you're looking at a group chart, click on Children to see a list of companies in the group.

Smart Money's Map of the Market

(*www.smartmoney.com* > Stocks > Stock Tools > Map of the Market)

A chapter on sectors wouldn't be complete without mentioning *Smart Money's* technological marvel, Map of the Market. Get there by clicking on the Map or the Market Symbol near the top of their Stocks page. If this is your first visit, be prepared to wait while Smart Money downloads the necessary software on your hard drive.

The map is made up of approximately 600 companies grouped by sector; for instance, technology, financial, healthcare, and so forth. Each sector is allocated real estate on the map proportioned to the market capitalization (size) of the companies making up the group. Within each sector are rectangles representing the largest individual companies within the sector. Again, the size of each company's rectangle is proportional to the firm's market capitalization. So you end up with an array of rectangles representing companies, organized by industry. The sectors are labeled with the industry names, and gray bars mark the sector boundaries.

DEFINITION PLEASE

Fundamental Analysis: Analyzing stocks by looking at earnings, sales, profit margins, etc.

Market Capitalization: Latest stock price multiplied by number of shares outstanding (shares issued).

Momentum Analysis: Usually involves looking for stocks in a strong uptrend (high relative strength) with strong earnings growth and increasing earnings forecasts. In today's market, may include relative strength only.

Sector Funds: Mutual funds specializing in a particular industry sector such as computers or health care.

The color of each company's rectangle is determined by price performance. Bright green means the price is up strongly, and bright red signifies a big drop in price. Several in-between shades of green and red designate lesser price moves. The map shows today's action when it is first displayed, but you can use the control panel to choose time spans going back as far back as 12 months.

The hot and cold sectors in the market can be seen at a glance just by looking at the colors. Move your cursor over a company rectangle and you'll see the company name and current quote information. Click on the company to bring up a menu to access selected research information.

It's all wonderful, even spectacular—but color me dubious—I've never figured out how I can use the map to make money.

BIG CHARTS (*www.bigcharts.com* > Industries)

Big Charts gives you the most flexibility of any site I've seen in terms of choosing a time frame for measuring sector (industries on Big Charts) performance. From the main page click Industries from the top menu to see a list of the top 10 best- and worst-performing industries sectors (they say industries) for the past three months. Then use the dropdown menu to select a performance time span ranging from one week to five years. After the top and bottom 10 performers appear, click on the group name to see a list of the 10 best- and worst-performing stocks in the group, over the selected time span.

Big Charts is about stock charts, so you can't do any research on the individual companies from here, other than to display their price charts. By the way, I couldn't resist looking up the best-performing industry over the past five years. It was semiconductors, up over 900 percent as a group. The strongest performer in the group was Vitesse Semiconductor, up more than 10,000 percent in five years. The worst-performing industry was precious metals, down 56 percent in the five year span—the worst stock in that group was Gold Standard, Inc., down 96 percent.

Industry group price trends tend to last for extended periods, typically several months, if not years. For instance the banking group was in an uptrend from January 1997 until early 1999. The distillers and brewers segment of the beverage industry was in a steep uptrend for all of 1998. Gold mining stocks were in a downtrend that started in the middle of 1996 and lasted until September 1999.

Best Investment Sites for Spying on Fund Managers

First Hand Funds (*www.firsthandfunds.com*): Shows you recent holdings, but the best part is a special tool that lets you see which stocks the fund bought and sold a month ago.

IPS Millennium Fund (*www.ipsfunds.com*): A diary of fund manager Robert Loest's thinking on practically every trade. Very valuable!

Munder NetNet Fund (*www.mundernetnet.com*): Munder tells you not only what they bought and sold last month, but why.

Open Fund (*www.openfund.com*): Open Fund displays their trades as they happen.

CHAPTER SEVENTEEN

Finding the Funds

S hould you buy mutual funds, or should you buy stocks? Many investors have pulled money out of funds in recent years because they think they can get better returns by picking their own stocks. Maybe, but there are some good reasons why you should still consider mutual funds:

Fund managers have better information. Mutual funds trade hundreds of thousands of shares of stock every month. Fund trading generates huge commissions for the brokers involved. It's no wonder that stock analysts advise mutual fund managers of changes in their outlook about stocks they're covering before they tell us. What's more, company executives often visit fund managers, toting new information about future products and strategies.

Diversification. Every investor, no matter how good their research and analysis, runs into the occasional disaster stock, the one that drops 25 or 30 percent before he or she can sell it. The same thing happens in a mutual fund, but the impact on the investor is much less. That's because most funds own 100 or more stocks, while you may only have 10 companies in your portfolio. A disaster in a single stock is a much bigger percentage hit to your portfolio than it is to a typical fund.

You don't have to watch your stocks every day. Successful investors need to stay abreast of new developments affecting their companies. Once you hire a good fund manager, it's the manager's job to keep up with the news and make adjustments to the portfolio as needed. We only have to check up occasionally to make sure the manager we hired is still at the helm and on track.

The Fund Raters

Morningstar, Value Line, and Lipper Analytical are the major companies in the business of rating mutual funds. Each company has their own methods of establishing ratings, but they're all based on historical performance. In fact, all mutual fund ratings boil down to two factors: historical returns and volatility.

- **Returns.** Fund shareholders make money in two ways: when stocks in the fund's portfolio increase in price and when the fund passes on dividends paid by companies in the portfolio. *Average annual return* measures the amount of money you would have made if you owned shares in the fund in past years, assuming you had reinvested any dividends received. Average annual return calculations also assume you've reinvested any capital gains distributions.

- **Volatility.** When statisticians describe average annual return, they're describing a straight line—it assumes fund share prices go up the same percentage day after day, and week after week. In reality, a fund's share prices go through varied and wild gyrations. Some weeks they're up strong, other times they nosedive, and you'll see your retirement nest egg going down the drain. These gyrations are termed volatility, and volatility is what keeps us awake nights. Volatility makes our stomachs churn. Volatility makes our spouses ask, "What were you thinking when you bought the fund?"

Fund Analysis (and It's Free!)

Although Value Line and Lipper Analytical do a good job of rating mutual funds, we're going to use the Morningstar Analysis for a number of reasons.

Morningstar is respected in the industry. If a mutual fund earns a high rating from Morningstar, they usually feature the rating in their advertising. All the information you need to evaluate funds is available free on Morningstar's site. No other Web site even comes close in terms of depth and scope of the information provided. Access to certain data on Morningstar does require a subscription—the cost is $9.95 per month, though AOL members pay $7.95 per month. But as you'll soon see, you can evaluate funds just fine on Morningstar using only the free information. It's an amazing deal considering many still pay $295 per year to receive Morningstar's monthly fund magazine. The mailed version includes more statistical data than available on the site, but nothing you need to evaluate funds.

START WITH A BIG SELECTION

I recommend that you analyze several mutual funds at one time, say 10 funds. That's because you tend to fall in love when you analyze one fund at a time. You will be more objective and

Best Investment Sites for Socially Responsible Mutual Funds

Citizens Funds (*www.citizensfunds.com*); **Good Money** (*www.goodmoney.com*); **Green Money** (*www.greenmoney.com*); and **S-R-Invest** (*www.tbzweb.com/srinvest*): All list socially responsible companies and/or mutual funds.

Social Investment Forum (*www.socialinvest.org*): General information on socially responsible investing.

SocialFunds.com (*www.socialfunds.com*): Tools for finding and comparing socially responsible funds.

analytical when you look at several funds at once. See the next chapter on screening for funds to learn how to find plenty of candidates for analysis.

Once you have 10 or 15 candidates, you want to eliminate the clunkers as soon as possible. There is no point wasting time analyzing funds you're not going to buy anyhow.

Start by going to the Morningstar site (*www.morningstar.com*) and entering the fund's ticker symbol into the box labeled Quotes & Reports on the left near the top of the page. Push "Go."

We'll divide our analysis into two sections: Quick Look and Detailed Evaluation. The point of the Quick Look is to identify and eliminate funds that won't be in the final contention. If you start with 10 funds—at most—only four or five will make it to the detailed evaluation stage.

The Quicktake Report consists of six major pages: Quote, Snapshot, Total Returns, Ratings and Risk, Portfolio, and Nuts and Bolts. Use the menu on the left to navigate to the various pages, or to specific sections within a page. You can easily see where you are because Morningstar highlights your current location in white. Links with a "+" require a subscription.

A Quick Look at a Fund

We'll look at five factors in the Quick Look.

- Morningstar star rating
- Load
- Morningstar return rating
- Morningstar risk rating
- Return/risk comparison

Generally, your candidate funds should pass all five to make it the detailed evaluation stage. Sometimes special circumstances warrant overriding certain requirements. Once you get the hang of it, the Quick Look shouldn't take more than five minutes per fund.

MORNINGSTAR STAR RATING

Morningstar uses a star system to rate funds. The best funds get five stars, and the worst one star. Morningstar requires at least three years' history to rate funds. Newer funds do not get a star rating, but you can still use information on the site to evaluate the funds.

Return vs. Risk

Like all fund-rating systems, Morningstar's ratings are based on a computer analysis of historical performance. The rating compares each fund's average annual returns to Morningstar's interpretation of the fund's historical volatility.

Volatility represents risk. Funds with high volatility are considered riskier than funds with low volatility. Funds with high annual returns combined with low volatility get the highest ratings. Funds with low annual returns and comparatively high volatility get low ratings.

We'll describe the rating system in more detail later. You'll find the Morningstar rating near the top of the page, on the right-hand side.

Portion of Morningstar's Mutual Fund Snapshot Page.

Eliminate Underperforming Funds Fast

I always end up eliminating one-, two-, or three-star-rated funds during the detailed evaluation. Consequently, I've made it a rule not to waste time analyzing them. As soon as I see funds with fewer than four stars I eliminate them. I suggest you do the same, with one exception. Large-capitalization growth stocks have left the rest of the market in the dust in recent years. Mutual funds specializing in anything other than large-cap growth stocks—say small companies, or value stocks or heaven forbid, small-cap value stocks—have dramatically underperformed the market.

A fund manager can be the best stock picker in the world, but he or she is going to have a terrible performance record if limited to buying stocks in an underperforming market segment. Now, many analysts are predicting small companies are ready to shine. If you believe that, and you want to participate in the predicted rally of small-cap stocks, you need to find good small-cap funds. However, you'll find few five-star small-cap funds, because the category has underperformed so consistently in recent times. In this case, you should widen your horizon to include lower-rated funds.

LOOK AT THE LOAD

Mutual funds come in two basic varieties: load and no-load. The load is a sales commission, usually paid to the financial advisor or stockbroker who sells you the fund.

Originally, all funds were load funds, because they were all sold through stockbrokers. Then no-load funds came along. No-load funds were sold directly from the fund to the shareholder, so no commissions were involved. Nowadays, you can still buy a no-load fund directly from the fund, but you can also buy them through discount brokers. They are still no-load funds, no matter where you buy them.

Discount brokers charge a transaction fee on certain no-load funds. The fee ranges between $10 and $100 or more, depending on the broker. If you buy funds in a lump sum, the transaction fees don't amount to much. However, if you're on a plan where you make regular monthly purchases, the transaction fees can be a significant drag on your returns. Your broker can supply you with a list of available funds, and any applicable fees.

Loads are usually a much more significant expense than discount broker transaction fees. Loads can be charged when you buy the funds—known as front-end loads—and/or when you sell the funds (deferred load). Front-end loads typically run about 5.75 percent.

Do loads hurt your returns? Let's look at a simple example:

Say you're planning to invest $1,000 in one of two funds. Fund A is a no-load fund, and Fund B charges a 5.75 percent front-end load. If you buy Fund A, the entire $1,000 goes into the fund. But what happens if you decide on Fund B? The load, in this case $57.50, goes to sales commissions, leaving only $942.50 going into the fund.

Now say Fund A returns 20 percent the first year, making your shares worth $1,200. If you do the math, you'll find that Fund B would have to return 27.3 percent for you to end up with the same $1,200 after the first year.

You'll find the load information listed under Sales Charge under Fund Details about halfway down the page on the left side. If you

---

Recommended Investment Sites

Tutorial Information

Insights by T. Rowe Price (*www.troweprice.com/mutual/insights/index.html*): Overview of everything from financial planning to derivatives.

Web Broker Ratings

Broker Trading Index (*www.keynote.com*): Measures Web broker response times.

Gomez's Internet Broker Scorecard (*www.gomez.com*): Ranks Internet brokers based on different criteria, such as costs, speed, and ease of use.

Motley Fool (*www.fool.com*): Active message boards on all aspects of online trading.

OnLine Investment Services (*www.sonic.net/donaldj*): Detailed reports including fees, commissions and charges, number of mutual funds offered, research options, and speed of the Web site. Most useful are lists of brokers for various categories of investing; for instance, the lowest-cost brokers for low-priced stocks, Canadian stocks, limit orders, and market orders. Check it out before you choose a broker.

(continued on next page)

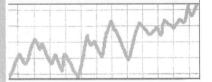

want no-load funds, look for both the front-end and the deferred charges listed as "None," meaning no-load.

Do load funds outperform no-load funds? There's no reason why they should. The loads are sales commissions. They don't go to the fund so they can hire better analysts, or more computers.

Sometimes, however, you may want to be in a particular market or industry, and you can't find any no-load fund in that sector. That would be a valid reason to pay a load—otherwise, eliminate load funds now.

MORNINGSTAR RETURN RATING

Morningstar rates mutual funds in two categories: return and risk. Select "Ratings and Risk" from the Quicktake menu to see Morningstar's ratings. Morningstar divides the mutual fund universe into four major groups:

- U.S. domestic stock funds
- International stock funds
- Taxable bond funds
- Municipal bond funds

Morningstar calculates a return rating for a particular fund by comparing the fund's average annual return to all other funds in the same group. They calculate a separate return rating for three-year, five-year, and 10-year periods. Of course, if the fund has been around only four years, you won't see a five-year or 10-year rating.

Morningstar's average annual return takes the fund's load charges and redemption fees into account. For instance, the three-year rating assumes you held the fund for three years and subtracts one-third of the load from the average annual return. This practice is both good and bad: it's nice to see the load-adjusted returns so you can compare load and no-load funds, but the results can be misleading. For instance, the 10-year return calculation subtracts only 10 percent of the load when computing the average annual return. You would get misleading results if you used the 10-year return to choose a fund, when you only planned to hold the fund for one year.

Recommended Investment Sites

(continued on next page)

Robert's Online Commission Pricer! (*www.intrepid.com*): Enter a stock price, number of shares, and exchange where listed, and the Pricer! lists commissions 100 different brokers would charge. Go to Robert's Financial Page to find it.

Smart Money (*www.smartmoney.com*): Thorough evaluation of brokers based on customer comments and their own research, but it's only updated once a year.

Smart Money's Broker Meter (*www.smartmoney.com*): Shows Web broker response times for seven different cities.

Web-Broker Comparison Tool (*www.xolia.com*): Compares features, fees, etc., on up to three brokers side-by-side. Very good.

Whisper Numbers
Earnings Whispers (*www.earningswhispers.com*): Whisper numbers are the earnings those in the know expect a company to report. Here's where to find them.

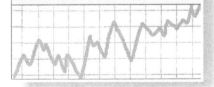

A Morningstar return rating of 1.0 means the fund's annual returns are exactly equal to the average of all funds in its group. If you're evaluating a U.S. stock fund with a three-year return rating of 0.90, that fund underperformed the average domestic equity fund by 10 percent. That's bad! Conversely, a return rating of 2.0 means the fund's annual returns over the period were double the average fund's return. That's good!

More Is Better

We buy funds to make money. Higher is better when it comes to returns. Avoid underperforming mutual funds as if they had the measles! You've heard the saying "Past performance does not predict the future." That's true sometimes, but a lousy stock picker will likely continue his or her losing ways. Stick with the winners!

Morningstar's five-year return rating, if available, works best for me. I look for funds with a minimum return rating of 1.5, meaning the fund returns beat the average by 50 percent, and I prefer at least 2.0. Your criteria may be different. For instance, risk-averse investors give higher priority to preserving their capital than to achieving high returns. These investors might settle for average returns—or even less, if the risk was low enough.

MORNINGSTAR RISK RATING

Mutual fund risk ratings are based on historical volatility. Rather than name it something simple—like volatility, for instance—mathematicians instead call it "standard deviation," a term meaning nothing to the rest of us. Despite the name, standard deviation is a powerful tool to help us evaluate mutual funds, and you'll learn how to use it later in this chapter.

Morningstar Ratings and Risk. Higher is better for return, and lower is better for risk.

Morningstar's risk rating is a variation of standard deviation. A fund's standard deviation increases when the share price makes a big move—up or down. Morningstar figures investors don't lose much sleep if their funds are volatile because they're going up. Investors only get upset when they're dropping. Thus Morningstar's risk rating only measures downward volatility. That makes sense, and I've found Morningstar's risk rating an important predictor of downside risk, especially in a bear market.

As with return, a Morningstar risk rating of 1.0 means the fund's historical downside volatility is average for its group (e.g., U.S. stock funds). Unlike return, lower is better for risk. A risk rating of 1.50 means the fund is 50 percent more volatile in a downdraft than the average fund—that's bad! A risk rating of .75 means the fund is 25 percent less risky when the market turns down—that's good.

I've found that the three-year risk rating works best. Lower is better for risk, and I stay below 0.90. Risk-averse investors should look for funds with risk ratings below 0.75.

Why do I use five-year return and three-year risk? Based on my experience, this combination has produced the best results. But we're talking about small differences. Your results wouldn't be much different if you used three-year or five-year ratings for both. Don't use 10-year ratings, though. I've found 10-year ratings are not as good predictors of future performance as the shorter-term ratings.

RETURN/RISK COMPARISON

It's important to compare risk to potential return, and Morningstar's ratings make it easy to do. What's a good return to risk relationship? Probably everyone has a different idea, but I require the return rating to be twice the risk.

It's incredibly simple to find out if the return is twice the risk. Divide the Morningstar return rating (five-year if available) by the risk rating (three-year). It's OK to use three years for both if five years isn't available. Here's an example:

Say the five-year return is 3.0, and the three-year risk rating is 0.9. Return divided by risk (3.0 ÷ 0.9) is 3.3, well above the minimum requirement. You don't have to be so mathematical; usually you can just look at them and quickly calculate whether the return is twice the risk.

Although conservative investors may accept funds with lower return ratings than I recommend to get lower risk, the comparison of return to risk ratings is still very important.

That's the entire Quick Look. Time to take the surviving candidates on to the Detailed Evaluation.

DEFINITION PLEASE

Closed-End Fund: Investors buy shares from other shareholders and sell shares to other investors. Share price is determined by supply and demand for fund shares (as opposed to Net Asset Value for open-end funds).

Geographic Funds: Mutual funds specializing in a specific geographic area, such as Europe.

Open-End Mutual Fund: Investors buy shares directly from the fund, and sell shares directly to the fund. Share price is the Net Asset Value (NAV).

The Detailed Evaluation
TRAILING RETURNS

Select Total Returns on the Morningstar Quicktake menu and scroll down to Trailing Total Returns.

Trailing returns are the average annual returns for one-, three-, five-, and 10-year periods—that is, if the fund has been around long enough to accumulate those histories. The section also includes shorter-term returns including one day, one week, and year-to-date.

Don't confuse trailing returns with calendar returns. Calendar returns are for specific years, e.g., 1998, 1999, or 2000. Trailing returns cover the period up to the report date; for example, if you are looking at a report dated October 6, 2000, the one-year trailing return goes back to October 7, 1999.

The trailing returns for all periods except 10 years are updated daily. The 10-year returns are updated monthly. The returns you see listed in the material distributed by the mutual funds is usually calculated as of the end of last year, or to the end of a recent quarter (March 31, June 30, or September 30). The trailing returns you see on Morningstar are more current, so they won't match the fund's literature.

Morningstar also shows you how the fund performed compared to the relevant index, usually the S&P 500, and how the fund ranked in its category. Trailing returns are the best way to look at a fund's history. Pay most attention to the three-year and five-year returns in comparison to the S&P 500 for three and five years. Since you can easily buy funds replicating the S&P 500, there's no point buying a fund that has substantially underperformed the S&P index. The S&P 500 has been on a tear in recent years and most funds haven't kept up. Don't eliminate a fund if its three- and five-year performance lags the index by 1 or 2 percent. Investors seeking value funds may have to accept 5 to 10 percent underperformance to find a sufficient selection.

Some investors also look at a fund's 10-year performance compared to the S&P 500. It's good if a fund shows outstanding longer-term results, but give more weight to three- and five-year performance.

If the fund still looks good, then look at the one-year performance. Cut them a little slack here. A fund can fall behind the S&P

500 because its investing style is temporarily out of style. For instance, in 1999 pharmaceutical and financial companies (banks, stockbrokers, insurance, etc.) were out of favor. Funds with large holdings in those industries didn't do well. That doesn't mean the fund manager has lost his or her touch. Eventually those sectors will come back, and those funds will outperform the market.

Most investors focus on year-to-date returns to select mutual funds. It's understandable. We all want to hop on the hot fund—you know the one, it's done 85 percent so far, and it's only halfway through the year! Try to avoid this trap. Whatever hot stocks these funds own are probably overextended and will start underperforming the market the day you buy the fund. It would have been nice if you had seen it coming, and jumped in at the beginning—but it's too late now.

STANDARD DEVIATION

Select Volatility under "Ratings and Risk" on the Quicktake menu. Standard Deviation measures volatility over the last three years. Why are we bothering with standard deviation when we've already eliminated volatile funds using Morningstar's risk rating? Stock market investing is tricky, and you have to have everything possible working for you. I've found that in certain market environments, standard deviation works better than Morningstar risk in helping you to avoid losing funds. I use both. Funds with standard deviations below 20 are the safest, and funds with standard deviations above 30 are high risk.

PRICE/EARNINGS RATIO

Select Portfolio on the Quicktake menu; "Price/Earnings" is listed under Investment Style.

So far our evaluation is based on historical performance. Price/Earnings ratio (P/E) gives us a clue to the future. Morningstar and other researchers have found P/E to be an indicator of future risk, especially in a weak or down market. In my own testing, I've found funds with P/Es above 30 are high risk, and those with P/E below 25 are low risk. These numbers apply only to general equity funds—funds specializing in specific sectors such as technology or healthcare always have higher P/Es. Most

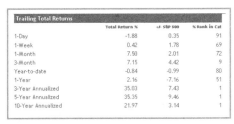

Trailing Total Returns			
	Total Return %	+/- S&P 500	% Rank in Cat
1-Day	-1.88	0.35	91
1-Week	0.42	1.78	69
1-Month	7.50	2.01	72
3-Month	7.15	4.42	9
Year-to-date	-0.84	-0.99	80
1-Year	2.16	-7.16	51
3-Year Annualized	35.03	7.43	1
5-Year Annualized	35.35	9.46	1
10-Year Annualized	21.97	3.14	1

The middle column compares fund's returns to the returns of the S&P 500 index. Pay most attention to three- and five-year data.

highflier funds are loaded with technology and Internet stocks that have high P/Es. It's difficult to find funds like these with P/Es below 30. You may have to accept the higher risk if you want to own these funds.

TOP 10 HOLDINGS

Select Top Holdings under Portfolio on the Quicktake menu. Morningstar shows you the 10 largest holdings in the fund's portfolio, based on the percentage of the fund's net assets.

Spend some time here. You can learn a lot about the fund and its probable future performance by looking carefully at its portfolio. If you've selected one of the recent top-performing funds, you'll probably see most of the recent highfliers in their portfolio. Granted, they are undoubtedly great companies, but they've appreciated enormously in value already and are selling at high valuations. You have to decide if you think they will continue to outperform the market in the future. There is no right or wrong answer to this question. If you think these recent highfliers have had their day, you would eliminate funds with a large weighting in these or similar companies.

Check the top holdings of funds you already own. Do they have the same companies in their portfolios as the fund you're considering? If so, you're not diversifying if you purchase another fund with similar holdings.

Look at the industries represented by the top holdings. For instance, say a fund owns several bank stocks, and you think rising interest rates will hurt future bank earnings. If you're right about interest rates, that mutual fund is destined to underperform the market in coming months. On the other hand, say the fund owns oil companies, or oil drillers, and you think demand for oil will continue to expand and push prices and profits up, then the funds may outperform the market.

You may find companies in the portfolio that you simply don't want to own. For instance, many value funds have large holdings of Philip Morris. You might avoid such a fund if you don't want to own tobacco companies.

Your analysis of the industries represented in the fund's portfolio is an important ingredient in picking winning funds. I can't

Smart Money Portfolios

Smart Money magazine features a new portfolio of mutual funds on an irregular schedule, but at least every three or four months. Each portfolio follows a particular theme—for instance, tax-efficient, low-risk funds with the best three-year returns, hot value funds, best new funds, etc. These portfolios are viewable on their Web site.

Most portfolios consist of four, five, or six funds, but sometimes they get carried away and feature 20 or more funds. In those cases, you'll have to do further research to bring the list down to a manageable number. To get there, from their Web site (*www.smartmoney.com*) click Mutual Funds on the top menu, then Magazine Portfolios from the menu on the left.

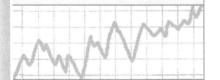

predict conditions at the time you read this chapter, but common sense goes a long way. You'll be amazed how good you'll get at analysis by keeping your eyes open to current events.

TURNOVER

Select Top Holdings under Portfolio on the Quicktake menu. Turnover is just above the Top 10 Holdings list.

Turnover (percentage) is a measure of a fund's trading activity. A fund has a turnover of 100 percent if, on average, the fund replaces all of its holdings in a year's time. We care about turnover for two reasons: taxes and management style.

Taxes

When a fund sells a stock at a profit, it incurs a capital gain. As sure as night follows day, capital gains beget income taxes. Funds have a choice. They can pay the capital gains taxes themselves, or they can distribute the gains to their shareholders and let us pay the taxes. Guess what? They *all* distribute the gains to shareholders. You don't gain anything from the transaction except a tax bill.

Say you own 100 shares of a fund with a share price (net asset value) of $20. Your holdings total $2,000. Now you receive a notice in the mail saying your fund is distributing $2 per share in capital gains. Sounds great—but the fund simultaneously reduces the share price by $2.

You probably don't see the $2 since most of us tell our mutual funds to reinvest the distributions. In this example, you would end up owning 111.111 shares (don't you love those decimals?) and since each share is worth $18, you still have $2,000 in the account. There's only one difference: now you get to report the $200 gain on your income taxes (no problem if you forget, the fund reports it to the IRS for you). Now here's the rub:

You owe the taxes even if you didn't make any money on the fund. You may have paid $25 per share, and now it's only worth $20, but you still have to pay taxes on the $200 distribution. You owe the taxes even if you bought your shares the day before the distribution was made. If taxes are a consideration, stick with turnover ratios below 50 percent.

Top Holdings Get Price Quotes			
Total Number of stock holdings	40	Turnover %	19
Total Number of bond holdings	0	Yield %	0.00

Top 10 Holdings:

Name of Holding	YTD Return %	% Net Assets
America Online	-17.63	12.40
Dell Comp	0.74	5.06
Gateway Inc	-23.33	4.87
Nextel Comms Cl A	4.43	4.59
WPP Grp	---	3.88
MCI WorldCom	-22.03	3.40
Citigroup	13.90	3.16
Nokia Cl A ADR	2.84	3.10
United HealthCare	27.83	3.09
Chase Manhattan	13.02	3.01
% Net Assets in Top 10 Holdings		46.56

Fund's top holdings; portfolio turnover is shown above holdings.

Taxes are not a consideration if your fund is in an IRA or other tax-sheltered account.

Management Style

Turnover tells you a lot about a fund manager's approach to investing. A turnover ratio of, say 250 percent, tells you the manager does a lot of trading. He or she probably is chasing highfliers and jumping off when they begin to falter. Conversely, a turnover of 20 percent says the manager follows a conservative buy and hold strategy, only occasionally selling existing holdings.

Which style is best? There's no right answer, because it depends on your preferences. The average annual turnover for a U.S. equity fund runs around 90 percent to 100 percent.

EXPENSES THAT COME RIGHT OUT OF YOUR WALLET

On to expenses. Select "Nuts and Bolts" from the Quicktake menu. Morningstar lists sales fees and all operating expense ratios in the "Fees and Expenses" section.

Sales Fees

Sales fees include the front-end and the deferred or back-end loads described earlier. The sales fees we haven't described yet are *redemption fees.*

A redemption fee is applied if you sell your shares before a specified minimum holding time. Funds use redemption fees to discourage short-term trading in the fund. Most funds don't assess redemption fees. For those that do, the minimum holding periods generally range from 60 days to six months. However, at this writing, Vanguard's Health Care Fund imposes a 1-percent redemption fee if you sell it within five years.

Fund Expenses

Funds spend money to hire analysts, rent offices, buy computers, advertise the fund, fly around the country visiting companies, and so forth. These expenses are labeled administrative expenses, management expenses, and 12b-1 fees. However they are labeled, they all come out of the fund's investment profits before you get yours.

The *Total Expense Ratio* totals all of the fund's expenses and it is the only number you have to look at. The expense ratio is expressed as a percent of the fund's total assets. For instance, if a fund owned $100 million of stocks, bonds, cash, etc., and spent $1 million on expenses last year, its expense ratio was 1 percent ($1 million expenses divided by $100 million assets).

Should you care about expenses? Let's look at an example comparing two funds, Fund A and Fund B. Let's make it simple and assume both funds own exactly the same stocks. The only difference is how much money it took to run each fund last year. Fund A's expense ratio was 2.5 percent, while Fund B spent only 0.5 percent of assets. Let's further assume that each fund's stock portfolio increased in value by 25 percent last year.

Let's see how each fund's shareholders fared. Remember, the expenses are deducted from the fund's profits before we get ours. Fund A's shareholders received 25 percent (portfolio returns) less 2.5 percent expenses—which adds up to 22.5 percent profit. Meanwhile, Fund B's shareholders received 24.5 percent return (25 percent less 0.5 percent). Maybe a 2 percent difference doesn't sound like much, but if you'd started with $10,000, after five years Fund A shareholders would end up with $76,096 compared to $89,473 for Fund B's shareholders (assuming the same expense ratios and 25 percent gross return for all five years).

Purchase Information

No-load funds can be purchased directly from the fund, or from certain discount stockbrokers. Funds typically set minimum requirements for share purchases. Morningstar lists the minimum requirements for three categories: general, IRA, and AIP.

The requirements for each category specify a minimum initial investment and minimum subsequent additions. Typically, you can add to your account in much smaller increments, once you've met the fund's initial investment requirements. Many funds have lower minimums for IRA and AIP accounts than for general accounts. (AIP indicates a fund's Automatic Investment Plan, an arrangement where you authorize the fund to make regular withdrawals from your bank account.)

The World's Best Mutual Funds

This is how *Money* magazine modestly describes their list of 100 recommended mutual funds. The funds are hand-picked by *Money's* editorial staff based on consistent performance over the past five years, reasonable expense ratios, and a consistent management team, among other criteria.

You might expect to find an abundance of technology funds in the specialty category, but T. Rowe Price's Science & Technology is the lone representative for this important market segment. I was surprised to see that three of the seven funds in the specialty portfolio were real estate funds.

To their credit, *Money* isn't swayed by recent performance—of the 16 funds in their small-cap portfolio, not a single one made money for their shareholders during the year prior to their selection.

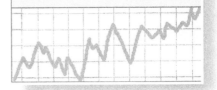

A fund's minimum investment requirements do not necessarily apply when purchasing through a broker. Web brokers often set different minimum investment requirements.

Brokerage Availability

You can purchase shares directly from the fund or from brokers listed in the Brokerage Availability section.

Management

Much of our evaluation is based on a fund's historical performance. That usually works because good funds tend to remain good performers, and inferior funds are apt to continue their losing ways. But a fund's performance is usually the result of its manager's stock picking ability. Our analysis doesn't mean much if the manager leaves.

Morningstar gives background on the fund manager (or managers) in the management section. The only important information in this section is right at the top—"Manager Start Date." Ideally, you'd like the fund manager to have been in place at least five years. If you're evaluating a newer fund, the fund manager should have been there from the fund's inception.

It's important to know if a fund you own or are evaluating has had a recent change in fund managers.

Sound the (Fund) Alarm

Morningstar does a lot of things well, but keeping us up to date on fund manager changes—and more important, their significance, isn't one of those things. For that we go to FundAlarm (*www.fundalarm.com*).

Fund Alarm's mission is to keep us informed of changes in fund management and to advise us of the significance of those changes. FundAlarm is fun to read; in effect, it's a gossip column for mutual fund investors.

Start with "Recent Manager Changes," a list of management changes for the past month. Below recent changes, on the same page, are changes announced during the past year.

Fund Alarm gives you considerable information about each change: who's leaving and why—and who's taking over and his or her background. The first part is mostly just the facts—who's coming and who's going.

What's most interesting are the "Fund Alarm Comments." This is where they put the change into context. For instance, *"This fund turned in two full, dreadful years . . . and there's no reason to believe it will change under the new manager."* Or *". . . he has no previous experience managing a diversified fund. . . ."* On a more positive note: *"Day-to-day management will remain in the hands of the same analysts who worked under . . ."*

This is news you can use!

The management change information and the entire site is updated once a month, on the first, and it's a good idea to check it once a month. There is an index on the Manager Changes page listing all funds with changes, but I never use it. The funds are listed in alphabetical order, and I can't resist scrolling down the entire list. It's interesting, and with only a dozen or so changes a month it takes maybe five minutes to read them all.

Below the current month's changes is an archive of changes going back 12 months. It's a good read, but if you're not interested, scroll down to Section 4, "Fund Companies Recently Sold." It's a short list—you'll be able to scan it in a few seconds. Management changes usually follow changes in ownership, so consider that if any of your funds appear on this list.

The "Highlights and Commentary" page is another must read. Here you'll find more fund news and gossip, along with lists of underperforming funds.

Fund Alarm also compiles lists: 3-Alarm funds are underperformers, and No-Alarm funds represent, in their view, the "Honor Role" of funds. They also compile a list called "The Most Alarming 3-Alarm" funds. None of your funds should fall into the 3-Alarm category if you've done your homework on Morningstar.

It's Not That Simple

Morningstar's return and risk rating calculations are more complicated than I've presented here. If you need more details about Morningstar's ratings or any other data items, click on the "Show Data Definitions" link at the bottom of the page containing the rating or data item. Morningstar's definitions will tell you more than you ever thought you wanted to know about each item.

More Mutual Fund Rating Services
VALUE LINE RATINGS

Morningstar and Value Line use opposite rating systems. Where Morningstar rates funds from one star to five stars, with five being the best, Value Line rankings range from one (best) down to five (worst).

Value Line rankings include an overall rank and a risk rank. The overall ranking compares a fund's historical growth and risk. The highest overall ranking (1) is awarded to the 10 percent of funds with the best combination of high growth and low risk. The lowest ranking (5) goes to funds in the bottom 10 percent.

Value Line's risk ranking evaluates the fund's volatility over three years. The funds with the lowest risk are rated one, and those with the highest risk are rated five.

Unlike Morningstar, Value Line doesn't make their rating information available on their own site. But you can find it on two sites that I know of: Quicken (*www.quicken.com* > Investing > Funds) and Stock Point. We'll use Stock Point for illustration.

Stock Point (*www.stockpoint.com* > Funds)

Select Funds from the menu on their home page, and then enter the fund ticker symbol or name where it says "Get Quote." Stock Point's quote includes quite a bit of information on the fund, including the Value Line rankings. Here are brief explanations of the significant information and how to interpret it. Click Help on the menu on the left for further information.

NAV Net Asset Value, the latest share price.

Assets Total amount of stocks, bonds, cash, etc., owned by the fund.

Turnover Percentage of the fund's assets traded in the previous fiscal year.

Distributions, dividends, and capital gains Total amount paid out on a per-share basis. Distributions are taxable, so you don't want any unless your fund is in a tax-sheltered account such as an IRA.

Overall rank 1 is best, don't settle for more than 2.

Risk rank Same criterion as Overall rank.

3- and 5-year performance Higher is better. Don't pay much attention to one-year, YTD (year-to-date), or 10-year numbers.

1998 bear market How much value the fund lost in the summer months of 1998. Pay more attention to the risk rank.

Maximum load Load paid when you purchase the fund; zero is best.

Deferred load Load paid when you sell; zero is best.

Redemption fee Penalty assessed if you sell the fund before a predetermined minimum holding period, zero is best.

Expense ratio Costs of running the fund, including the 12b-1 and management fees. Lower is better—don't go above 1.75 percent.

Minimum initial investment Minimum opening balance the fund will accept—not necessarily an issue if you buy the fund through a broker.

Minimum subsequent investment Minimum amount you can add if you already own shares in the fund—again, not an issue if you buy through a broker.

Sector distribution Shows you how the fund's assets are distributed among industry sectors. This is very important. Make sure you are comfortable with the outlook for sectors in which the fund has most of its assets.

Portfolio composition Most stock funds keep more than 90 percent of assets invested at all times. If the fund you're looking at has more cash, it means the fund's manager thinks the market is overpriced, or the manager can't find enough stocks meeting his or her investment requirements.

Top 10 holdings (select from menu on left) The fund's largest holdings. Look at these carefully.

LIPPER ANALYTICAL

Lipper does not calculate fund risk and return ratings in the same manner as Morningstar and Value Line. Instead, Lipper ranks funds compared to their "peer group." The peer group is all other funds with the same stated objective, e.g., growth funds. Though theoretically valuable to investors following an asset allocation strategy, in practice the definition of peer groups is arbitrary and not very useful.

Lipper's ratings are available on CBS MarketWatch (*cbs.marketwatch.com*). From the main page, select Mutual Funds and then enter the fund name or ticker symbol in the data box on the left.

Load or No-Load?

What are the advantages of load vs. no-load mutual funds? In most instances, the load is merely a marketing cost, the money doesn't go toward the fund's operating expenses. Load funds don't necessarily have more analysts or better computers. On the other hand, stockbrokers and financial advisors have to get paid somehow.

If a broker or advisor turns you on to a moneymaking investment, it's worth it to you to pay the load. Sometimes you'll find a mutual fund that has special qualities you can't find in a no-load fund. Maybe it has a manager who is especially good at picking stocks in a market segment you want to be in. If you want to be in that sector, and you can't find an equally good no-load fund manager, it could still be worth your while to pay the load and ride the hot manager's picks.

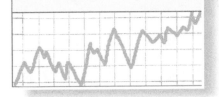

ASSET ALLOCATION: CBS MARKETWATCH PORTFOLIO BUILDER

CBS MarketWatch (*cbs.marketwatch.com*) takes an interesting approach to selecting mutual funds. All we have to do is decide on an investing style. MarketWatch decides the types and asset allocation of funds we should have in our portfolio, and gives us a list of the top 25 funds in each category.

From the main page, select Mutual Funds, then click Portfolio Builder under Tools.

First determine the portfolio category closest to fitting your situation (listed in order of increasing risk).

- *Income Preservation* portfolio is designed for investors who will need to take their money out of the market within two years. For instance, say you are planning to buy a house or start a new business, etc. These investors do not have the liberty of waiting for the market to recover from a downturn before pulling their money out. The portfolio is invested mostly in fixed-income bond funds, with a small weighting (20 percent) in blue chip stock funds and in cash (20 percent).
- *Conservative Income* portfolio is for investors who want a steady income flow but are willing to take some modest risks. The portfolio is heavily weighted in bond and blue chip stock funds.
- *Growth & Income* portfolio is structured for investors with a four to seven-year time horizon. They can wait out short-term market downturns. The portfolio consists of mostly stock funds, but a substantial amount is held in bond funds and cash.
- *Wealth Builder* portfolio is designed for investors with a 10-year time horizon. The portfolio emphasizes building future wealth over current income. The portfolio holds mostly stock funds with relatively small holdings in bond funds and cash.
- *Aggressive Growth* portfolio is designed for long-term investors with a high tolerance for risk. Mostly blue chip stock funds, but about a third of the portfolio is made up of growth-oriented stock funds.

Click on a portfolio to see the details. Each portfolio tells you how you should allocate your money between stock funds, bond funds, and cash or money market funds. Within stock funds, it gives you a distribution between general equity, small cap, and international funds.

Bond funds include intermediate and long-term categories. As with stock funds, MarketWatch tells you how to allocate funds between these categories. Click on a subcategory, such as General Equity Funds, to see a list of the top 25 funds in that category ranked by three-year return. Most of us aren't going to buy 25 funds in each category, and unfortunately MarketWatch doesn't give any guidance as to how to select funds from the list of the top 25 funds.

ASSET ALLOCATION: CNBC PORTFOLIO BUILDER

CNBC (*www.cnbc.com*) has a page dedicated to helping investors determine the type of mutual funds they should select based on their age and risk tolerance. From the main page, select Funds, and then click on Techniques. Select your age range from the following choices:

Early	20s & 30s
Middle	40s
Maturing	50s
Retirement	60s
College Funding	

(saving for your children's college tuition and expenses)

For each age range, CNBC displays suggested fund allocations for three investing styles: conservative, moderate, or aggressive. The allocations are divided between balanced, growth, income, and growth and income funds. Unfortunately, that's as far as CNBC takes it. They don't recommend specific funds in any of the categories. Even so, the page is worth looking at.

KIPLINGER'S (*www.kiplinger.com*)

Kiplinger's makes selecting mutual funds as easy a pushing a button. To get there, select Investments from the Kiplinger's page,

X Marks the Fund

Mutual fund ticker symbols are always five characters long, and always end with the letter "X."

then Funds, and finally click Kiplinger's Portfolios from the Quotes & Portfolios menu. They've defined three mutual fund portfolios:

1. Long-Term: Designed for investors who won't need to withdraw their funds for at least 10 years. Most of the portfolio is in growth or technology funds.
2. Medium-Term: A mixture of growth, value, foreign stock, and bond funds for investors with a five to nine year time horizon.
3. Shorter-Term: For investors needing to take their money out within five years. About 60 percent of the portfolio is in large-cap stock funds, the balance in bond funds and real estate investment trusts (REITs).

Select the portfolio of interest and Kiplinger shows you a list of four to eight suggested funds, depending on the portfolio selected, and the percentage of your total investment you should allocate to each fund. That's all there is to it. Kiplinger updates the portfolios in March of each year. To see how the most recent year's selections performed, click on "Full Story" on the Kiplinger's Portfolios page and then click on "Update: Feast and Famine."

No-Load Funds: Buy Direct or Through a Broker?

When no-load mutual funds started, they were available only from the fund itself. That was the whole point of no-load funds. When you buy shares in a load fund, the load charge is typically paid to the broker or financial advisor selling you the fund. That's how they get paid.

No-load funds were developed to help investors by selling shares directly to investors, eliminating the middleman, and along with it, the sales commission, or load. Instead of going through a broker or advisor, you buy directly from the fund itself.

Then Charles Schwab, and later other brokers, came up with the mutual fund supermarket idea. Now you have a choice, you can buy funds from a broker, or from the fund itself. Here's a comparison of buying fund shares directly from the fund versus buying them from a broker.

INITIAL PURCHASE

- **Direct**—The process of buying a fund direct starts with obtaining a prospectus. You can get a copy mailed to you by calling the fund, or in many cases you can download it from the fund's Web site. Once you've read the prospectus, you buy shares by filling out an application and mailing it, together with a check, to the fund. Your purchase is completed a week or so later, and you receive a confirmation in the mail.
- **Web Broker**—Assuming you already have an account, you enter your purchase using their Web site. The purchase is completed when the market closes that day if you entered the transaction before a predetermined cut-off time, or the next day if not.

TRANSFER OR SALE OF FUNDS

- **Direct**—Transfers between funds can be handled by a single telephone call if you're moving your funds between mutual funds in the same family—say if you're selling the Vanguard 500 Index fund and buying the Vanguard Health Care fund. Transferring between fund families is another matter. Say, for instance, you want to sell the Vanguard 500 and replace it with the Janus 20 fund. First you call Vanguard and wait for the check to arrive in the mail: allow one to two weeks. Then fill out a Janus application and mail it along with a check to Janus. The entire transaction, selling Vanguard and buying Janus takes around three weeks.
- **Web Broker**—Log on, enter the trades, and log off. Both trades will be completed that day, or the next, depending on the time of day you entered the transactions.

STATEMENTS

- **Direct**—Each fund family sends you a periodic statement. You'll receive five statements if you hold funds in five different families.
- **Web Broker**—You'll receive one statement covering all of your holdings.

DEFINITION PLEASE

Asset Allocation: The process of dividing your funds among different classes of investments such as stocks, bonds, or real estate. You could further allocate your stock funds into value, growth, foreign, etc.

Redemption Fee: Fee charged when you sell a mutual fund, if you haven't held the fund for the prescribed minimum time.

Screening: Searching the entire universe of mutual funds or stocks meeting user-specified criteria.

TRANSACTION CHARGES

- **Direct**—No-load funds do not assess charges unless you violate their rules, such as selling too soon, or trading too often.
- **Web Broker**—Depending on the fund, brokers may charge a transaction fee for buying or selling, anywhere from $10 to more than $100. Some brokers list applicable fees for each fund on their Web site.

MINIMUM PURCHASE AMOUNT

- **Direct**—No-load funds typically require a minimum opening purchase amount to open an account, anywhere from $1,000 to $100,000. Once open, they usually require a lower minimum to add to your holdings. Funds often establish reduced minimums for tax-sheltered accounts such as IRAs.
- **Web Broker**—Many brokers do not adhere to the same minimums established by the funds. For instance, Fund X might require $25,000 to open a direct account, but Charles Schwab might only require $2,500. Brokers are reluctant to publicize their minimum requirements for specific funds. You usually have to call them to find out, although some post the requirements on their Web site.

Direct Investing

If I had to pick one thing that I wished somebody had pounded into my head when I was younger, it would be the power of compounding. Say you set aside $50 every month in an investment returning 15 percent annually. After 10 years, you'd have $13,761. If you kept going, you'd have $33,425 in 15 years and $74,862 after 20 years.

Is 15 percent annual return an unreasonable expectation? The U.S. stock market, as measured by the S&P 500 index, averaged roughly 18 percent average annual returns for the past 10 years. Say you got lucky and beat the market with 20 percent annual returns. Then your $50 monthly contribution turns into $55,785 in 15 years and $155,483 after 20 years.

Yet, it's difficult to find places to invest relatively small amounts efficiently. Even a deep discount $10 commission takes too big a bite out of a $50 purchase. Many mutual funds are set up to handle regular contributions starting as low as $100, and that kind of investment plan makes a lot of sense.

What if you want to pick your own stocks instead of investing in mutual funds? If you do, direct investing plans are designed for you There are two types: dividend reinvestment plans (DRIPs) and direct stock purchase plans (DSPs). DRIPs are designed for investors who already own shares of stock in a dividend paying company. DRIP plans do not necessarily allow investors to make their initial purchase through the plan. DRIPs let existing shareholders collect dividends paid by the issuing company in shares instead of cash. DSPs allow you to purchase shares directly from the issuing company instead of going through a broker. It can be a one-time or periodic purchase.

Two good places for basic training on direct purchase plans is Drip Central (*www.dripcentral.com*), part of Invest-O-Rama, and Motley Fool (*www.fool.com* > Fool's School > Drip Investing). They both offer an assortment of tutorials and message boards.

Drip Central, run by Douglas Gerlach, Invest-O-Rama's founder, has better tutorials, especially their "Guide to DRIP Investing," and "Ask Doug—Answers to Frequent Questions." Motley Fool's message boards are more active and much easier to navigate than the boards on Drip Central. I suggest getting up to speed on Drip Central, and then hanging out on the Fool's boards to stay current.

NETSTOCK DIRECT (*www.netstockdirect.com*)

When you're ready to get serious about investing via DRIPs and DSPs, Netstock Direct's role in life is to help you find companies with DRIP or DSPs meeting your needs and then facilitate enrolling in the plans online. The best way to start is to use Netstock Direct's screening program to search through the entire list of companies offering DRIPs and DSPs to find plans you like the best.

Select "Find Plans" on the Netstock page to use the screening program. Check out the Quick Search menu on the left to see if any of these ready-made searches fit your needs. If not, use the screening program to find exactly what you want. Use of the program is self-explanatory. Here are a few suggestions:

When Will I Become a Millionaire?

(*www.buyandhold.com* > Resources > Calculators > Savings)

It's a question I'm sure all of us have pondered from time to time, and BuyandHold.com illustrates the power of compounding combined with a regular investment program to get to the $1 million goal.

It's a fill-in-the-blanks calculator. Enter your current age, how much money you're starting with, and how much you can invest monthly, along with your expected annual return. They also ask for your income tax rate and the predicted inflation rate. Don't stress over these two, just use the default values. Try varying the return rate. Enter the age you want to become a millionaire, and click on results.

The calculator tells you not only how long it will take you to become a millionaire with the values you entered, it tells you what you have to change to reach $1 million at the age you chose.

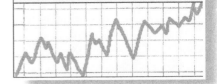

DEFINITION PLEASE

Direct Stock Purchase Plan (DSP): A plan implemented by a corporation allowing the purchase of shares, or fractions of shares, directly from the company, usually on a regular basis.

Discount Broker: A stockbroker charging lower commissions than full-service brokers. Discount brokers do not give investment advice.

Dividend Reinvestment Plan (DRIP): A plan implemented by a corporation to allow investors to collect dividends in shares (usually fractions of shares) of stock rather than in cash.

- Search the entire market or select particular industries. I suggest limiting your search to industries with strong growth prospects such as pharmaceuticals, technology, telecommunications, and the like.
- Look for companies offering either DSPs, DRIPs, or both. Many newer companies don't pay dividends, and a DRIP plan doesn't necessarily allow you to make your original purchase, so a DSP (Direct Stock Plan) is your best choice.
- Search for U.S. companies, international companies, or both. I prefer U.S. companies because it's often difficult to get enough information on foreign companies to adequately follow them.

Plan features include "Offers automatic deductions from my bank account." Automatic deductions are essential, they're the key to keeping you on a plan when you're tempted to use the money elsewhere.

Administering DSPs is a money loser, and only about 600 companies offer the plans. Some plans aren't practical for many investors because the fees and/or the minimum investments are too high. Now thanks to the Net, there's another approach—a sort of a "cyber-direct investment plan."

CYBER-DIRECT INVESTING

A least two Web sites let you buy stock direct in companies, whether or not they offer DSPs. These services establish lists of eligible stocks, and then allow members to invest as little as $20. The site buys the shares on the open market and transfers a fractional ownership to your account. For instance, 0.5 share is added to your account if the market price of the stock you're buying is $100 per share, and you invest $50. You can split your investment among several stocks. It's not possible to implement such a plan through a conventional Web broker because they have no facility for selling fractional shares, and their commissions would take an unacceptably large bite out of your monthly investment.

BuyandHold.com (*www.buyandhold.com*)

BuyandHold.com offers a selection of more than 1,200 stocks in a variety of industry sectors. You can also buy foreign stocks. There is something for every investing taste, everything from Amazon.com to Hilton Hotels, from Citigroup to Harley-Davidson.

BuyandHold.com offers another option that may make more sense than buying individual companies. Unless you're well diversified, you run the risk of one bad stock ruining the performance of your entire portfolio.

Therefore index investing is a safer approach. For instance, the NASDAQ 100 index reflects the performance of the 100 largest companies listed on the NASDAQ market, mostly high-tech companies. By the end of 1999, this index had, on average, risen more than 57 percent annually for five years. Sure, there's some risk, but that seems to me to be a safer investment than trying to pick the next hot tech stock.

In addition to the NASDAQ 100, BuyandHold.com offers securities representing the Dow Jones Industrial Average, the S&P 500 or S&P MidCap 400 indexes, and indexes representing nine S&P industry sectors such as consumer services, financial, technology, and so forth.

You can open an account on BuyandHold.com by filling out an application online, then printing and mailing it in, along with a check for at least $20. Once you've opened an account you can add to it by check or bank wire, but the best way is to use their "E-ZVest" feature to set up periodic purchases. You can specify weekly, monthly, or quarterly investments, and E-ZVest automatically withdraws the funds from your bank account, or from your BuyandHold.com account.

How much does all this cost? BuyandHold.com charges a $2.99 commission for each transaction. For instance, if you set up your account to buy two stocks once a month, you would pay $5.98 commission every month. That's too much if your total investment is $50. If you plan to invest $50 monthly, invest in only one stock, or set it up for $150 quarterly, and buy at most, three stocks. Sell orders also cost $2.99 per trade. Dividends are reinvested at no cost.

BuyandHold.com is set up for long-term investing, not for rapid trading. You can enter new buy or sell orders anytime, but the trades are only executed twice daily.

ShareBuilder (*www.sharebuilder.com*)

ShareBuilder.com works in much the same way as BuyandHold.com. They offer a larger selection of stocks, but no indexes. They charge less when you buy, $2.00 instead of $2.99 for BuyandHold.com, but they make it up by charging $19.95 when you sell. They also charge an $11.95 annual membership fee starting with your second year. Single (non-periodic) purchases cost $5.00.

You can enter new buy orders at anytime, but ShareBuilder only trades once a week for $5.00. You can trade in real time if you pay $19.95.

Universal Stock Access (*www.universalstockaccess.com*)

Universal Stock Access, an offshoot of The Moneypaper, the widely advertised DRIP investing service, was not yet operational when I wrote this chapter in April 2000. They plan to execute periodically scheduled trades for no commission if you pay them $199 once a year to be a member, plus $3 to set up each new stock. For that money, you could do 67 trades on BuyandHold.com.

Universal Stock Access will handle your buy transactions for $2 each if you don't pay the $199 annual fee. They charge $10 for each sale transaction. All buy and sell orders are executed on a fixed date, once a week.

CLOSED-END FUNDS

Most investors buy open-end mutual funds. You buy shares of an open-end fund directly from the fund, and when you sell, you sell them back to the fund. An open-end fund can sell as many shares as investors want to buy, there is no limit. The value of shares (net asset value or NAV) in an open-end fund is simply the total assets of the fund (stock, cash, etc.) divided by the number of outstanding shares.

A closed-end fund issues a fixed number of shares when the fund starts business. Once these shares are sold, the fund doesn't sell any more shares. If you want to buy shares in the fund, you must buy them from a shareholder who wants to sell. Conversely, you have to find a buyer before you can sell your shares.

When a holder of an open-end fund redeems shares, the fund must raise cash to repurchase the shares, sometimes forcing the fund manager to sell stock that he or she otherwise wouldn't sell. Closed-end fund managers can make long-term investment decisions without having to worry about raising cash to redeem shares, theoretically, giving them an advantage over open-end managers.

Closed-end fund shares trade on the open market just like a stock. Unlike an open-end fund where the share price exactly equals the net asset value, open-end fund shares may trade above or below the net asset value. The forces of supply and demand set the share price. If shares are trading above the net asset value, they are said to be trading at a premium, if they are trading below net asset value, they are said to be trading at a discount.

A good place to learn about closed-end funds is the Web site operated by the Closed-End Fund Association (*www.closed-end-funds.com*), a trade association representing the closed-end fund industry. You can find detailed information about all closed-end funds including a description, returns, current prices, and the fund's premium or discount. You can compare the premium or discount to the average, maximum, or minimum values for the current year, as well as the average premium or discounts over the past 10 years. You can also see the top 10 holdings in the fund's portfolio and the sector allocation of the portfolio.

Use the Custom Fund Search to find the funds with the best returns, the biggest discounts, or the highest premiums to net asset value. Check out the Education Center to get up to speed on closed-end funds.

Dollar-Cost-Averaging

You are dollar-cost-averaging if you invest a fixed amount in a single security on a regular basis. It's similar to the regular investing plans as in a DSP, except dollar-cost-averaging implies investing in the same stock, index, or mutual fund every time.

When you dollar-cost-average, the number of shares you get for each purchase depends on the current price. For instance, if you invest $100 and the share price is $10, you get 10 shares. If by the next month, the share price dropped to $8, you'd get 12.5 shares. If the price goes up to $15, you get only 6.7 shares.

With dollar-cost-averaging, you buy more shares when the shares are relatively cheap, and less when they're expensive. It's a gimmick of sorts—what's important is to keep putting that money in month after month after month. . . .

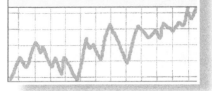

CHAPTER EIGHTEEN

Screening for Top Mutual Funds

The Best Fund Search Tool

QUICKEN (*www.quicken.com* > Investing > Fund Finder

Quicken offers the best all-around mutual fund search tools. Quicken uses data provided by Morningstar, including their star ratings. You might think that Morningstar, being the source of Quicken's data, would have the best fund screening tools, but Quicken's screening programs are better.

Quicken gives you three ways to search for funds: popular searches, easy-step searches, and full searches. Popular searches utilize easy-to-use predefined screens. EasyStep searches are custom searches that you define using a wizard-like question-and-answer approach. The full search shows you all of the available screening variables on one page.

Quicken Popular Searches

Selecting Popular Searches displays a list of 11 searches divided into five categories:

1. *Morningstar's Best*

- Ranked by 5-year performance—lists all funds with Morningstar's top rating (five stars) ranked by 5-year average annual return.
- Ranked by 10-year performance—lists Morningstar five-star funds ranked by 10-year average annual return.

These are the best overall searches. Limiting the search to Morningstar five-star funds ensures a selection of quality funds. Use the five-year version because five-year returns are a better indicator of future performance than 10-year numbers. The search will not list any funds that haven't been around at least five years. The search doesn't limit results to no-load funds, so you'll have to do that manually, or use the full search, if that's an important criterion for you.

2. *Best of the No-Load, Low-Expense Funds*

- Equity Funds—no-load funds investing primarily in stocks with expense ratios less than 0.75 percent, ranked by 5-year average annual return.

- Bond Funds—no-load bond funds with expense ratios less than 0.3 percent, ranked by 5-year average annual return.

It makes sense to seek out low-expense funds, but I think Quicken has gone overboard here. When I ran this screen, the expense ratio limit tossed out the 25 top performing no-load funds with average annual returns ranging from 29.1 percent to 50 percent. Screening is just the first step in the evaluation process. I would rather consider the expense ratio further along in the process—when you are comparing two otherwise similar funds.

3. *Best Small Funds*

- Under $100M in Assets—very small funds, ranked by 3-year performance
- Under $250M in Assets—small funds, ranked by 3-year performance.

Some market experts say smaller funds have an advantage because they can take advantage of opportunities that would be too small to have an impact on the performance of larger funds. I don't know of any studies that have proven this theory one way or the other.

4. *Best of the Market Cap Segments*

- Large-Caps—funds that specialize in companies exceeding $5 billion in market capitalization, ranked by 5-year average annual return.
- Mid-Caps—funds that specialize in companies with market capitalization in the $1 billion and $5 billion range, ranked by 5-year average annual return.
- Small-Caps—funds that specialize in companies with less than $1 billion in market capitalization, ranked by 5-year average annual return.

Large company funds have outperformed mid- and small-cap funds in recent years. This search is for you if you think it's time for smaller companies to shine. Be sure to do your research;

Quicken lets some funds sneak onto the listings whose holdings don't appear to match the screen definitions.

5. *Best Getting Started Funds*

- Minimum Investment $250—no-load funds requiring a minimum investment of $250 or less, ranked by 5-year performance.
- Minimum Investment $500—no-load funds requiring a minimum investment of $500 or less, ranked by 5-year performance.

The fund's minimum investment requirements don't necessarily apply if you're buying the fund through a broker. For instance, Schwab requires $2,500 minimum for all funds.

RUNNING THE SCREENS

The searches run automatically when you select them. The Fund Finder displays the first 25 funds, sorted according to 3-year, 5-year, or 10-year average annual return, depending on the search you selected. When you first run a search, Quicken displays the results in a default, or basic, format.

The first two columns show the fund name and ticker symbol. The third column contains a link to detailed information about the fund (Quote Plus), including a current quote, the manager's name and tenure with the fund, the fund size, front-end load, and the minimum investment required to buy shares directly from the fund. The fund's performance, and its performance compared to the S&P 500 index for the past one, three, and five-year periods, and year-to-date is shown. Quicken also shows you the Morningstar star rating, Morningstar risk and return ratings, and the category, such as specialty-technology, large-cap growth.

QUOTE

You can link to the Quote display from the Mutual Fund Finder's fund list, or access the display directly by requesting a quote on a mutual fund from various locations including the Investing main page.

The Quote link displays some basic information about each fund. You can use Quote data to rule out some candidates at this point. Here are some tips to guide you:

Category: Eliminate funds that don't fit your investment requirements. For instance, there is no point in going any further if the fund specializes in large growth companies and you're looking for a fund in the small value sector.

Load: Eliminate load funds here if you want no-loads.

Expense Ratio: Eliminate funds with expense ratios higher than 2.0 percent.

Manager Tenure: Anything less than three years makes the ratings based on historical performance meaningless.

Long-Term Performance: Growth investors should require 3- and 5-year performance at least close to, if not better than, the S&P 500 index. You can determine that by looking in the S&P 500 Index row. Negative numbers means the fund underperformed the index in the period.

Morningstar Ratings: Stick with four- or five-star overall ratings. The box includes simplified versions of Morningstar's return and risk ratings. Growth investors should look for a combination of above average return and average or below average risk. Conservative investors should insist on low risk above all.

ELIMINATE FUNDS NOW

The purpose of doing the analysis using the Quote display is to reduce the number of candidate funds down to a manageable number. Don't make a final decision until you've completed the full analysis.

Depending on the fund, there could be more links leading to a fact sheet, prospectus, family page, etc. These are all links to the fund's, or fund family's, Web pages.

The Mutual Fund Finder's Basic display also shows the Morningstar Rating, Front-End Load, Expense Ratio, Manager Tenure, and overall size (net assets) of the fund. Print out the first page (25 funds) and cross out the funds of no interest. For instance,

DEFINITION PLEASE

Expense Ratio: All expenses incurred by mutual fund management in operating and marketing the fund. Includes management and 12b-1 fees. Doesn't include loads or redemption fees. Expense ratios are deducted before computing fund returns.

Morningstar: Mutual fund rating service.

I eliminate funds with front-end loads, expense ratios greater than 2.0 percent, and manager tenures of less than three years. You may have different criteria.

DISPLAY OPTIONS

You can use the Fund Finder's Display dropdown menu to select five additional display formats:

1. Performance—shows the year-to-date; three-month; one-, three-, five-, and 10-year annualized returns; and the dividend yield.
2. Expenses—shows the front (end) load, expense ratio, (deferred) sales charge, redemption and 12b-1 fees, and the five-year annualized return.

   - The deferred sales charge, also known as the back-end load, is a fee imposed when you sell your shares back to the fund. The percentage usually declines the longer the shares are held.
   - The expense ratio is the percentage of the fund's assets taken out to run the fund.
   - The redemption fee is being imposed by more and more funds to discourage short-term trading. The redemption fee, usually about 1 percent, is assessed when you redeem your shares if you held them less than a specified minimum time, typically, a few months to a year.
   - The 12b-1 fee is a marketing charge. The expense ratio includes the 12b-1 fee, so there is no point to considering it again, or you'll be counting it twice.
3. Rating—shows the Morningstar Rating, manager tenure, and five-year annualized return.
4. Portfolio—shows the average market capitalization and the average price/earnings and price/book ratios of stocks held in the portfolio. Once again, the five-year annualized return for the fund is shown here also.

   - Check the market capitalization to determine if the fund meets your needs in terms of company size.

- The price/earnings ratio is an important indicator of future risk. For general equity funds, above 30 is high risk, and below 25 is low risk. These rules do not apply to industry-specific funds such as pharmaceutical or technology funds (see page 224 for details).
- Price-to-book ratio is often used to determine if a fund is holding mostly value stocks (P/B below 3), or mostly growth stocks. I haven't seen any evidence that low price/book ratio funds are less risky than other funds.

5. Operations—shows the minimum purchase requirements, manager tenure, and size of the fund (net assets). Don't confuse the net asset value, or fund size, with the market-capitalization of the fund's portfolio holdings. The net asset value is the total value of the fund holdings. Funds with assets less than $100 million are considered small funds, and those with assets exceeding $1 billion are considered large funds. The market-capitalization of a fund expresses the size of the companies the fund owns. A small fund (assets less than $100 million) could still own large-cap stocks.

The Fund Finder usually sorts the funds found by a search according to five-year average annual return, with the highest returns on top. You can use the Sort dropdown menu to sort the list using one-, three-, five-, or 10-year average annual returns, or by expense ratio or fund name. Leave the dropdown menu to the right of that set to "Desc" (descending) if you want the funds listed with the highest values at the top (returns), or select "Asc" (ascending) if you want the lowest values listed first (expense ratio or fund name).

Quicken EasyStep Search

Quicken's Fund Finder EasyStep Search leads you through the creation of a custom mutual fund screen one step at a time. It doesn't offer as many choices as the Full Search, but it's simple to use, and is a good middle ground between the simplicity of the Popular Searches and the flexibility of the Full Search. Here's how to use it.

Step 1: Morningstar Categories

Categories describe the types of stocks a mutual fund prefers to own. Sometimes the category defines the size and valuation of companies in the portfolio, such as mid-cap growth, or it could refer to a particular industry, such as specialty-health. You can select more than one category by holding down the Ctrl key while you click on the categories. Push Next to advance to Step 2.

Step 2: Morningstar Rating

Pick the minimum Morningstar Rating you want to see from the drop-down menu. Select "any" if you don't care.

Step 3: Five-Year Total Return

Enter a minimum acceptable value for five-year average annual return, or select from the choices in the dropdown menu:

- Beats S&P 500—average annual return must be greater than the return of the S&P 500 index. Select the S&P when you're screening for U.S. funds. Anything you type in the "Min" box will override the dropdown menu. So be sure to delete anything you've entered there if you change your mind and decide to use the dropdown menu.
- Beats MSCI World—return must outperform the Morgan Stanley Capital International World Index, an index tracking the performance of stock markets in 22 countries including the U.S. Select this index when you're screening for international funds.
- LB Aggregate—return must exceed the return of the Lehman Brothers Aggregate Bond Index, a combination of government, corporate, mortgage-backed, and asset-backed bonds and other securities indexes. Use when searching for bond funds.

Step 4: Expense Levels

Select a maximum acceptable front-load from the top dropdown menu. Choices are 2.0 percent, 3.0 percent, 5.0 percent, any, or none. The typical front-load is 5.75 percent. So select "any" if a load fund is acceptable, otherwise select "none."

Select a maximum acceptable expense ratio from the lower dropdown menu. Your choices are 0.3 percent, 0.5 percent, 0.75 percent,

1.0 percent, 2.0 percent, or "any." Screening for 1.0 percent or less would cut out most of the best performing funds of recent years.

Step 5: Operation Variables

Pick a value for maximum fund size as measured by total net assets. Choices are $100 million, $250 million, $1 billion, $5 billion, or "any." If you're looking for very small funds, pick $100 million. If you want to avoid the very largest funds, select $5 billion, otherwise pick "any."

Pick a value for minimum manager tenure, that is, how long the same person has been managing the fund. Choices are 1 year, 3 years, 5 years, 10 years, or "any." Longer is better, but most funds haven't been around more than five years. Picking too long of a minimum, say 10 years, would eliminate most funds.

Select Finish to get the results. You have the same display options as described for Popular Searches.

Quicken Full Search

Quicken's Fund Finder Full Search gives you more control over the screening parameters than the EasyStep Search.

Section 1: Morningstar Information

- Morningstar Categories: You can select more than one category by holding down the Ctrl key when you click on a category. I usually leave it on the default: all categories.
- Morningstar Rating: I usually select "at least 4 stars."

Section 2: Performance Data

- Returns: Here is where you specify minimum acceptable returns for periods ranging from three months up to 10 years. Returns for one year or more are always expressed as average annual returns. For instance, a 25 percent five-year return means an average 25 percent each year for five years. You can enter a specific minimum amount, or require returns to exceed a specified index's return. I usually use

DEFINITION PLEASE

Load: A sales commission paid when you buy (front-end) or sell (back-end) a mutual fund.

No-Load Mutual Fund: No sales commission is charged if you buy shares directly from the fund. There may or may not be a commission charged if you buy the fund through a broker.

REIT: Real estate investment trust. A special form of mutual fund investing only in real estate. REITs must pay out most of their earnings as dividends to share owners.

Best Investment Sites for Company Research

Biospace
(*www.biospace.com*): Caters to biotech investors.

Equity Insights
(*www.equityinsights.com*): Displays sophisticated fundamental analysis results in an easy-to-interpret bar-chart format. A must for fundamental research.

Equity Web
(*www.stockfever.com*): Good place to research a specific company. Enter a stock symbol, then you're presented with links to a multitude of sources for news and research on the company.

Free Edgar
(*www.freeedgar.com*): Best place to access SEC reports. You can set up a portfolio and Free Edgar will send you e-mail when a company in your portfolio issues a report.

Hoover's
(*www.hoovers.com*): Good site for easy-to-understand company

(continued on next page)

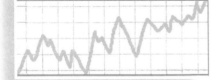

the index comparison: S&P 500 for U.S. stock funds, MSCI World for International funds, and the LB Aggregate for bond funds. It's easy to get carried away here. Try to avoid the temptation to search for the current hot funds: three and five-year returns are the most significant.

- 12-Mo Dividend Yield: Dividend yield is the share price divided by the dividends paid during the last 12 months. Investors seeking income can use the Dividend Yield to refine their search. Remember, dividends are taxed as ordinary income, so tax sensitive investors might want to require a maximum dividend yield of zero. The search uses the dropdown menu value unless you've typed a number in the "Min" or "Max" boxes. You don't have to specify both a minimum and a maximum. If you typed "2" in the Min box and left the Max box blank, the program would search for funds with a minimum 12-month dividend yield of 2 percent with no maximum limit. Be sure you remove all typing from the Min and Max boxes if you want the program to use the dropdown menu values.

Section 3: Expenses

- Front Load: See comments in EasyStep section.
- Expense Ratio: See comments in EasyStep section.
- Deferred Sales Charge: A type of load fee assessed when you sell the fund. The percentage typically decreases the longer you own the fund. Since you're not given enough information here to determine how long the fee applies, select "any" or "none."
- Redemption Fee: A fee instituted to discourage short-term traders. The fee usually disappears after a specified time, but from the information given here you don't know how long. I suggest "any" or "none."
- 12b-1 Fees: These are marketing fees already included in expense ratio. Select "any."

Section 4: Operations Data

- Minimum Initial Investment: The minimum investment required if you buy directly from the fund in a regular account. Funds often offer reduced minimum requirements for IRA accounts, and brokers may have different minimums. Setting requirements here may unnecessarily eliminate funds. Select "any."

- Total Net Assets: The size of the fund. Some say smaller funds do better than larger funds, but I've seen little evidence to support that theory. See comments in EasyStep section.
- Manager Tenure: See comments in EasyStep section.

Section 5: Return

This section is misnamed; it would more accurately be called "risk factors."

- Price/Earnings Ratio: An important measure of future risk. The dropdown menu gives you a choice of 15, 20, or 25 for the maximum allowable price/earnings ratio. If you're searching for value funds, use 25, otherwise use the max box. I suggest a maximum price/earnings of 35 if you're looking for general funds. Select "any" from the dropdown menu if you're searching for high-tech funds. Don't be confused by the "%" indicator after the Min and Max entry boxes—it is an error; price/earnings is not expressed in percent.
- Median Market Cap: Market capitalization of an individual stock is the number of shares outstanding multiplied by the stock price. If a company's stock price is $10, and it has one million shares out, its market capitalization would be $10 million. A mutual fund's median market capitalization is the average of the market caps of the stocks in the portfolio. You can select either Small, Medium, or Large Cap using the dropdown menu, or you can specify minimum and max-imum values separately. Try setting the minimum value to 5000 million (5 billion). You will get the larger medium-cap and all of the large-cap funds. Don't type in a comma when you enter "Median Market Cap"—it confuses the program.
- Price/Book Ratio: The price/book ratio of a stock is the stock price divided by the book value. Stocks with price/book ratios less than 3.0 are said to be value-priced. The price/book ratio of a fund is the average of the price/book ratios of the stocks in the portfolio. I've never

Best Investment Sites for Company Research

(*continued from previous page*)

descriptions and by far the best source for a list of competitors.

Market Guide (*www.marketguide.com*): Concise summary of funda-mental data plus income state-ments, balance sheets, and cash-flow statements in an easy-to-read format. Start your fundamental analysis here.

Morningstar (*www.morningstar.com*): Fundamental data plus stock grades with Morningstar's assessment of a company's fundamentals in four categories.

Quicken's Industry Comparison (*www.quicken.com*): A good way to see how a com-pany fits in its industry. Get a stock quote, then click on "Compare Stock to Competitors" to see a list of the company's competitors listed in order of company size. Then you can compare companies in a variety of categories.

found a way to make money using price/book ratio as a selection factor. I suggest "any."

Section 6: Display Options

See the discussion in Popular Searches section.

RUN THE SEARCH

Press Show Results to run the search. Typically, you'll be unhappy with your first results. Either you'll get too many or too few funds, or the funds listed won't be what you want. If you don't get enough funds, try widening or eliminating search parameters one-by-one until you find the culprit. Narrow the parameters if you're getting too many funds. Ideally, you'd like to come up with about 20 reasonably good candidates that you can analyze further.

E*Trade Searches

(*www.etrade.com* > Mutual Funds > Power Search)

E*Trade is a leading Web broker. Most Web brokers feature a selection of research features for their customers. E*Trade does too, but they also have some research tools available to everybody—customer or not. E*Trade's mutual fund Power Search is one. Registration is required to use many of E*Trade's free services.

Power Search is easy to use and has features I haven't seen anywhere else. Here's how to use it.

- Fund Family: If you're interested in specific fund families, use the menu to select them (Hold down the Ctrl key while you click to select multiple families), otherwise leave the selection at the "Any Family" default.
- Investment Objective: Use this menu if you want to select a particular industry sector such as health or technology funds, or a specific type of bond fund. Leave it set at the default "Any Objective" if you're looking for general U.S. stock funds.
- Historical Performance: You can specify a minimum average annual return for one-, three, five-, and 10-year periods. I prefer funds with at least a five-year track record, so I would

pick the "5-year" period. You may find this restriction eliminates too many funds for your taste. Select the minimum return from the dropdown menu from values ranging from 2.5 percent to 50 percent. I suggest starting with "at least 25%" for any period less then 10 years. Select "at least 15%" for the 10-year period.

- Fund Assets: You can choose from a maximum fund size of $10 million, $100 million, $500 million, and $1 billion. I suggest the default "Any Amount."
- Age of Fund: You can select a minimum age of three, five, or 10 years from the dropdown menu.
- Minimum Initial Investment: Many funds have different required minimums for IRAs than for regular accounts. This is the only search I've seen that allows you to choose between an IRA and a regular account type when you specify the minimum investment. You can choose a maximum required investment of $250, $500, $1,000, $2,000, $5,000, $10,000 or "any" minimum from the dropdown menu.
- Commission Type: This is another feature I've seen only on E*Trade. Brokers allow you to select from a long list of mutual funds; some are no-load and others are load funds. Some of the no-load funds still incur a transaction fee, typically ranging from $10 to $100 when you buy or sell the fund. Other funds have no fees whatsoever. E*Trade allows you to search for these funds by selecting "No transaction fee" from the dropdown menu. The other choices are no-load with transaction fee, load, or any commission type. Even if you specify "any," the program displays the commission type in the report. I suggest selecting "any," otherwise you could miss out on a good fund over a $25 fee.
- Annual Expense Ratio: Choose from maximum values in the range of 0.25 percent to 3.0 percent. I suggest 2.0 percent, or "any."
- 12b-1 Fee: You can pick from selections between 0.0 percent and 2.0 percent. Leave this set at the "any" because this fee is also included in the expense ratio.
- Qualified In: A list of U.S. states. Relates to tax exempt bond fund searches. Select "any."

DEFINITION PLEASE

12b-1 Fee: Annual marketing fee charged by some mutual funds. Named after SEC regulation allowing such fees.

Alpha: A statistical concoction that's supposed to measure the excess performance of a mutual fund compared to the performance expected for its beta. Higher is better.

Sharpe Ratio: An attempt to compare a fund's performance to risk. Higher Sharpe Ratio funds are said to be better performers than lower-ratio funds.

(continued on next page)

- Portfolio Management Strategy: This section is a continuation of the Investment Objective selections. There's a mishmash of selections here, many of them not available on other screening sites, including emerging market stock funds specific to Africa/Middle East, Asia, and Latin America; an emerging market bond category; index and enhanced index funds; socially responsible funds; tax-managed and micro-cap funds.
- Annual Turnover: Turnover is a measure of a fund's stock trading. See page 226 for information on how to interpret turnover. The choices include maximum turnover ratios in the 50 percent to 400 percent range. Given these choices, choose 50 percent for funds in taxable accounts.
- Fund Manager Tenure: You can select between choices on one-, three-, five- and 10-year minimums, or "any." I suggest three years.
- Risk Measures: This section should really be titled "statistical measures," because not all the variables here measure risk. These measurements are related to Modern Portfolio Theory, developed by Nobel Prize–winning economist William F. Sharpe and his associates. I find Morningstar's return, risk, and star ratings do a better job of helping me select winning mutual funds than do the measures in this section.
  - Alpha measures a fund's risk-adjusted return somewhat similar to Morningstar's return rating. In theory, higher is better, but I've never made money selecting high alpha funds. E*Trade gives you a range from minus 10 to plus 10. I suggest "any."
  - Beta is a measure of a fund's volatility compared to an index, typically the S&P 500. In theory, high beta funds are more volatile, and likely to produce bigger returns in a strong market and bigger losses in a weak market. I suggest "any."
  - Sharpe Ratio is a comparison of risk adjusted return to volatility, somewhat similar to the formula Morningstar uses to calculate their star ratings. This indicator is named after its inventor, William F. Sharpe. I suggest "any."

- R-Squared is a measure of how a fund's price moves in tandem with its appropriate index (S&P 500 for large funds). The range is 0 to 100. A value of 100 means the fund's price movements are entirely explained by the appropriate index. Theoretically, you can't use alpha and beta unless R-Squared is high. I suggest "any."

RUN THE SEARCH

Press Search when you've finished to get the list of funds meeting your requirements. Before showing you the list, E*Trade tells you how many funds it found and asks you how you want to sort the list and how many funds you want to see on one screen.

You can tell the program to sort the funds by returns for 1, 3, 5, or 10 years, or by expense ratio. Select No Preference if you want to see them listed alphabetically. I suggest sorting by three- or five-year average annual returns.

You can also choose how many funds you want to see listed on a page. Your choices range from 10 to 150 funds per page. Your primary consideration here is the speed of your connection and your patience. I've found 150 funds take too long to download into my browser, so I usually elect to see 50 funds at a time.

Other Good Fund Screeners

SMART MONEY FUND FINDER (*www.smartmoney.com* > Funds > Fund Finder in Fund Tools section)

Smart Money's Fund Finder has some unique features worth mentioning. Smart Money has its own rating system, awarding grades from A to F, based on their assessment of risk and reward with a small adjustment for Drag on Returns; that is, loads, expense ratio, and portfolio turnover.

Smart Money grades funds by comparing them to their peer group, which are funds with similar objectives. For instance, large-cap value funds are compared to other large-cap value funds, technology funds to other tech funds, etc. This in an important distinction from the way Morningstar does it. Morningstar compares

---

Best Investment Sites for Finding Ideas—Web Pundits
(*continued from previous page*)

Motley Fool (*www.fool.com*): Home of the Rule Maker, Rule Breaker, Foolish Four, and other portfolios.

MSN MoneyCentral (*moneycentral.msn.com*): Jim Juback and a variety of other pundits offer picks.

PaceSetters Database (*www.prars.com*): A selection of 15 to 29 stocks best meeting classic fundamental criteria. Very good.

Sivey on Stocks (*www.money.com*): Michael Sivey is a Warren Buffett–style stock picker.

Smart Money (*www.smartmoney.com*): Stocks picked by *Smart Money* magazine's editors.

Value & Growth Stock Review (*www.vgsr.com*): A list of undervalued stocks starting to move up.

ValueStocks.net (*www.valuestocks.net*): Stocks selected using strategies inspired by Benjamin Graham.

a stock fund to all other U.S. stock funds, not just funds with similar objectives.

Smart Money's peer group approach is important to investors following an asset allocation strategy, but a disadvantage for others who want to find the best funds, regardless of their stated objectives.

CNBC'S WHAT'S WORKING?

(*www.cnbc.com* > Funds > Best Searches under Other Links)

We all say we're long-term investors, but in our heart of hearts we know we'd love to find funds likely to produce blowout performance as soon as we buy them. CNBC gives us a shot at finding out what today's hot funds have in common.

Select Best Searches on the Mutual Fund page to display a list of fund searches that produced the best returns in a variety of categories over the past six months. That is, the results displayed assume you selected the funds six months ago. The hope is, as long as market conditions stay the same, these searches will continue to find outperforming funds. The list displays the average returns of the top 25 mutual funds meeting the search requirements. The searches with the best returns are listed first. When I looked, a search called Strong Growth/Income funds topped the list, producing an 84 percent return in six months.

This kind of information only helps if you think market conditions haven't changed much in six months. If so, the selection strategies that worked then would probably continue their success.

What if you think the market is changing quickly, and tests run six months ago are ancient history? No problem. Use the drop-down menu to pick two months, or even one month, and CNBC will show you the searches that produced the best results then. If you're looking for longer-term trends, select 12 months for your testing period.

SIMPLE FUND SEARCH

(*www.cnbc.com* > Funds > Fund Screener > Mutual Funds)

CNBC has a Screener Tool that is deceptively easy to use, but produces worthwhile results. Click Fund Screener from the Funds page and select Mutual Funds from the list inside the Screener Tool.

You'll see a choice of performance ratings ranging from one week to five years. Pick one and be prepared to wait. The screener may take a minute or so to display the results.

In the meantime your screen will appear frozen. Eventually, you'll see a list of 25 funds with the best performance for the period you selected. Above the list is a chart showing the returns you would have received if you had bought the 25 top-rated funds using the same search criteria at times ranging from one to 12 months back. The best searches will show consistently increasing returns as you go back in time. A list of the components used in the screen is shown to the left of the Returns chart.

CNBC also shows you the current share price (Net Asset Value) and a trend arrow indicating whether the fund's share price is currently in an uptrend or a downtrend.

ADVANCED FUND SEARCH

(*www.cnbc.com* > Funds > Fund Screener > Advanced Search)

CNBC also offers an Advanced (mutual fund) Search accessible from the Screener Tool. The Advanced Search allows you to

screen for funds using a variety of sophisticated performance and risk criteria such as "up-market premium," "risk-free probability," and the like.

The Advanced Search is, in my view, the most powerful mutual fund screening program available on the Web.

DEFINITION PLEASE

Net Asset Value: Value of all stock and other assets owned by mutual fund divided by the total number of shares the fund has outstanding.

Portfolio: A group of stocks, mutual funds, or other securities.

Standard Deviation: A measure of a mutual fund or stock's historical volatility.

Turnover Ratio: The frequency with which a mutual fund changes its portfolio holdings. 100 percent turnover means a fund, on average, changes all the stocks in its portfolio once a year.

CHAPTER NINETEEN

The IPO
Gold Rush

When a company sells their stock to the public for the first time, it is called an Initial Public Offering (IPO).

Until recently, companies raised capital from venture capitalists and other private sources to get started. Then after establishing a track record of increasing sales and profits, the company would "go public" by offering shares to investors. The venture capitalists and other original investors could "cash out" by selling their stock on the open market after a predetermined waiting (lockup) period. Venture capitalists reaped large profits from successful start-ups, but they typically had to wait three or four years before the company's business progressed to the point that it could be taken public. The original investors often lost their entire investment because the start-up never did grow to the stage where it could be taken public.

Now venture capitalists have discovered they don't have to wait more than a few months because investors will rush to buy practically any IPO with a catchy name. There's not much risk for the venture capitalists because the new company doesn't need a track record, and nobody knows if it will be successful when the company goes public. Since venture capitalists have invested only a few cents per share, even the biggest IPO bomb will net them huge profits. The result is a gold rush for venture capitalists, and new issues are flooding into the market. The glut seems not to matter, and many IPO's issue prices increase substantially from the first day of trading and often for weeks to come.

The IPO Process

Companies could sell shares to the public by themselves, but most go public with the assistance of underwriters. Underwriters are usually brokerage houses experienced in creating the forms required by the SEC and in marketing the new shares to the investment community.

Companies doing the underwriting are called investment bankers. Underwriting is extremely profitable, so investment bankers actively court companies considered candidates to go public. The investment banker selected to bring the company public is called the lead underwriter.

The lead underwriter, with the help of accountants and lawyers, prepares and files a preliminary prospectus with the SEC describing the business, how the money raised by the offering will be used, the salary and business experience of key officers, etc. The preliminary prospectus also specifies the estimated share price and number of shares to be sold. These estimates can be, and often are, changed in the final version of the prospectus.

The lead underwriter invites other investment bankers to participate, thus forming a syndicate of investment bankers. The members of the syndicate present the company in a "road show" to prospective buyers: mostly mutual funds, trust funds, and other institutional buyers.

The lead underwriter along with the issuing company decide on the price and number of shares to be offered to the public, based on interest expressed by the institutional buyers. Setting the issue price is tricky. They want it to be low enough so all the shares are sold and the price pops up the first day, but not so low as to leave too much money on the table. The shares are made available for trading after the SEC approves the prospectus.

OPENING DAY

If it's a hot IPO, demand exceeds supply, and buyers, even large institutions, end up with fewer shares than they requested. Brokers divvy out shares to their best customers—those generating large commissions. Individual investors seldom see any allocation of hot IPOs from traditional brokers.

If the share price does pop on the opening day, institutions often sell their IPO shares on the open market on the first day of trading—a process termed "flipping." Individual investors lucky enough to get shares at the issue price are usually discouraged from flipping their shares by their broker.

LOCKUP PERIOD

Company insiders including venture capitalists, officers, and other large shareholders are typically prohibited from selling their shares during the lockup period. Typically 180 days, the lockup period is not required by law. It's determined by the lead underwriter, and can be shortened by agreement between the underwriter and the issuing company.

IPO Terms

aftermarket Trading of shares after the IPO date.

allocation The number of shares you're allowed to purchase, usually a small percentage of your requested amount.

book A list of buy orders kept by the lead underwriter.

bucket shop An underwriter with a reputation for handling penny stocks.

direct public offering IPO handled by issuing company without using underwriters.

due diligence The process whereby the underwriters conduct an in-depth examination of the company's business prospects.

effective A registration is declared effective when the offering receives final approval from the SEC, usually the night before trading begins.

fallen angel An IPO trading below its issue price in the aftermarket.

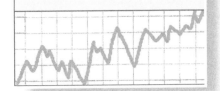

QUIET PERIOD

The company, its officers, and analysts associated with the underwriters are forbidden by the SEC from saying anything about the company not included in the prospectus until the "quiet period" ends, 25 days after the stock starts trading.

Finding and Evaluating IPOs

It looks like, before long, individual investors will have more opportunities to get in on IPOs at the issuing price. That doesn't mean you will automatically make money on every IPO offered to you. Some IPOs see spectacular price increases on the first day of trading, but others go down. Here are some ideas on finding and evaluating IPOs.

Your first step is finding the list of companies planning to go public.

PRELIMINARY PROSPECTUS

The clock starts ticking when a company files a preliminary prospectus. It usually takes about two months from the initial filing until the shares start trading. The process of filing the preliminary prospectus is called the "initial filing." You can see a list of filings on IPO.com (*www.ipo.com*). Click "Filings" on the top menu to see the filings sorted with the most recent on top. IPO.com displays the filing date, lead underwriter, the estimated offering price, number of shares to be offered, and the estimated value of the total offering. Click on the company name to get more information. The information is helpful if you want to get a head start on researching new issues.

Researching an IPO can be frustrating because the majority of companies issuing IPOs in the current market don't have enough of an operating history to analyze. Long-term business prospects generally don't matter much in the first few weeks an IPO trades. They do later, especially when the lockup period expires and insiders are free to sell their shares.

In the meantime, the laws of supply and demand determine IPO share prices. Let's look at these factors.

Supply

The supply side of the equation is easy to determine—it's the number of shares that will be available for trading. During the first 180 days of trading, the shares issued in the IPO are the only shares available for trading. After the lockup period expires, the supply includes shares owned by original investors looking to cash out.

Type the company name or ticker symbol into Ostman's Alert IPO (*www.ostman.com*) Search window at the top of the main page. Be sure to select "ticker" from the dropdown menu if you enter the company's ticker symbol instead of the name. Press Search to display the company profile. Click on the company name and then on Offering to display the information you need.

- Status/Tentative Pricing shows the date the shares are expected to start trading.
- Lead Underwriter is important information you'll need later, so make a note of it.
- Shares is the number of shares expected to be sold during the IPO, that is, the supply of shares during the first 180 days of trading.
- Over-Allotment is an additional number of shares that may be sold at the discretion of the lead underwriter if the IPO is extremely popular. The over-allotment is usually 15 percent of the IPO shares and is sometimes called the "Green Shoe."
- Post-Offering Shares is the number of shares that will be outstanding after the IPO shares are sold.
- Lockup Period is the time agreed to by the issuing company and the lead underwriter before insiders can begin selling their shares.

What's the optimum number of shares available for trading? Lower is better. What's low and what's high depends on the awareness of, and excitement for, the company by the market. Nine of the 10 best performing IPOs of 1999 sold 10 million shares or less in their initial offering.

Of course, you won't know if the original investors and other insiders will necessarily start selling their holdings when the lockup

IPO Terms

fast track An underwriter brings an IPO to market in less than the typical eight weeks.

final prospectus Contains updates from the preliminary prospectus and the final price and quantity of the shares issued.

flipping A practice whereby buyers of the IPO at the issue price sell their shares on the same day.

float Number of outstanding shares not owned by insiders, and thus available for trading.

green shoe An agreement allowing the lead underwriter to buy up to an additional 15 percent of shares at the offering price for several weeks after the IPO. The term, also known as over-allotment, is named after the Green Shoe Company the first company to offer the option.

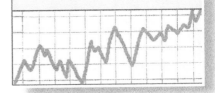

period ends. Much of that depends on who's holding the shares and upon their assessment of the company's future prospects. This is an area where knowledge of the company's long-term growth prospects and competitive position will help you make a better decision.

Demand

Figuring out the supply side of the equation is easy, demand is another story. There are two factors we can look at to help us estimate demand for an IPO: market excitement and the reputation of the lead underwriter.

MARKET EXCITEMENT

Mutual funds and other institutional investors don't care about a company's fundamental prospects if they're only planning to own the shares for a few hours. Same thing with most short-term individual investors who will buy shares the opening day from institutions dumping the stock. They're in it for the ride and could care less about how many widgets the company will sell next year.

What is important? The degree of market excitement or "buzz" about the stock. We can't measure buzz directly, but there are a few places we can look to get a handle on it.

Red Herring (*www.redherring.com* > IPO News > View IPO Calendar)
Red Herring is a magazine focusing on the business aspects of technology. Red Herring is also the nickname for an IPO's preliminary prospectus, so it's a fitting site to research IPOs. Click on View IPO Calendar on their IPO News page.

Red Herring's IPO Calendar shows you a list of upcoming IPOs with the estimated prices and, more important, their Street Poll. Red Herring's Street Poll is their reading of the market enthusiasm for the new issue. The Street Poll ratings run from Red Hot down to Cool. Red Herring gives little detail on how they come up with their Street Poll rating, saying only that it's derived from "various Wall Street sources." Pay attention to these ratings because Red Herring's mission and reputation is built upon staying on top of business buzz.

IPO Terms

gross spread The discount, typically 7 percent to 8 percent, between the issue price and the price the underwriter actually pays the issuing company for the stock.

indication of interest Tentative orders by institutional investors, possibly based on issue price, received during the road show.

insiders Directors, officers, and investors holding more than 5 percent of the company's outstanding shares before the IPO.

lead manager The underwriter in control of the offering.

lockup period A period, usually 180 days, based on agreement between the lead underwriter and the issuing company when insiders are not allowed to sell their shares. The lockup period may be changed by agreement between the issuing company and the underwriter.

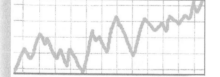

You can get more information on any offering by clicking on the company name. Each listing shows the lead underwriter for the offering. Jot it down if you don't have it already, because you'll need it soon.

Ostman's Alert IPO (*www.ostman.com* > Bull/Bear Rank)

Ostman's Alert IPO gauges market excitement with their Bull/Bear IPO Rankings. They only rank IPOs due out within seven days. They track changes in the number of shares offered and estimated issue price to compute a Bull/Bear score. Positive scores are bullish, and negative scores bearish. The range of scores isn't fixed, but typically stays in the −3 to +3 range. They say they've "seen deals as high as +5, however."

UNDERWRITER: HOT BECAUSE YOU'RE HOT

The success or lack of success of an IPO is due, in part, to the reputation of the lead underwriter. Certain underwriters are considered hot because their recent IPOs sizzled. Institutions are more likely to buy issues taken to market by hot underwriters because they made money on their prior offerings. Success begets success. Hot underwriters have their choice of the best IPOs, because the new companies know of their earlier successes and seek them out.

To find the hot underwriters use IPO.com (*www.ipo.com*). Select Underwriters from the menu on the left side of the main page to display the information. IPO.com shows you two lists: the 10 underwriters bringing the most IPOs to market and the 10 underwriters whose IPOs, on average, increased the most in share price during recent months.

In 1999, Credit Suisse First Boston, Goldman Sachs, and Morgan Stanley Dean Witter were the leading investment banks in terms of number of IPOs brought to market. Together, these three accounted for 16 of the 25 best performing IPOs brought to market in 1999 (data from *www.ipohome.com*). These three investment bankers, together, were lead underwriters for only two of the 25 biggest losers of 1999. Of the 25 best performers in 1999, investment bankers listed in IPO.com's top 10 in terms of number of IPOs brought 24 to market. By contrast, underwriters not appearing in the top 10 list brought 13 of the 25 worst performing IPOs in 1999 to market.

IPO Terms

offering price The price, usually set the night before the sale, that initial buyers pay for the stock.

offering range The expected offering price specified in the preliminary prospectus, typically a spread of $2 to $3. The offering range often changes upward if the road show indicates heavy interest in the issue, or downward if there is lack of interest.

opening price The first public trading price.

over-allotment See Green Shoe.

oversubscribed Orders exceed number of available shares. Most issues are oversubscribed, otherwise the offering is canceled.

penalty bid A charge by your broker if you sell shares you received from the initial offering too soon.

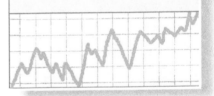

The Aftermarket

Whether you're a mutual fund or an individual investor, you won't get as many shares of an IPO at the offering price as you wanted. If you want more, you'll have to buy them after they start public trading—that's the aftermarket.

How do you know which recent IPOs are going to shine, and when to buy them? Some investors look at the "opening day pop." That's the difference between the issue price and the close on the first day of trading. An IPO with an issue price of $10 and a closing price of $20 on the first day of trading had a 100 percent opening day pop.

Does it work? I used data available on Renaissance Capital's IPO Home site (*www.ipohome.com*) to see what happened in 1999. Here's what I found:

- Nine of the 10 hottest performers in the aftermarket in 1999 had opening day pops greater than 100 percent. Five of them had pops exceeding 200 percent. One, Liberate Technologies, had a pop of only 27 percent.
- Eight of the 10 worst aftermarket performers had pops of less than 10 percent; in fact, seven had no gain, or dropped on the first day of trading. Only one, Value America, had a first day pop exceeding 100 percent. That accounts for 9 of the worst 10 performers. The tenth, Prism Financial, ended the first day 30 percent above the issue price.

Does this mean all you have to do is buy companies with big opening day pops? Unfortunately, it's not that easy. At the end of 1999, some of the stocks with the biggest opening day pops, including VA Linux, Cobalt Networks, MarketWatch, and CacheFlow, were trading near or below their opening day closing price.

Timing

When is the best time to buy aftermarket stocks? Most, but not all, drop in price for the first few trading days after the IPO before heading up. Problem is, what's a few days? Sometimes it's two, most often it's four or five trading days. Sometimes they just go straight up without any pause. There's no hard and fast rule, but if you do see a hot IPO drop the day after the opening day, you have, on average, two or three trading days before it starts up again.

QUIET PERIOD EXPIRATION

Analysts working for an IPO's underwriters are obligated to cover the new stock, meaning they will write reports forecasting earnings and making buy, hold, or sell recommendations. The underwriter is expected to support the stock after the IPO. Supporting the stock implies keeping the share price up by a number of means, including circulating positive analyst reports.

The analysts can't publish their reports, however, until the expiration of the quiet period, usually 25 days after the stock went public. Since there are usually three investment bankers involved in an IPO, that means that you can expect to see three analysts' reports issued within a day or two of the expiration date. Usually you see three new buy recommendations on the company in the space of a day or two.

You can see where an unsuspecting investor, cruising the headlines, would be impressed by analysts from three different prestigious brokerage houses all issuing buy ratings at the same time.

You can view a list of quiet period expiration dates on Ostman's Alert IPO (*www.ostman.com*) by clicking Quiet Period in the News section of IPO Data on the menu on the left. Quiet periods can expire any day of the week, even Sunday, so allow a day or two after the listed date for the analysts' reports to appear.

Is this the Holy Grail? No way! Many investors are on to what's happening, and sometimes the analysts don't come through with strong buys as expected. For instance, Martha Stewart doubled the first day of trading on October 19, 1999. Despite their obligations, analysts just couldn't come up with enthusiastic recommendations for a stock they apparently thought was already fully priced, and issued ratings like outperform, accumulate, and market perform. The stock price continued on a downtrend already in place.

Sometimes investors expecting a rash of strong recommendations push the price up in anticipation of the Quiet Period expiration. Whatever the reason, it's hard to discern any predictable stock price pattern related to Quiet Period expiration.

IPO Terms

pinks A form of the preliminary prospectus without specifying an initial price range or number of shares to be offered.

pipeline Companies that have filed a prospectus, but have not yet issued their shares.

post-offering shares The total number of shares outstanding after the IPO.

postponed Issue date is delayed due to lack of buying interest or other unfavorable market conditions.

preliminary prospectus Document prepared by the lead underwriter and associated lawyers and accountants describing the company, its business strategy, previous financial results, management, ownership, competition, etc.

premium Difference between the issue price and the first trade, also called the "pop."

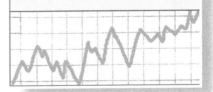

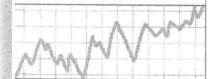

LOCKUP EXPIRATION

Most companies issuing IPOs sell 4 to 12 million shares in the initial offering, a small fraction of the maybe 50 million shares outstanding. Who owns the balance? Early investors, venture capitalists, officers and directors, etc., all waiting for a market price to be established so they can cash out. They can't sell, though, until the lockup period expires.

You can see a list of expected lockup expirations from Ostman's (*www.ostman.com*) by selecting Lockups just above Quiet Period. Tracking lockup expirations doesn't appear to work any better than tracking Quiet Period expirations.

Just because insiders can sell doesn't mean they will sell, at least not anytime soon. If anything, traders anticipate the expiration and dump the stock a week or so before the date.

All that said, insider selling can force an IPO's stock price down for weeks or months if there is enough of it. For instance, market maker Knight/Trimark's share price fell around 46 percent when its lockup expired on July 13, 1999, and insiders dumped almost 1.5 million shares by August 15.

The only way to forecast insider selling after lockup expiration is to scrutinize insider trading reports for planned sale notices, watch SEC filings for planned secondary offerings, and keep an eye on news and analysts' reports.

Analyze the Business

You will find it beneficial to your financial health to learn something about the issuing company's business prospects before buying an IPO.

According to SEC regulations, everything there is to know about a company before the initial shares are sold and during the quiet period after the offering is supposed to be included in the prospectus. The underwriters, their analysts, or anyone else connected with the offering are not allowed to issue additional information of any type.

Company officers and representatives from the underwriter do present additional information verbally to institutional investors during the road show preceding the offering. As of this writing, individual investors are precluded from seeing the information presented at these shows, but pressure is mounting to change the rules.

HOOVER'S ONLINE (*www.hoovers.com* > IPO Central)

Hoover's is in the business of profiling all sizable U.S. companies, whether publicly traded or privately held.

In most cases, Hoover's is the only source of information about an IPO company, besides the information found in the prospectus.

Hoover's doesn't evaluate a company's future prospects, but they do give you important information about its business and competition. A big advantage of Hoover's is they present the information in plain English, and they avoid usage of meaningless phrases like "solutions," and "mission critical," so prevalent in the prospectus and other reports filed by high-tech companies.

You can get a list of scheduled pricings for the current week and six weeks ahead by selecting IPO Central from Hoover's home page, and then clicking on the week of interest. Hoover's displays the usual information: company name, symbol, estimated number of shares and price range, and the total amount expected to be raised by the offering. From there, click on the company name to access Hoover's report.

Alternatively, enter the company name or ticker symbol on Hoover's main page if you already know it.

- **Company Capsule:** The capsule starts with a paragraph describing the company's business, including a list of their major customers in a descriptive paragraph. It's well done, and it's a must read for every IPO investor. Equally important is the list of Top Competitors. Most lists of competitors found on the Web are inadequate, listing companies that aren't competitors and overlooking the important rivals. Hoover's isn't perfect, but they're the best I've found on the Web. I always research the competition to see if one of them might be a better investment.

- **Financials:** Most IPOs issued in the current market environment haven't been in business long enough or sold enough of their products or services to have a financial statement worth analyzing. In those cases, you might as well skip this section. Hoover's shows you the quarterly income statement

and balance sheet going back five quarters. It's easy to read; however, I prefer the statements in the prospectus because they include a cash flow statement.

- **News & Analysis:** Hoover's stands out because you can't find news on IPOs on sites like Yahoo!, Quicken, and CBS MarketWatch. Those sites access all stories by ticker symbol, and ticker symbols don't go into their database until the stock starts trading. You'll see some headlines when you select the News & Analysis page, but click on Hoover's News under News & Commentary and Hoover's Research Center for the best stories.

- **Industry:** This page includes links to Primary Industry, a list of companies in the same industry, and Hoover's Industry Snapshots. The primary industry list is too long, and too varied, often listing more than 100 companies, and most of them aren't really in the same industry. Hoover's Industry Snapshot is well done and interesting, but isn't focused enough to be of much value. For instance, I looked up Lexmark, the maker of inkjet and laser printers, and got a discussion of the entire computer hardware industry. Next, look up the prospectus if you're interested in doing further research after reviewing Hoover's information.

OSTMAN'S ALERT IPO (*www.ostman.com*)

The prospectus is filed with the SEC, so you can view it on Free Edgar or similar sites, but I find Ostman's Alert IPO the easiest to use. Enter either the company name or proposed ticker symbol into the IPO Search box and click Search.

- **Intro:** Ostman's displays an overview page with a one-line description of the company's business and other basic information. News headlines about the offering are listed at the bottom. The headlines are basic, listing filing dates, price and number of share revisions and the like. There is no link to related information.

- **Offering:** This section rehashes some of the same information included in the Intro, but adds details on the over-allotment, post-offering shares, and the lockup period. The post-offering shares number is the total number of shares that will be outstanding after the offering is completed. This is an important number because it represents shares owned by insiders including investors who may want to cash out when the lockup expires. The section titled "Use of Proceeds" describes how the proceeds from the offering will be used. It usually says the proceeds will be used for general corporate purposes. It's a danger sign if it says the money will be used to pay off the original investors, or to pay down debt.

- **Company Description:** Describes the company's business in techno-babble. You don't need to read this section if you've already done your research on Hoover's.

- **Financials:** Most IPOs won't have meaningful information here because they haven't been around long enough. If you are researching an established company, follow the same analysis procedure outlined in Part 3, Chapter 8.

- **Management:** This is where they list the titles and ages of officers and directors, tell you how much money they're making, and give you a short resume for each officer. Once I get past that these people are younger than my kids, I review their resumes. Successful people are likely to repeat, so look for officers who have been in key management positions at other successful companies. Ideally, members of the board of directors should be people who have held top management positions in large, successful companies, not necessarily in the same business.

- **Shareholders:** This section lists insiders—that is, holders of at least 5 percent of the existing stock before the IPO. Ideally, you would like most of the shares to be in the hands of officers, who may keep their holdings indefinitely, but in most cases you'll see banks and investment firms with large holdings. The shareholders list is interesting to read, but you probably won't learn much that would affect your decision to buy the stock.

- **Competition:** This section lists all current and potential competitors in each of their target market segments. They tend to be all-encompassing, but check the list to see if there is anyone significant that Hoover's didn't mention.

IPO Terms

red herring A nickname for the preliminary prospectus derived from the fact that certain information in it is printed in red ink.

registration statement (S-1) A notice, including the preliminary prospectus, filed with the SEC of intent to issue an IPO.

road show Presentation made by underwriters and company officers to institutional investors.

roll-up Several independent companies merge into a single company at the time of the IPO.

selling shareholders Insiders selling their shares at the time of the offering. It's not good news if you see much of this.

spinning Underwriters allocate shares of hot IPOs to prospective customers.

spin-off A public company sells shares in a division to the public.

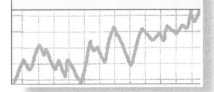

- **Underwriters and Experts:** These two sections list the underwriters, lawyers, and accountants involved in preparing the offering. The name of the lead underwriter is important. The names of lawyers and accountants is not of much value.
- **Risks:** The company describes all conceivable risks, whether due to failure of the company to develop competitive products or due to external factors such as interest rate increases, economic depressions, floods, or plagues. The idea is to name everything, so you can't sue them, no matter what. A lot here is boilerplate, but you should read it just in case they mention something important.

The purpose of analyzing the information found in the prospectus, and at Hoover's, is to determine if the company is in a business that makes sense, and that the company has the personnel to make it happen. Many companies are being rushed to market that don't stand a chance of success. Most of them are in technical fields that most of us don't understand enough to judge their merits. If that's the case, supplement the research outline here by looking for commentary on the company on sites like Red Herring or Upside.

It you feel uncomfortable with your knowledge level, consider waiting until the expiration of the quiet period before making your final decision. Then you might find analysts' reports that will give you further insights into the company's operations and chances for success.

Buying IPOs

THE OLD-FASHIONED WAY—KNOW SOMEBODY

Buying shares of a hot IPO at the issue price is not easy for anyone, institutions or small investors.

Your best bet is to be an active trader, with a big balance, in an account with an underwriter of the IPO. If you fit that description, then it becomes a matter of how many shares your broker has to allocate, and your relationship with your broker. Long-established active brokers get bigger allocations than new brokers, but probably have more clients wanting shares.

THE WEB WAY

Web brokers are starting to get IPO allocations. This trend will continue, and there will undoubtedly be more brokers involved by the time you read this. Offerings are usually limited to U.S. residents.

E*Trade (*www.etrade.com* > IPOs)

E*Trade provides customers with a shot at buying IPOs at the offering price. E*Trade doesn't get allocations of all IPOs, and doesn't get sufficient allocations of those it is involved in, to satisfy the requests of its customers. Here's how the system works.

Start at the IPO Center. The Current Offerings section lists IPOs open for conditional offers. Review the current offerings and complete an eligibility profile for offerings of interest. You must complete a separate eligibility profile for each offering. The profile inquires about your income, net worth, total investment portfolio, investment experience, knowledge, and objectives.

Your eligibility profile is scored by a computer program and you receive an immediate response. The eligibility requirements are E*Trade secrets. However, you can assume that E*Trade would not want to sell an IPO to low-income, inexperienced investors with less than "aggressive growth" financial objectives. You *cannot* submit another profile for the same IPO from the same account if your profile is rejected. However, you can submit a new profile from another account.

You can submit a conditional offer after your eligibility profile is approved, and you acknowledge having been provided with a preliminary prospectus. You specify the maximum number of shares you want to purchase, and the maximum price you will pay in the conditional offer. You must have sufficient funds in your account to cover the purchase. You cannot purchase IPO shares from E*Trade on margin.

You can cancel or change your conditional offer until you are notified that you have received an allocation. E*Trade keeps you up to date on the status of the IPO via e-mail and on the IPO Bulletin section of the "IPO Center" page. The IPO pricing is usually finalized the night before the issue begins trading. Conditional offers must be reconfirmed if the final offering price falls outside the expected price

IPO Terms

stabilization Members of the underwriting syndicate buy shares on the open market after the issue in an attempt to keep the share price from falling below the issue price.

stuffed Institutions get stuffed when they unexpectedly get all of the shares of an IPO they requested.

syndicate The group of underwriters formed to market an IPO.

tombstone Advertisements by the selling syndicate that appear after the issue of an IPO notifying the public of their involvement.

tranche A "multi-tranche" distribution is an IPO marketed in more than one country.

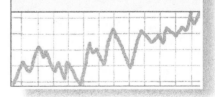

range. You have two hours after the final pricing to change or cancel your offer. You receive notice of your allocation after that period.

Shares are allocated using a lottery system; however, Power E*Trade Platinum customers have a priority allocation. An account with a history of selling previous IPOs within 30 days (flipping) will be penalized in the allocation process.

Wit Capital (*www.witcapital.com*)

Wit Capital's IPO procedures are simpler than E*Trade's and there is no eligibility profile required. You can sign up to receive IPO Alerts via e-mail, or you can monitor the list of current offerings on the site. Both the e-mailed IPO Alert and the Current Offerings page have links to a special page they call "cul de sac" listing information about the offering.

You can submit a conditional offer after acknowledging you've received the preliminary prospectus. You can specify a maximum price you're willing to pay (limit), or accept any price within the offering range. Unlike E*Trade, Wit Capital doesn't require the funds to be in your account, and allows margin purchases. Their only requirement is that you have assets worth $2,000 in your account.

You can modify or cancel your conditional offer through your Open Orders page in the Manage My Account section. Modifying an order doesn't affect your first-come first-served priority. Wit Capital sends you a confirmation request via e-mail when the IPO price has been finalized. You must type "confirm" in the subject field and reply to the request if you're still interested in the offering.

Wit Capital allocates shares on a first-come, first-served basis. Accounts that have received allocations of previous offerings and sold within 60 days are deemed flippers and are not eligible for an allocation. Wit sends you an e-mail notification advising you that you did (or did not) receive an allocation, and the number of shares if you did. Unlike normal stock purchases where you have to settle within three days, Wit gives you six to eight days to pay for the shares.

OpenIPO (*www.openipo.com*)

OpenIPO is a new kind of investment banker. It's run by W. R. Hambrecht and Co. Bill Hambrecht was a founder of Hambrecht & Quist, a leading investment banker. OpenIPO is pioneering a new approach to investment banking and IPO share distribution. There is no road show, and no allocation of shares to institutions, large investors, VIPs, or anyone else. Everyone—mutual funds and individual investors alike—bids at the same auction. The system is called a Dutch Auction.

In a Dutch Auction, your bid specifies how much you're willing to pay for how many shares. For instance, you may bid $15 per share for 500 shares. For this example, say the issuing company wants to sell 5 million shares. A computer keeps track of the bids and determines the highest price at which all of the shares will be sold. If participants bid for 5 million shares at prices of $16 and higher, the price would be set at $16 and you wouldn't get any shares. If the price came out at $13, you would get 500 shares at $13 per share. All buyers pay the same price, and you never pay more than your bid.

You can open an account at Hambrecht, or you can purchase through a participating broker.

Bidding starts within two business days of the filing of the preliminary prospectus, and goes until the registration is declared effective (approved) by the SEC, typically a period of 6 to 10 weeks. Your bid can be above, below, or within the range estimated in the preliminary filing. You can make multiple bids at different prices. Say 200 shares at $15, 100 shares at $16, etc.

All bids are secret; no one can see yours, and you can't see any others. You can cancel or change your bids at any time prior to the notice of effectiveness from the SEC.

Bids may also be cancelled within one hour of the notice, but new bids or modifications cannot be made during that hour. You must have sufficient funds in your account, and you cannot buy on margin.

OpenIPO sends you a funding reminder by e-mail about two weeks prior to the anticipated date of the offering. They send you a reconfirmation by e-mail about two days before the anticipated approval by the SEC. You have 48 hours to mark a box in that e-mail and reply to stay in the auction.

OpenIPO sends you yet another e-mail when the offering has been declared effective by the SEC. Finally, you receive an Auction Results e-mail notifying you of the clearing price. You get all the

IPO Terms

underwriter An investment banking firm that enables the IPO by producing and filing the prospectus, creating interest in the stock, and then buying the shares from the issuing company and reselling them to investors.

unseasoned Stocks that have not traded for a sufficient length of time to establish a track record.

venture capitalist Typically, a private firm investing in start-up companies in exchange for an ownership interest.

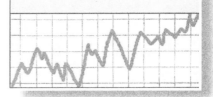

shares you offered to buy if your bid was above the clearing price, and none if it was below. If you bid was at the clearing price, you get an allocation depending upon how many other shares were bid at that price.

OpenIPO has no restrictions on holding time or flipping. You can sell your shares the same day without being excluded from future auctions. So far IPOs offered via the Dutch Auction process have been few and far between. It's not clear if OpenIPO will continue to bring IPOs to market via this path.

E Investment Bank (*www.einvestmentbank.com* > Offering Center)

E Investment Bank gives you a chance to buy IPOs underwritten by Wedbush Morgan Securities. The site allows you to open a temporary account online enabling you to immediately place indications of interest. That's important because they allocate shares on a first-come, first-served basis.

Enter an Indication of Interest indicating the number of shares you want to buy. You can specify a maximum price (limit) or elect to pay the final offering price without limit. You can modify or cancel the order until the issue is priced.

E Investment Bank doesn't send you any reconfirmation requests or notifications. You have to look in your E OrderBook to see your allocation, if any. E Investment encourages you to hold your IPO shares for at least 60 days and threatens to exclude you from future offerings if you don't.

Direct Stock Market (*www.dsm.com*)

Companies can issue IPOs without hiring an underwriter. Why would they want to do that? Probably their business, or business plan, hasn't developed enough to attract investment bankers. Direct Stock Market features direct offerings, but doesn't sell stock; they merely post a profile of each company and a link to their site. You buy the shares directly from the issuing company.

Many of the securities listed here can only be sold in a few states, and you would probably have difficulty finding buyers if you decide to sell.

CHAPTER TWENTY

Investing Supersites

The goal of investing supersites is to provide everything investors could possibly desire, so you'll never have to leave the site. Here's a rundown on where the major investing portals are:

CBS MarketWatch (cbs.marketwatch.com)

CBS MarketWatch is excellent for news and commentary. CBS financial reporters cover breaking news as it happens and the selection of commentary from highly regarded market gurus is superb.

The only downside is the layout. The site is the hardest to navigate of any I've seen. Major features can be almost impossible to locate, and the links to them elusive. To make matters worse, once you find a feature, there are no navigation clues at the top of the page to show you how you got there.

The main page displays major headlines and the major market indexes. Click on the Personal Finance link at the top for in-depth features on a variety of investment topics, all written by CBS MarketWatch reporters. Click on the Mutual Funds link for in-depth stories on funds—again, this is all original material by their own reporters.

The best way to find the balance of CBS MarketWatch's plentiful features is to select "Regular Features" just below the headlines on the main page. If you know what you want, select features of interest directly from this page, otherwise, click on "Feature Descriptions" for a single sentence description of each feature.

There is plenty of good information here, more than most of us have time to read. Here are my favorites.

NEWS FEATURES

- "ADR Report" is a brief rundown on markets around the world.
- "Earnings Surprises," a column by Barbara Costanza, isn't your usual cryptic list of positive and negative surprises. It's a detailed summary of what happened, and how the stock price reacted.

- "Internet Daily" keeps you updated on events in this fast-moving sector.
- "IPO First Words" interviews executives of recent IPOs. They're not allowed to discuss their company's prospects during the "quiet period" following the IPO, typically 25 days, and this column tries to catch them soon after the quiet period expiration. Several additional IPO related features are also listed here.
- "Ratings Changes" lists the day's changes in analysts' buy/hold/sell recommendations, including comments, and changes in price targets.
- "Ratings Game" is an in-depth look at one or two recent analysts' ratings changes, often including an interview with the analyst.
- "Silicon Stocks" and "Software Report" reviews each day's happenings in the technology sector.

COMMENTARY

CBS MarketWatch features columns authored by a variety of well-known and respected market mavens. You can access them from the "Commentary" link under News on the main page or via the Regular Features page. See Chapter 5 for a rundown of who's online here.

Yahoo! Finance *(finance.yahoo.com)*

Yahoo! combines much of the information you need to research, analyze, and track your investments on one site. The categories may not be the best of everything, but the combination keeps me on Yahoo! more than any other site.

One of Yahoo!'s strongest features is My Yahoo!, the ability to tailor Yahoo!'s main page to your needs. We'll describe My Yahoo! in the next section, but first I'll describe my favorite features included in the abundance of information accessible from the Yahoo! Finance main page.

Yahoo! doesn't waste your time downloading fancy graphics. The links to market information are grouped under simple headings

Quicken
(www.quicken.com)

Quicken is more of a tool box than a full-service portal. You can look up news, quotes, and charts for any stock. But they don't have general news headlines, nor very much commentary.

Quicken's forte is research. They are one of the few sites carrying Dow Jones news. They're my favorite resource for analysts' forecasts and recommendations. They offer a variety of fundamental analysis tools. They're especially good at comparing two or more competing companies' fundamentals on the same display.

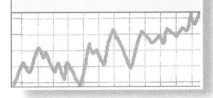

such as U.S. Markets, World Markets, etc. There are many more links under each heading than I have room to describe here.

U.S. Markets

IPOs lists recent IPO pricings, filings, withdrawals, and news all on one page. You can also see lists of best performers and worst performers, and IPO lists by underwriters.

Research (Earnings):

> **Dates** lists earnings reports expected current day and two days before and after. The list includes the forecast earnings and the scheduled conference call date (see Chapter 21 on conference calls).
>
> **Calls** links you to a calendar of conference calls available for listening through Yahoo! Simply click on Listen from Archive to hear the call. Click on Recent Additions near the top of the page to display another calendar listing calls available from other conference call sites such as Street Fusion and Street Events, as well as Yahoo!'s calls.

The link by Industry lists more than 75 industry sectors. If you're interested in companies involved in Fiber Optics, click on that link to see the companies in the sector including the last quarter's actual earnings, the next quarter's forecasted earnings, and the average analyst buy/hold/sell recommendation.

Reference

The calendars link splits Calendar list companies with scheduled stock splits during the current month.

Editorial

Links to articles from Motley Fool, TheStreet.com (including James Cramer's Wrong!), Individual Investor, Worldly Investor, Forbes.com and the Industry Standard. Here are my favorites.

- **TheStreet.com:** Jim Cramer is TheStreet.com's main attraction. Cramer comanages a hedge fund, appears on TV frequently, and writes columns for financial magazines. Cramer's columns are mostly about short-term trading.

They're outspoken and interesting, even if you're not interested in the short-term.

"View From TheStreet.com" is a daily column spotlighting a specific company or industry. The columns are insightful and worthwhile.

"Silicon Valley" columns by Adam Lashinsky and other reporters cover the Net. Anyone interested in investing in Web stocks should read these columns.

- **Individual Investor:** The magazine of the same name has its own free site carrying the same columns available on Yahoo!, still, it's convenient to scan them here. "Stock of the Day" favorably describes one company each day. It's a place to get ideas, but be sure to do your own research. "Mutual Funds" interviews a different fund manager each day. The columns typically say something about how the manager picks stocks and names their current favorites. "Industry Analysis" covers industry segments such as computer gaming, semiconductors, oil and gas, etc., giving you their take on who's hot and who's not.

Financial News

By Industry lists major industry sectors such as Food, Restaurants, Transportation, Airlines, and so forth. Clicking on a selection brings up a slew of news stories for companies in the industry sector. The menu is a little tricky. It doesn't show all of the sectors of each industry. You have to click on the link under the major industry name to see the complete list.

Alta Vista Money

(*money.altavista.com*)

Alta Vista features quotes, charts, news, and portfolios. The site amalgamates features from CBS MarketWatch, Briefing, Raging Bull, and other sites, saving you the trouble of hopping around.

My Yahoo! (*my.yahoo.com*)

The customizable combined news and portfolio feature is the best thing about Yahoo! Once you've set it up, you can see at a glance how your stocks are doing and view the news headlines for your portfolio.

Many of Yahoo!'s features can be easily tailored to your needs. For instance, when you ask for a quote, you can choose to see the

usual: last trade, high, low, volume, and so forth, but you also see a thumbnail-size price chart along with the quote. You can click on the thumbnail to see a larger chart, and you can select time spans from one day to as long as the stock has been trading.

Once you're at the quote display, you can get news and a lot more. For instance:

- **News:** You can see headlines going back about three months from the press release distribution services, Reuters, and Associated Press, plus analysis from CBS MarketWatch, Motley Fool, and others. You won't find news from Dow Jones or Bloomberg on Yahoo!, but this is a good start.
- **Research:** A compilation of analysts' buy/hold/sell recommendations and earnings forecasts going back 90 days. Yahoo! also shows you the earnings surprise history going back five quarters.
- **Insider Trading:** A list of recent trades by corporate officers, board members, and other insiders.
- **SEC:** Displays the management discussion sections of recent quarterly and annual reports filed with the SEC.
- **Messages:** These are the wild and unruly stock forums peculiar to Yahoo! You may learn something about the company here, but try Motley Fool, Silicon Investor, or Raging Bull first.
- **Financials:** Contains recent income statements, balance sheets, and cash flow statements taken from quarterly and annual reports filed with the SEC.
- **Profile:** A compilation of useful data about a specific company. A good place to see an understandable description of the company's business.

Setting Up My Yahoo!

My Yahoo! displays the stocks in your portfolio in a column on the left side of the page. It displays current prices and today's price change—more details than that if you desire. Stocks up for the day are shown in green, stocks down in red. Therefore, you can see how you're doing at a glance just from the colors on your screen.

Yahoo! displays news headlines for each stock in your portfolio on the right. You can set it up to see just today's headlines, or show headlines as far back as one month. You can set it to list one to 10 headlines for each company.

CREATING YOUR PORTFOLIO

Start at Yahoo!'s finance page (*finance.yahoo.com*). Click Register/Sign In to set up a login name and password. Be sure to enter your correct e-mail address when you register in case you forget your password. Most sites send your password to your e-mail address if you ask them.

Click "Continue to Yahoo! Finance" after you've registered and select "Portfolios – Create." Pick a name for your portfolio and enter a few ticker symbols separated by spaces not commas. Don't worry about entering all the symbols now, it will be easy to make changes later. You can look up ticker symbols by clicking the "Look Up" link on the right. If you do, use your browser's Back button to return to the "Edit Your Portfolio" page. Scroll down to basic features after you've entered the ticker symbols.

It's important to click "Finished" when you're done instead of using the browser Back button. Click Finished on the "Edit Portfolios" page (top right).

Now you'll see the beginnings of your personalized view, but it probably won't be all that you want. The left side contains a default Quotes portfolio, your portfolio, and below that, some features that you may or may not want. Yahoo! displays news stories on the right, none related to your portfolio.

Click the "Edit" button in the Portfolios section, and then select "Customize Display Options." It didn't used to be much of a problem to convert prices expressed in fractions such as 1/2 or 1/4 to understandable numbers. But now quotes often look like this: 231/256, so you'll probably want to display the decimals. Select "Decimals (dollars & cents)" and click Finished at the top to return to the Edit Portfolios page. Delete the Quotes portfolio, then select "Edit" for your portfolio. Check any indexes you want displayed from the selections below your ticker symbols and click Finished

near the page bottom. Select Finished on the Edit Portfolios page to return to your customized view.

Use the Edit button in the Portfolios section anytime you want to add or delete entries in your portfolios. If you don't see your changes when you return to your custom view, it's because you used the Back button on your browser instead of clicking "Finished" somewhere along the way.

CUSTOM VIEW OF NEWS

Now select headlines you want displayed in your custom view.

Select "Content" in the Personalize section near the top left to display a list of everything Yahoo! has to offer for this page. Restraint is called for, or you'll end up with more stuff than you'll ever look at.

Check the categories you want and uncheck the others. You can change your selections at any time. The L or R after the category indicates whether the item will be displayed on the left or right hand side of your custom page. Here's my take on the selections.

- **My Yahoo! Essentials:** Stock Portfolios must be checked to display your portfolio. Leave everything else unchecked, otherwise your page will be too cluttered.
- **Business & Finance:** Company News must be selected to see headlines for the stocks in your portfolio. Upgrades/Downgrades lists stocks with changes in analysts' buy/hold/sell recommendations. You don't need to check this to see changes for stocks in your portfolio, they'll be included in the Company News section. Earnings Surprises lists stocks with the biggest percentage surprises, both positive and negative. As with upgrades and downgrades, you don't need to select this category to see surprises for your portfolio, it will be in the headlines. Click Finished when you've selected all the items of interest.
- **Company News:** Select "Edit" in the Company News header section to select the news sources you want to use, and to determine how many headlines you want displayed, and for how long.

DISPLAY OPTIONS FOR COMPANY NEWS

You can choose to have headlines displayed for periods from a day to a month. Your choice depends on how often you plan on looking at your custom display. I look almost every day, and two days works the best for me. You can also choose how many headlines you want to see displayed. You don't lose news because it's not displayed. You can always click on the underlined ticker symbol to see a complete list of everything Yahoo! has on the company.

Yahoo! organizes the headline source selection by category:

Multimedia: Select these sources if you'd rather watch and listen to news than read it.

Financial News: Everything in this category is valuable except for Standard & Poor's.

Financial and Earnings:

- EDGAR Online abstracts information from reports companies file with the SEC, mainly financial statements. Check it only if you're interested in analyzing financial statements.
- NetEarnings lists earnings report and conference call dates. Earnings reports move stock prices. You should know when they're coming, even if you don't look at them.

Editorials: The category contains hard news from Reuters Business News and analysis and commentary from other sources.

- Individual Investor is a full-fledged investment site. They analyze one company each market day. Keep this selected because you should know what they're saying about companies you follow.
- Motley Fool's feeds are mostly market recaps naming winners and losers without much detail.
- Online Investor highlights a different stock every market day. They're good at what they do, so you want to know when they talk about one of your stocks.
- Reuters Business News presents good summaries of earnings reports and other market moving news affecting specific companies.
- TheStreet.com is a subscription site featuring good analysis by a variety of knowledgeable reporters. But most of the time when you click on one of their links, you get a message saying you can't see it because you're not a subscriber. Skip it.

America-iNvest.com

(*www.america-invest.com*)

America-iNvest.com provides a good selection of news, commentary, quotes, and charts. Features include market news reports by their own reporters and a variety of commentary:

- Guru Picks of the Day features three or so analysts' ratings changes, including a fairly lengthy explanation of the analysts' reasoning.
- What Word on the Web quotes a half-dozen or so writers from other Web sites on their views of current market events.
- Insider Trading features an in-depth look at a company with strong insider buying or selling by insider-trading guru Bob Gabele.
- MicroCap Model Portfolio includes 15 or so recommended stocks from their MicroCap 1000 index.
- "The Technical Trader" column by money manager Harry Boxer analyzes individual stocks and the major market indexes from a technical analysis perspective.

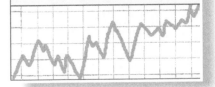

Company Press Releases: There is no way to tell Yahoo! that you only want to see the important press releases. So keep all of these selected and ignore the headlines of no interest.

External (Non-Yahoo) Sites: This category is similar to Editorials.

- CBS MarketWatch is the best source of breaking and interpretive news. Be sure it's selected.
- CNET News.Com is a new player in the news business. They get their news from Bloomberg, so it could be a good source. So far, though, not much has come from CNET. Keep it selected, just in case.
- Red Herring is a source of news and gossip relating to technology companies, with an emphasis on the Internet and related communications products. It's a good source if you're interested in the subject.
- Motley Fool is also listed in the Editorials category.
- TheStreet.com is also included in the Editorials section.
- *Upside Today* is a leading magazine covering technology, especially from an investing perspective. Keep this selected if you're interested in the field.
- ZDNet is another good source of technology news. Select it if you're interested in technology.

FINAL LAYOUT

We have just one more step in customizing your display and you'll be finished. When you're back at your custom page, click Layout in the Personalize section to arrange the order of display on your page. Highlight any item and use the up or down arrows to change its position on your page. You can use the "X" button to delete highlighted items. Be sure to click Finished when you're done making changes.

Be sure to bookmark your custom view. Almost everything on your display can be customized, including the colors. The best place to do it is at *edit.yahoo.com/qcustom.html.*

CHAPTER TWENTY-ONE

Staying Connected: News and Communications

K eeping up with the news online serves two distinct purposes for an investor:

1. Keeping up with the market: the big picture, what's driving the market today. Where's the hot money going? Who's up, who's down, and why? This is how you stay up with trends in the market.
2. What's moving your stocks—stocks you own, or stocks you're following: How do earnings reports, analysts' ratings changes, strategic moves, acquisitions, etc., impact on these stocks?

The best sites for keeping up with the market don't work well for keeping you informed on a specific list of stocks. You'll want to employ different sites for each purpose. Before getting into the specifics, let's review the types of news available on the Web.

Press Releases

Most news headlines you see on Web sites are actually press releases. These are stories written by public relations professionals hired by a company to announce anything the company thinks is worth the effort and expense. You can count on the press release to put the best possible spin on any story, no matter how dismal the reality.

Despite the inevitable spin, press releases are important because they are often the first word out on breaking news. Quarterly reports are especially important because they usually give you enough information to check revenue growth rates, operating margins, etc.

Two major services, Business Wire and PR Newswire, distribute these releases to Web sites and to other media such as newspapers, radio, and TV stations.

Scan the headlines of all press releases, but ignore announcements of new products, partnerships with other companies, and the like. Large companies tend to make announcements like these practically every day.

Pay close attention to announcements of a high-level executive leaving the company, especially the chief financial officer. It's uncanny how the resignation of the CFO so often signals a future stock price drop.

READING AN EARNINGS REPORT PRESS RELEASE

The first news on reported earnings always comes in the form of a press release—before the conference calls, analyst meetings, etc. Analysts scrutinize every word, looking for clues pointing to changing trends in sales, profit margins, or earnings. You can do the same thing. Here's how:

Download the press release distributed by Business Wire or PR Newswire—not the summary distributed by Reuters, AP Financial, or Standard & Poor's. You'll find it easier to print out the release, rather than working from your monitor screen.

ADTRAN, Inc. Reports First Quarter 2000 Results

HUNTSVILLE, Ala.--(BUSINESS WIRE)--April 10, 2000--ADTRAN, Inc. (NASDAQ: ADTN - news) reported results for the first quarter of 2000. Sales for the first quarter increased 28.9% to $99,470,000 from sales of $77,163,000 for the first quarter of 1999. Net income for the quarter increased 84.3% to $16,795,000 compared to $9,111,000 for the first quarter of 1999. Earnings per share, assuming dilution, increased 77.6% to $.42 compared to $.24 for the first quarter of 1999.

Commenting on the results, Mark C. Smith, Chairman and Chief Executive Officer, stated, "This was the best first quarter performance in ADTRAN's history. We are especially pleased with the strong sequential revenue growth in our Systems product lines led by Total Access, ATLAS and the MX 2800. Revenues from Systems product sales in the current quarter increased nearly 27% compared to the fourth quarter of 1999."

Addressing overall operating trends Mr. Smith noted that, "Shipments increased throughout the period and expenses remained at planned levels resulting in favorable operating margins. Continued penetration in the CLEC market and the growing strength of our Systems products cause me to believe that ADTRAN is poised for continued success."

ADTRAN, Inc. designs, develops, and markets a broad range of high-speed digital transmission products utilized by Telcos, corporate end users and OEMs to implement digital data service over existing telephone networks.

This press release contains forward-looking statements that reflect management's best judgment based on factors currently known. However, these statements involve risks and uncertainties including the successful development and market acceptance of new products, the degree of competition in the market for such products, the product and channel mix, component costs, manufacturing efficiencies, and other risks detailed in our annual report on Form 10-K for the year ended December 31, 1999. Such risks and uncertainties could cause actual results to differ materially from those in the forward-looking statements included in this press release.

Condensed Statements of Income
For the periods ending 03/31/00 and 03/31/99

First Quarter   First Quarter
2000   1999

A company always releases its earnings report via a press release.

Access Market Guide (*www.marketguide.com*) and note the following before examining the press release (see Chapter 8 for information on using Market Guide reports):

- The Operating Margin from the Profitability section of the Snapshot page. The number reflects results from the four previous quarters.
- The 1-Year Sales % Growth Rate from the Growth Rates section of the Highlights page.

Now look at the press release. Among other information, most earnings reports include:

- Earnings for the most recent quarter and the percentage increase compared to the same year-ago quarter.

- Sales increase for the most recent quarter compared to the same year-ago quarter.
- A condensed income statement, sometimes called an operations statement or something similar.

The market will react immediately to the reported earnings. It's too late for you to act on this information, so there are other factors you should look at:

Revenue Growth

Compare the most recent quarter's sales (revenue) growth announced in the press release to Market Guide's 1-Year Sales % Growth Rate. Here's how to interpret the comparison:

- Latest quarter sales growth rate exceeds 1-year sales growth: that's good news. Sales growth is accelerating.
- Latest quarter sales growth rate equals 1-year sales growth: that's OK, especially if the growth rates exceed 15 percent for value stocks, and 20 percent for growth stocks.
- Latest quarter sales growth rate is less than 1-year sales growth: that's bad, especially if the latest growth rate is significantly less, e.g., half the 1-year rate.

Margins

Find the income statement (a.k.a. operating statement) for the most recent quarter (use annual or year-to-date figures if the latest quarter isn't included in the release). The very top number (top line) on the income statement is the sales for the period. Locate "operating income." It may also be labeled operating profit, operating earnings, income from operations, etc.

Compute the operating margin by dividing the operating income by the sales and converting to percentage. For example, if the operating income is $50 and sales are $100, divide 50 by 100 (50 ÷ 100) and multiply by 100 to get 50 percent.

Compare the computed operating margin (latest Q Operating Margin) to Market Guide's Operating Margin. Here's how to interpret.

- Latest O.M. higher than Market Guide O.M: that's good. Rising margin trends point to increases in consensus future earnings forecasts.

- Latest O.M. equal to Market Guide O.M: that's OK
- Latest O.M. less than Market Guide O.M: that's bad. Declining margins lead to cuts in earnings forecasts.

Hard News

Hard news is stories written by reporters working for major news services. The emphasis is on reporting the bare facts, sometimes with interpretation. The news services strive to be objective in their reports. These are the major sources.

Reuters Business News and **Reuters Securities** report the news without much interpretation. Sometimes they simply summarize a press release. Sometimes they'll compare a company's reported earnings to analysts' forecasts in their report.

Dow Jones, publisher of the *Wall Street Journal,* doesn't report every event at every company, but when they do a story, they do it better, in more detail, and with more background quotes from analysts and other observers than anyone else. Sometimes Dow Jones will be the only service with a story explaining a recent stock move. Make it a point to check Dow Jones news on companies of interest on a regular basis.

Bloomberg News, like Dow Jones, often reports stories you won't find anywhere else. Unlike Dow Jones, though, Bloomberg stories on individual companies tend to be bare-bones reports with just a terse outline of events. Still, Bloomberg is a source you should check regularly.

Associated Press reports are similar to Reuters Business News stories: they report the hard news without much interpretation.

Standard & Poor's issues terse summaries of earnings reports.

Interpretive News

Interpretive news helps to put the hard news into context. Is it significant, or a nonevent? How does the company's news relate to the competition?

DEFINITION PLEASE

Book Value: Total shareholders' equity from the balance sheet divided by the number of shares outstanding.

Bottom Line: After-tax earnings. Literally, the bottom line on an income statement.

Cash Flow: After-tax income minus preferred dividends and general partner distributions plus depreciation, depletion, and amortization (Market Guide definition). See Operating Cash Flow and Free Cash Flow.

Dividends: Cash or stock paid to shareholders, usually on a quarterly schedule.

CBS MarketWatch is the best source for an interpretive take on breaking news affecting a specific company. CBS MarketWatch has real reporters, and they stay on a story with frequent updates until it's over.

Bloomberg Keeps Up with the Market

(*www.bloomberg.com*)

Bloomberg is an institution in the world of finance, providing news, data, and analytical data to stockbrokers, institutional managers, and analysts around the world. Bloomberg is a 24-hour a day operation; their reports are updated around the clock.

Bloomberg's site is hard to navigate. Their main page is a hodgepodge of headlines, ads for Bloomberg services, and market data. Much of the good information is hidden, and you have to search around to find it.

Current News & Columns

Select News (called Top Financial News on all other menus) from the menu on the left to see current major financial news. These look like the same kind of headlines you see on other sites, but once you click on "more" you'll see the difference. Bloomberg's market news stories are lengthy, detailed, and provide considerable background information.

- *Top World News* includes a handful of stories from the U.S. and abroad, some business-related and some not.
- *Stock Market Update* overviews current market action and highlights the top market-related stories.
- *After-Hours Trading* highlights trading action when the major U.S. markets are closed.
- *Technology* features about a dozen news stories on high-tech companies.
- *Economy and Politics* describes government actions affecting business in the U.S. and around the world.
- *Columns* features a dozen different writers covering stocks, bonds, mutual funds, and markets and finance in general,

in the U.S. and abroad. Some are daily columns, some weekly, and some monthly. Bloomberg lists columnists' names only, not their area of interest. Stock columnists include John Dorfman, Kathryn Harris, and David Pauly. Chet Currier writes about mutual funds. Carolyn Baum covers the U.S. stock market in general. Mark Gilbert and Joe Mysak focus mainly on currencies and bonds. There are a multitude of other columns listed here worth your time including *Taking Stock, Insider Focus, Company Spotlight,* and *Industry Spotlight.*

Other news categories of interest accessed from the menu on the left include:

- *Stocks on the Move:* During regular market hours, and after hours, Bloomberg shows you the stocks making significant moves. Bloomberg displays a stock chart and background on each featured company.
- *Movers by Exchange* lists the volume leaders and highest percent gainers and losers either by exchange or in composite form.
- *Industry Movers* lists the S&P industry groups with the highest percentage gains and losses for the day.
- *Most Active Options* lists put and/or call options with the highest volume, and the highest percentage gainers and losers.
- *Regional Indexes* tracks the performance of stocks of major companies in almost 100 regions in the U.S. Regions can be cities such as San Francisco, areas such as the San Francisco Bay Area, or entire states, such as California.

Where to Keep Up with Your Stocks

Several sites allow you to set up a portfolio of stocks you want to follow, and then collect news headlines for those stocks. Yahoo! does the best job of combining quotes and news in one display.

Sources Not Covered by Yahoo!

Yahoo! does not provide Dow Jones or Bloomberg news feeds. But you can fill in the blanks.

- **Bloomberg News:** You can get Bloomberg stories on their own site (*www.bloomberg.com*), but it's faster and easier to go to CNET Investor (*investor.cnet.com*).
- **Dow Jones:** Dow Jones news stories are carried on Dow Jones.com (*www.dowjones.com*), Smart Money (*www.smartmoney.com*), and Quicken (*www.quicken.com*). Quicken's site is faster and easier to use than the others.

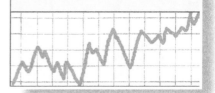

DEFINITION PLEASE

Operating Cash Flow: Surplus cash generated from company's basic operations without regard to income tax entries such as depreciation and amortization. Changes in levels of inventories, accounts receivable, and accounts payable also affect cash flow. Also see Free Cash Flow.

Operating Income: Sales minus all expenses except income taxes and other items not related to the basic business.

Operating Margin: Operating income divided by sales.

YAHOO! (*finance.yahoo.com*)

I set up Yahoo! as my home page. That means Yahoo! shows up automatically when I start my browser. I do that because I can set up Yahoo! to display prices and news headlines for all the stocks I'm following on a single page. Then I can see what's going on with all of my stocks at a glance. See Chapter 20 for instructions on setting up a personalized stock page on Yahoo!

Yahoo! news includes the usual press releases, plus hard news from the Associated Press and Reuters. Yahoo! gets interpretive news feeds from a variety of sources—CBS MarketWatch, Motley Fool, *Individual Investor* magazine, and several others. Yahoo! also gets news feeds from several technology-oriented sites such as ZDNet, Red Herring, and Upside Today. Yahoo! also displays analyst recommendation changes from Briefing.com.

News by E-Mail

INFOBEAT (*www.infobeat.com*)

The problem with news on the Net is there is just too much of it. Well-known companies are mentioned in several stories every day. InfoBeat solves the problem the old-fashioned way. They hire editors to read the news for you. The editors throw out the irrelevant and send you summaries of important stories. You can click on a link included with each summary to read the full story if you need further details.

You won't find the stories on their site—InfoBeat e-mails the news to you. Sign up on the site and then set up portfolios for stocks or mutual funds and select the reports you want to receive. Choices include:

- *Morning Call:* a market update and news highlights, not necessarily about your stocks, sent about 90 minutes before the markets open.
- *Midday Update:* market update and news highlights sent around 1:30 P.M. ET.
- *News Alerts:* major news moving one of your stocks. The alert is delivered throughout the day.

- *Closing Bell:* closing prices and news briefs for your stocks, including changes in analyst recommendations and forecasts.
- *Weekender:* Your stocks' 52-week highs/lows and P/E ratios.

Additional available reports not related to your portfolios include Internet news, summaries of selected Raging Bull discussions, and currencies and commodities reports. You can also sign up to get general news and news on entertainment, sports, and weather.

FINANCIAL TIMES' FT.COM (*www.ft.com*)

The Financial Times site has free e-mail daily newsletters covering banking and finance, energy, Internet and e-commerce, IT industry, media and entertainment, personal finance, and telecommunications, plus "Today's FT in Brief," covering companies and markets or world news and comment. They also have a weekly news summary.

Message Boards

A message board is a location on a site dedicated to discussion of a particular topic, usually a single stock or industry sector. Messages can be posted on the board by anyone who registers with the site. You can read messages in chronological order of posting, and contribute your own comments if you like.

Message boards are populated by people with a variety of agendas. Some are short sellers trying to frighten shareholders into selling. Others are scammers pumping penny stocks so they can dump them later. Some are hyping other Web sites. Then you have the cheerleaders—shareholders who, without any apparent knowledge, are constantly talking up the company and predicting a doubling of the share price by Christmas. They stand ready to personally attack anyone who dares post a comment even remotely questioning their rosy forecasts. Mixed in are legitimate investors hoping to share or gain some knowledge about the company.

Message boards can be helpful, despite the negatives. They serve two useful purposes.

1. Say you're researching a stock and you want to see if you've overlooked any competitors. There are always plenty of short sellers more than eager to name other firms who are "eating this company's lunch." If you don't find such a message, post a question asking about competition.
2. Sometimes a stock makes a sudden move without apparent reason. You can't find any news, and/or changes in analysts' opinions or earnings forecasts. Head for the message boards when that happens. Possibly, someone will mention a news story you didn't see. These posters often include a link directly to the story.

Message boards have no value to you unless you can find messages about your stocks. There are probably hundreds of sites with message boards, but only four attract enough traffic to be of use: Yahoo!, Motley Fool, Raging Bull, and Silicon Investor. Here's how many messages were posted on each site's Microsoft's board by 2:00 P.M. Pacific Time on a typical day in February 2000.

Yahoo!	385
Motley Fool	43
Raging Bull	83
Silicon Investor	43

You can access each of these boards separately when you need information on a company, but there's an easier way.

COMPANY SLEUTH
(*www.companysleuth.com* > Company Reports)

Company Sleuth tracks more than 20 categories of items about most listed stocks including news, Internet domain name registrations, trademarks, changes in analysts' reports, insider trading, SEC filings and more. You can set up a portfolio on the site and they'll send you an e-mail when new information concerning your stocks is listed. Among the other items they track are message board postings.

The advantage of using Company Sleuth is you can check all of the major message boards from one place, whether or not there has been recent activity on the boards. When you access the site, Company Sleuth displays the previous day's activity—e.g., the number of new messages on Motley Fool—for the stocks in your portfolio.

Click on Reports on the top left to change to a display listing all of Company Sleuth's resources in a single menu on the left. You can enter a ticker in the entry box near the top right to see the same display for any stock. Clicking on any link takes you to the selected resource, regardless of whether any recent activity is listed.

Clicking on "Raging Bull Msg," for instance, takes you to the Raging Bull message board for the stock. When you're done, click on "Back to Company Sleuth" at the top and then select another site, e.g., Motley Fool, from the menu on the left.

The advantage of using Company Sleuth is you can see which boards have recent activity on your stock, and you don't have to log in and navigate through each site, Company Sleuth takes you directly to the board. Here's a rundown on each major site:

YAHOO! (*finance.yahoo.com* > Quote > Msgs)

The easiest way to get to a message board is to first get a quote on the stock and then click on "Msgs" under "More Info." One reason Yahoo!'s boards get so much traffic is they're not moderated, meaning no one from Yahoo! monitors the boards and removes blatant advertising, nasty language, insults to other posters, and so forth. The boards are truly a walk on the wild side. You have to wade through a lot of garbage to find worthwhile information. Still, the boards are easy and fast to navigate, so you can quickly scan many postings.

THE MOTLEY FOOL (*www.fool.com* > Messages)

The Motley Fool is the antithesis of Yahoo! in important ways. The Fool's boards are tightly monitored. Offensive posts are removed, and the perpetrator is de-registered. A Fool-registered member can easily alert monitors to an offensive post by clicking on "Problem Post," or conversely, draw other Fool's attention to especially helpful posts by clicking on "Recommend It."

These efforts rid the Fool's message boards of the hucksters and the unruly tone prevalent on Yahoo! Some posters still insult

Rumor Buzz

Rumors could be why your favorite stock just zoomed up or down for no apparent reason. Rumors are always buzzing through the market, causing wild gyrations in stock prices. Sometimes rumors accurately predict future events, but most turn out to be just *rumors,* and nothing ever happens.

You can tune into the rumor buzz at *www.StockSelector.com.* StockSelector.com gives you a good rundown on the rumor along with the date and time they first posted it.

Click "Rumors" on the menu on the left to read the rumors going back about a month or so.

The best way to keep up with rumors is by e-mail. StockSelector.com will send you each day's top rumors. It's free; just sign up by selecting "Subscribe" on their main page.

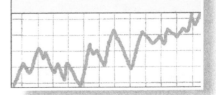

each other, but most posts address company-related issues instead of other posters' background and sexual habits.

The Motley Fool site emphasizes fundamental analysis in its tutorials and model portfolios. Consequently, site visitors in general, and message board posters in particular, have the same fundamental analysis inclination. It shows in the quality of the postings.

The Fool's boards are the best of the major sites in terms of quality of discussion, but they don't get as many posts as Yahoo! That's not a problem for highly visible stocks such as Microsoft or Intel and the like, but it is an issue for lesser-known companies. You'll probably have to rely on Yahoo! or other boards for discussions of less popular stocks.

RAGING BULL (*www.ragingbull.com*)

Raging Bull's messages lack the fundamental analysis bent of Motley Fool. There's quite a bit of serious discussion regarding a company's merits, but they tend to focus on analysts' comments and analysis of the stock charts.

Most of Raging Bull's posters are interested in technology, so you'll find better coverage of small- and mid-cap tech stocks here than on Motley Fool. Raging Bull's messages are mostly civil and nearly all postings are on topic.

SILICON INVESTOR (*www.siliconinvestor.com*)

You can read messages for free, but Silicon Investor requires a paid subscription to post messages. Silicon Investor is much like Raging Bull, with an emphasis on technology.

The postings are similar in quality and tone to Raging Bull's messages. It's worth checking Silicon Investor if you can't find enough messages on Motley Fool or Raging Bull.

CLEARSTATION (*www.clearstation.com*)

ClearStation doesn't get the traffic of the bigger boards, but it's a favorite site of technical analysts—that is, investors using stock charting as part or all of their decision making process. As expected, ClearStation's message board postings mostly discuss a stock's current chart.

The postings are relevant and free of personal attacks or huckstering of any kind. In fact, they're usually succinct and straight to the point, often including a buy or sell recommendation.

Conference Calls

Did you ever wonder why your favorite stock went down after announcing great earnings that beat expectations? Chances are, while you're reading that glowing press release, company executives are busy revealing different news to big shareholders and analysts—news that wasn't included in the press release. Maybe they expect sales to be soft in the next quarter, or development of that hot new product is going slower than expected, or worse, profit margins are coming down.

How does this important information get out to analysts and large shareholders? Conference calls!

Conference calls are typically scheduled shortly after the earnings report is released. While the earnings press release typically includes minimal detail and puts the best possible spin on the results, the conference call tells the real story.

In the past, conference calls were restricted to institutional investors and analysts employed by brokerage firms. Now pressure from government regulators is forcing companies to rethink that policy, and more of them are making the calls accessible to the public.

Until recently, you could only listen to these calls by calling a special telephone number. Now most publicly available calls can be accessed via the Internet. You can listen to the calls live, or listen to archived calls. The calls are usually archived for a month or longer, so you can review older calls.

You need compatible audio player software (and hardware) in your computer to listen to the calls. If you don't have the software, you can download it from most conference call sites. Reporting companies have to pay broadcasting services such as Vcall, StreetFusion, Yahoo! Broadcast, Street Events, and others to make the calls available on the Internet.

DEFINITION PLEASE

Conference Call: A multi-party telephone call hosted by a company, primarily for analysts, and held shortly after making an earnings announcement.

Insiders: Officers, directors, and anyone else owning more than 10 percent of stock outstanding.

Institutional Ownership: Shares owned by pension funds, mutual funds, banks, etc.

Revenues: A company's sales.

WHO LISTS CALLS

BestCalls (*www.bestcalls.com*)

BestCalls specializes in keeping track of planned conference calls. You can enter your portfolio and BestCalls will send you e-mail notices of upcoming calls. You can also check lists of scheduled calls on the site.

Information for each call includes the date and time of the live call and who's invited to listen. If the public is invited, you can listen in by clicking on the "Click to Listen" link. BestCalls also lists the time replays will be available, and a link to listen to them as well.

Yahoo! (*quote.yahoo.com* > Research > Earnings > Calls)

Yahoo! has their own "Yahoo! Broadcast" conference call center where you can listen to live or archived calls. Their Conference Call Calendar only lists calls hosted by Yahoo! Broadcast. Click on "Listen" to hear those calls. Click on "Recent Additions" near the top of the page to display calls broadcast by Street Fusion and Street Events, as well as Yahoo! Broadcast. Yahoo! has no facility for searching for scheduled conference calls by company name or ticker symbol. That's a big negative in my book.

WATCH THE NEWS!

Neither BestCalls nor Yahoo! list all scheduled calls available to the public. Finding out about conference call availability is sort of hit or miss. If you're interested in a specific company, your best bet is to directly contact investor relations at the company.

Your next best bet is to watch the news headlines on companies of interest. The companies themselves may not publicize a conference call, but the Web sites carrying the calls issue press releases that you will pick up when you scan the headlines.

LISTENING IN

I have mixed feelings about conference calls. They take around 45 minutes. They always start with a prepared statement from the CEO followed by a prepared statement by the CFO. Both of these are usually delivered in a monotonous, droning style and are full of jargon particular to their business. The only times I have ever fallen asleep at my desk have been when I was listening to these calls.

Some calls broadcast by Street Fusion allow you to listen to selected segments such as the earnings statements, or the question and answer period. On some calls, Street Fusion supplies a written transcript. That's the best solution. You can scan a transcript in far less time than it takes to listen to the call. It costs the reporting companies more to broadcast the calls when Street Fusion breaks them into segments or provides a transcript, so the practice isn't widespread.

Like many other activities, the more you do it, the better you'll get at interpreting conference calls. There's a certain language and protocol that analysts follow when questioning company executives. Many experienced call listeners feel they get the most valuable information from the question and answer period that comes near the end of the call. You can gain experience in what you want to listen for by listening to archived calls.

Chat Rooms: Not Really Worth It

Chat rooms are different from bulletin boards. With bulletin boards, someone posts a message, and waits until another person sees their message and replies. That could take hours, if not days.

Chat rooms on the other hand are real-time. Once you enter a chat room, you type a message into a box labeled "Chat" near the bottom of the screen and click the "Send" key. Your message is displayed to everyone in the room. Yahoo! designates rooms for different interest areas such as sports, music, or computers, and there are several for stocks (*finance.yahoo.com* > Community > Stock Chat).

Stock chat room conversations may revolve around stocks, but they often veer off into other subjects. They're not a productive use of your time and I doubt that serious investors spend time there.

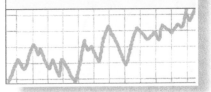

Appendices

Analyze a Stock in 30 Minutes

FINDING INVESTMENT CANDIDATES

The first step in the investment process is finding stocks to analyze.

You probably already get investment tips from friends, family, and people you meet in business or at the supermarket. Great! More is better. Take tips from them all because you'll be able to quickly separate the investments worth researching from the frauds, scams, and just plain bad ideas.

But don't rely solely on tips from amateurs for your ideas. You can use the Web to find worthwhile tips and ideas from analysts, fund managers, and other experts who are "in the trenches" making daily decisions that—if they are wrong—will be hung out there for the whole world to see. You can emulate the investing styles of famous gurus like Peter Lynch and Warren Buffett to choose investment candidates. Chapters 4 and 5 tell you where to look.

YOU CAN MAKE YOUR OWN TIPS

By the time you've finished this book, you probably have your own ideas about what makes a good investment candidate. If so, you can employ powerful, readily available, screening tools to search the entire market in seconds for quality stocks meeting your particular investment style. Chapter 6 tells you how.

Seasoned investors know that all investment ideas, no matter the source, Warren Buffett or your gardener, are all tips that must be systematically evaluated. Here's a plan to do that evaluation, and do it fast with the skills you've learned from this books.

We've given you a handy Checklist for Finding Winning Stocks beginning on page 309. Make copies of the checklist and fill it out as you go through the evaluation process. Use a separate checklist for each stock you're ana-

lyzing. You'll be amazed how just filling out the checklist will make you a more disciplined and better investor.

FIRST STEP: ELIMINATE

Nobody wants to spend all of their free time in front of a computer screen analyzing stocks. So, your goal when evaluating investment candidates is to eliminate as many as you can, as soon as possible. There's no point in wasting time researching stocks that you're not going to end up buying, or at least seriously considering.

Chapter 8 shows you how to use information available on Market Guide's (*www.marketguide.com*) site to dispose of stupid investment ideas in minutes.

Start with the Snapshot

Fill in the information on the top line of the checklist.

Write in the market capitalization and circle one of the choices: small-cap, mid-cap, or large-cap. Now answer this question: Is this the size company I want to invest in? Disqualify this stock if the answer is no.

Fill in the price/earnings and price/sales ratios. Pay most attention to price/sales. Is this stock within the valuation range you're looking for? If not, eliminate this stock now.

Look at the stock price chart on the Market Guide Snapshot. Is the stock price trending up, down, or in consolidation? If the chart shows a downtrend, either eliminate the stock, or put it aside and look at it in another month or so.

Record the average daily volume and eliminate the stock if the volume is less than 0.04 million (40,000).

Note the cash flow per share and eliminate the stock if the cash flow is a negative number. Record the current ratio and eliminate the stock if less than 1.5.

Record the Total Debt/Equity but don't eliminate the stock at this point based on debt/equity.

Record the Gross Margin and Operating Margin. You'll use these to compare this company with any competitors you may discover when you look at Hoover's or the SEC reports.

Now use the menu on the left to display the Market Guide Performance page for the company, and scroll to Institutional Ownership.

Note the institutional ownership and the Three Months' Net Purchases. Eliminate the stock if less than 40 percent institutional ownership, or if the net purchases are negative indicating institutions are selling the stock.

Note the Insider Trading activity. Do the net transactions exceed one million shares? If so, you'll want to look at the details of who is doing the trading later on.

Now switch to the Market Guide Highlights page.

Record the average annual percentage sales and earnings growth for one, three, and five-year periods. Eliminate the stock if the one-year growth rate doesn't equal or exceed the three-year growth, and/or the three-year growth rate is less than 15 percent.

The earnings growth rate should more or less track the revenue growth rates. Eliminate companies with erratic earnings growth rates.

Note the names of any brokerage firms with significant holdings of the company's shares in the "Equity" paragraph below the earnings per share by quarter display. This information will help you put any buy/hold/sell recommendations you see from these broker's analysts into perspective.

You can use these simple checks to dispose of stupid investment ideas in minutes. If you're good at it, at most, five out of 20 candidates will survive this quick examination. If you're really disciplined, only one or two will survive. You won't waste much time on losers; the entire process for 20 companies should take you no longer than 30 minutes.

Check the News

I really feel stupid when, after spending an hour researching a company, I discover the CEO was fired three weeks ago for cooking the books, or because the board of directors just realized nobody wants to buy that fantastic new buggy whip they spent millions developing. Five or 10 minutes spent checking the news now could save you from wasting time researching a stock that you won't buy anyway. Chapter 21 tells you where to look.

WHAT DO THEY DO?

Take the survivors to Hoover's (*www.hoovers.com*) to learn what the company does for a living, and just as important, who else is doing the same thing.

The latter is critical. By this time, you've only invested maybe 15 minutes of your time on this company. It's not too late to change horses. What would make you do that? You've found a stronger competitor in the same field. You'll be a happier camper if you always pick the best company in any industry sector.

In this step you'll learn what the company does, discover the competition, and add any equal or stronger competitors to your candidate list. If you're lucky, you can accomplish this in five minutes, if not it could take 15.

Display Hoover's Company Capsule and read the description of the company's business.

Does the business make sense to you? Is the company in a business where at least 15 percent annual sales growth is plausible? If not, eliminate the company.

Record the names of the three top competitors listed below the description and look up their Company Capsules by clicking on the links.

Are they really competitors? Sometimes Hoover's lists companies that are only marginally in the same business. Record the names of any substantial competitors and research them on Market Guide. Normally, you want to pick the best company in an industry sector. The best company is typically the one with the highest profit margins and the highest sales.

ANALYSTS' CONSENSUS RECOMMENDATIONS AND FORECASTS

Momentum-oriented investors don't spend much time evaluating a company's balance sheets or sales growth. They focus on earnings growth, and more specifically, future earnings growth prospects. They know the market fixates on earnings: stocks soar when earnings expectations rise and nosedive when expectations go the wrong way. You may not be a momentum investor, but you're not here to lose money either. Ergo, you'd better check the same things they do before you go further. This will take less than five minutes for each stock.

Chapter 10 describes how to interpret Quicken's analysts' recommendations and forecasts.

Note the analysts' current Consensus Buy/Hold/Sell recommendation on the stock. The acceptable rating range depends on your investing style (value, growth, or momentum) and is shown on the checklist. Confirm that the current rating fits your requirements. Eliminate the stock if the consensus recommendation doesn't meet your criterion.

Record the Consensus EPS Growth estimates for the current and upcoming quarter and year. As with the buy/hold/sell recommendation, the acceptable varies with your investment style. Eliminate the stock if the forecast earnings growth doesn't meet your criterion.

Record the number of analysts making current buy/hold/sell recommendations and eliminate stocks with fewer than five analysts.

Record the trend of earnings forecasts for the current fiscal year. An increasing trend means the forecast earnings are higher now than they were 30 days ago, and 30 days ago is higher than 60 days ago, etc. Ignore $0.01 changes. All investors should disqualify companies with negative trends, and momentum investors require positive trends.

Look at the Quarterly Earnings to evaluate the earnings surprise history. All investors should eliminate companies with a history of negative surprises, and momentum investors should insist on a history of positive surprises.

READ ANALYSTS' RESEARCH REPORTS

Analysts produce copious research reports with good background information on a company and its industry. You may or may not agree with their buy/hold/sell recommendations, but it pays to read their reports. This will take around 10 minutes, 30 if you get lucky and find several worthwhile reports. Chapter 10 tells you where to find these reports.

CHECK INSIDER TRADING

It should make you nervous if key executives are dumping shares of a stock you're considering buying. Look at what those in the know are doing, especially if Market Guide indicated significant insider trading activity. Chapter 11 tells you where to get the information. Allow about 5 minutes for this check.

GET A SECOND OPINION

Everything has checked out so far. You think you've discovered a winner. Why not get another opinion, just in case you overlooked something? It's easy and will take about 15 minutes. Chapter 14 tells you how.

CLUES TO FUTURE DISASTER

You have a serious contender if you've reached this stage. Now is the time to make sure you're not buying a future disaster.

Disaster is when you turn on the TV and hear them talking about your beloved stock losing 30, 40, or 50 percent of its value, because earnings came in far below expectations or the company warned of an upcoming slowdown in growth. Stocks rarely recover quickly—if ever—from this sort of drubbing. Shareholders are usually in for months, if not years, of underperformance. Chapter 13 explains how to detect stocks heading for disaster.

Start with Morningstar's Grades (*www.morningstar.com*).

The acceptable grades for value and growth investors are shown on the checklist. Momentum investors don't care about these fundamental criteria.

Next check Equity Insights (*www.equityinsights.com*).

First look at the trend in Economic Margins for the company. Focus mainly on the two right-most bars representing the current and next fiscal years. The trend should be flat or up. Equity Insights is a tough grader, so give a company a little slack here. Avoid companies with noticeable downtrends in economic margins from the current to next fiscal years.

Next look at the sales growth trend for the latest quarter compared to the sales growth for the same year-ago quarter. Eliminate companies with a substantial drop in sales growth rates as indicated on the checklist.

Record the accounts receivable (DSO) for the latest quarter and the same year-ago quarter. Eliminate companies with increasing DSOs as indicated on the checklist. Use Inventory turns instead of accounts receivable when analyzing retail stores.

FINAL CHECKS

Take a quick look at the stock chart (Chapter 12) and check for last-minute news headlines before you buy. These two steps should take about one minute each.

That's it. You're done!

FINDING WINNING STOCKS USING MARKET GUIDE SNAPSHOT

GENERAL

Company: _____

Ticker Symbol: _____ Date: _____ Recent Price: _____

COMPANY SIZE

Market Cap (check one):

❏ Small-cap (below $2B) ❏ Mid-cap ($2B to $8B) ❏ Large-cap (over $8B)

VALUATION

Price/Earnings (P/E): _____

Price/Sales (P/S): _____ (below 2 = value, 2 to 10 = growth, 10+ = momentum)

TIMING AND LIQUIDITY

Price Chart (check one):

❏ Uptrend   ❏ Downtrend   ❏ No Trend (consolidation) _____

Average Daily Volume: (0.04 mil minimum) _____

FINANCIAL

Cash Flow per Share _____ (avoid if negative)

Current Ratio: _____ (1.5 minimum)

Total Debt/Equity: _____ (0 is best, below 0.50 preferred; depends on industry)

PROFITABILITY

Gross Margin: _____%

Operating Margin: _____% (margins are needed for competitive analysis)

FINDING WINNING STOCKS

PERFORMANCE

Institutional Ownership: _____ % (avoid below 40%)

Institutional 3 Mo. Net Purchases: _____ (avoid if negative)

Insider Trading Net Shares Purchased: _____

(Note only net transactions exceeding one million shares)

HIGHLIGHTS

Sales %

1-yr _____   3-yr _____   5-yr _____

(15% min for growth, s/b greater than 3-yr)   (15% min, s/b equal or greater than 5-yr)

EPS %

1-yr _____   3-yr _____   5-yr _____

(should track or exceed sales growth)

INSTITUTIONAL OWNERSHIP:

_____

_____

_____

BROKERAGE FIRMS OWNING STOCK:

_____

_____

_____

FINDING WINNING STOCKS: THE COMPETITION

Hoover's:

_____

_____

_____

Other Sources:

_____

_____

_____

FINDING WINNING STOCKS
WITH ANALYSTS' RATINGS AND FORECASTS

Consensus Buy/Hold/Sell: _____

(Value investors 2.5 to 5.0; growth investors 1.0 to 2.0; momentum investors 1.0 to 1.5)

Consensus EPS Growth:

This Q: _____%   Next Q: _____%   TFY: _____%   NFY: _____%

(Value investors 20% max; growth investors 20% minimum; momentum investors 30% minimum)

Number of Analysts: _____ (5 minimum)

FINDING WINNING STOCKS: ADVANCED MOMENTUM FACTORS

Consensus EPS Trend _____

(All investors avoid negative trend; momentum investors buy on positive trend only.)

Surprise History: _____

(All investors avoid negative histories; momentum investors buy on a history of positive surprises only.)

FINDING WINNING STOCKS WITH MORNINGSTAR GRADES

Growth: _____ (Value investors ignore; growth investors A- or better)

Profitability: _____ (Value investors and growth investors A- or better)

Financial Health: _____ (Value investors and growth investors A- or better)

Valuation: _____ (Value investors A or A+; growth investors ignore)

FINDING WINNING STOCKS THROUGH CLUES TO FUTURE DISASTER

Economic Margin Trend: ❑ Up   ❑ Down   ❑ Flat

(All stocks: Flat or up OK; avoid down)

Sales Trend: Year-ago _____ %   Latest _____ %

(Drop of 50%, e.g., from 70% to 35%, is a clue to future disaster)

Operating Margin: Year-ago _____ %   Latest _____%

(Drop of 20%, e.g., from 14% to 11%, is a clue to future disaster)

Accounts Receivable (DSO): Year-ago _____   Latest _____

(Manufacturing companies only: downtrends are good, uptrends bad. Increase of 25%, e.g., from 20 days to 25 days, is a clue to future disaster.)

Inventories (Turns): Year-ago _____   Latest _____

(Retail stores only: uptrends are good, downtrends bad. Decrease of 25%, e.g., from 10 turns to 8 turns, is a clue to future disaster.)

Analyzing Mutual Funds in 30 Minutes

FINDING FUND CANDIDATES

Just like stocks, you will get the best results if you analyze several mutual funds at the same sitting. Otherwise, you'll usually find a reason to fall in love with each fund if you research them one at a time. Examining 10 to 20 funds together forces you to focus on eliminating the weakest candidates.

You'll have no problem coming up with enough fund investment candidates using the screening programs described in Chapter 18.

ANALYZING THE FUND CANDIDATES

Chapter 17 describes a quick and effective method for analyzing mutual fund investment candidates. Your goal should be to eliminate the weakest candidates as you proceed through the analysis. It should take you about five minutes to do the Quick Look analysis, and most of your candidates should be eliminated there. Only your strongest funds should make it to the Detailed Evaluation.

We've included a Checklist for Finding Winning Mutual Funds on page 314 to help you with your evaluation. Make copies of the checklist. Use a separate copy for each fund that makes it past the Star Rating and Load requirements. Refer to Chapter 17 for a detailed explanation of each step. All but the last step of the analysis is done using Morningstar (*www.morningstar.com*). Morningstar displays the fund Snapshot page after you enter the ticker symbol.

Disqualify all funds with fewer than four Morningstar Stars, except for the rare special conditions outlined in Chapter 17.

Eliminate load funds unless there are no equivalent no-load funds.

Fill out the top three lines on a checklist for funds passing the above requirements.

Use the menu on the left to switch to the Ratings and Risk page.

Record the Morningstar Return Rating. Use the five-year rating if available. Growth investors should eliminate funds with return ratings less than 1.5. Aggressive growth investors should require a minimum 2.0 return rating.

Note the Morningstar three-year Risk Rating. Risk averse investors should disqualify funds with risk ratings above 0.75. Growth investors should stay below 0.90. Aggressive growth investors should look more at the comparison of the return and risk ratings, rather than the risk rating by itself.

Calculate the return/risk comparison ratio by dividing the return rating by the risk rating. All investors, whether risk averse, growth, or aggressive growth in orientation, should disqualify funds with comparison ratios less than 2.0.

You've completed the Quick Look. It should take less than five minutes per fund, once you get the hang of it. Hopefully, you eliminated a significant chunk of your original candidates in this step. Stack the survivor's checklists with the highest return/risk comparison ratios on top. These are your best candidates.

DETAILED EVALUATION

Switch to Morningstar's Total Returns page and scroll to the Trailing Returns section.

Record the three- and five-year returns compared to the S&P 500 index (middle column). Growth investors should eliminate funds underperforming the index. Value style mutual funds have underperformed the overall market in recent years, so value investors can accept funds underperforming the index as shown on the checklist.

Return to the Ratings and Risk page.

Note the standard deviation listed under Volatility Measurements. Acceptable values depend on your risk tolerance. Standard deviation is a measure of volatility, and the recent overall market volatility may make it difficult to find low volatility funds.

Switch to the Portfolio page.

Note the Price/Earnings ratio in the Investment Valuation section. Use the checklist guidelines. At this writing in April 2000, it's difficult to find funds meeting the low-risk guidelines.

Note the Turnover Percent in the Holding Details section. Tax sensitive investors should eliminate funds with turnover ratios exceeding 50 percent.

Look closely at the fund's Top 10 Holdings using the considerations outlined in Chapter 17. Portfolio analysis doesn't lend itself to a simple entry on the checklist, but don't skip it. This is the most important step in your evaluation.

Switch to Nuts and Bolts and scroll to Fees and Expenses.

Record the Total Expense Ratio. Disqualify funds with expense ratios exceeding 1.95%.

Check the fund manager's start date in the management section. Morningstar's return and risk ratings may be irrelevant if the fund manager has held his/her job less than three years.

You have just one more step remaining. For that, you'll need to go to the Fund Alarm site (*www.fundalarm.com*).

Search for the fund as explained in Chapter 17. Look for Fund Alarm's analysis to see if there has been a change in fund management within the past three years.

The information in Morningstar's Management section may not be up to date. So check for recent management changes on Fund Alarm.

That's all there is to it. You should be able to do a complete fund analysis in 30 minutes.

FINDING WINNING MUTUAL FUNDS: QUICK LOOK

Star Rating: _____ stars (Select 4- or 5-star funds only)

Load: ____% (No-load only)

Morningstar Return Rating: _____

  (Use 5-year rating, if available, 1.5 minimum, 2.0 or higher preferred; higher is better)

Morningstar Risk Rating: _____ (Use 3-year rating; 0.90 maximum; lower is better)

Return/Risk Comparison: _____ (2.0 minimum; higher is better)

FINDING WINNING MUTUAL FUNDS: DETAILED EVALUATION

Three-year return compared to S&P 500: _____%

  (Growth funds: equal to, or better than, S&P 500; value fund: within 10%)

Five-year return compared to S&P 500: _____%

  (Growth funds: equal to, or better than, S&P 500; value funds: within 5% to 10%)

Standard Deviation: _____ (Below 20 is low risk, above 30 is high risk)

Price/Earnings Ratio (P/E): _____

  (Below 25 is low risk, above 30 is high risk; applies only to general funds, not industry-specific funds such as high-tech or health care)

Turnover: _____% (Stay below 50% if taxes are a consideration)

Total Expense Ratio: ____% (1.95% maximum, lower is better)

Fund Manager There at Least Three Years? ❏ Yes   ❏ No

Glossary of Investment Terms

10-K: Annual report required by the SEC.

10-Q: Quarterly report required by the SEC.

12b-1 Fee: Annual marketing fee charged by some mutual funds. Named after SEC regulation allowing such fees.

Accounts Receivable: Money owed by customers for received goods or services. Customers must have been billed for items to be included in receivables.

Aftermarket: Public trading of a company's shares after its IPO.

Alpha: A statistical concoction that's supposed to measure the excess performance of a mutual fund compared to the performance expected for its beta. Higher is better.

Analyst: Someone typically working for a brokerage house who publishes buy/hold/sell recommendations and earnings forecasts for a stock. Buy-side analysts work for institutional buyers, and sell-side analysts work for brokerages.

Arbitrage: The act of taking advantage of the difference in price of the same security traded on two different markets. For instance, if Nortel Networks were trading at $100 (U.S.) on the Toronto exchange and $99 on the NYSE, an arbitrageur would buy shares on the NYSE and sell them on the Toronto exchange.

Ask Price: The price you are asked to pay when you buy a stock.

Asset Allocation: The process of dividing your funds among different classes of investments such as stocks, bonds, or real estate. You could further allocate your stock funds into value, growth, foreign, etc.

Average Daily Volume: Average number of shares traded per day over a specified period.

Average P/E Ratio: Average price/earnings ratio of stocks owned by a mutual fund.

Backtesting: Determining the results of using particular screening criteria, as if the screen had been run at some point back in time, and the selected stocks or funds were held for a predetermined time period and then sold.

Basis Points: One basis point is 0.01 percent. Usually used to describe changes in bond yields. For instance, a 10 basis point increase means the interest rate went up 0.10 percent. A 100 basis point change is 1 percent.

Beta: Compares a mutual fund or stock's volatility to a benchmark (usually the S&P 500 Index). A beta greater than 1 is more volatile than the index. For instance, a beta of 1.5 means the fund or stock is historically 50 percent more volatile than the index.

Bid Price: The price you're offered when selling a stock.

Big Board: The New York Stock Exchange.

Blue Chips: Large, stable companies.

Boiler Room: A high-pressure, often fraudulent, telephone sales operation.

Book-to-Bill Ratio: The ratio of a company's new orders to shipments in the same period. A book-to-bill ratio greater than 1.0 indicates sales growth. Ratios less than 1.0 reflect shrinking sales. Used mostly in the semiconductor industry.

Book Value: Total shareholders' equity from the balance sheet divided by the number of shares outstanding.

Bottom Line: After-tax earnings. Literally, the bottom line on an income statement.

Breakout: A charting (technical analysis) term meaning a stock price has moved above or below a previous trading range.

Bulletin Board System: Stocks that don't qualify for NASDAQ listing are traded here or by Pink Sheets. Stay away!

Buy-Side Analyst: Analyst working for mutual fund or other institutional investor. We don't usually get to see their reports.

Call Option: An option to buy 100 shares of a specified stock at a predetermined price. See LEAPs and Put Options.

Capitalization-Weighted Index: Largest companies have most influence on index price action.

Cash and Cash Equivalents: Cash in the bank and all securities that can readily be converted to cash.

Cash Flow: After-tax income minus preferred dividends and general partner distributions plus depreciation, depletion, and amortization (Market Guide definition). See Operating Cash Flow and Free Cash Flow.

Charting: Making buy and sell decisions based entirely on stock price and volume history (same as technical analysis).

Chat Room: A real-time message area usually dedicated to a particular topic.

Closed-End Fund: Investors buy shares from other shareholders and sell shares to other investors. Share price is determined by supply and demand for fund shares (as opposed to Net Asset Value for open-end funds).

Commodities: Minerals such as gold or silver, food such as corn or wheat, animal products, and the like.

Common Stock: Shares of a publicly held corporation; usually includes voting rights. Common stock has lower priority in the event of a liquidation than preferred shares.

Conference Call: A multi-party telephone call hosted by a company, primarily for analysts, and held shortly after making an earnings announcement.

Consolidation: A charting term meaning a stock price is in a trading range, not moving significantly up or down.

Contrarian: Similar to value investor. Looks for stocks with prices beaten down out of proportion to fundamentals.

Current Ratio: Current assets (cash, inventories, and accounts receivable) divided by liabilities due within one year.

Day Sales Outstanding: A measure of accounts receivable compared to sales. Higher DSOs means a company's receivables as a percentage of sales have increased; not a good sign.

Debt to Equity (Long-Term): Total long-term debt divided by total shareholder equity.

Debt to Equity (Total): Total (short- and long-term) debt divided by total shareholder equity.

Derivatives: Options and other instruments whose value depends on an underlying security. For instance, the value of a call option on Cisco Systems (derivative) fluctuates with the price of Cisco Systems' stock.

Diluted Earnings (a.k.a. fully diluted earnings): Total of after-tax (bottom-line) earnings divided by number of common shares, including unexercised stock options, unconverted preferred stock, and convertible bonds. Undiluted earnings would be after-tax earnings divided by issued stock only, not considering outstanding options, etc.

Direct Stock Purchase Plan (DSP): A plan implemented by a corporation allowing the purchase of shares, or fractions of shares, directly from the company, usually on a regular basis.

Discount Broker: A stockbroker charging lower commissions than full-service brokers. Discount brokers do not give investment advice.

Dividend Reinvestment Plan (DRIP): A plan implemented by a corporation to allow investors to collect dividends in shares (usually fractions of shares) of stock rather than in cash.

Dividend Yield: The annual dividend paid divided by the latest share price.

Dividends: Cash or stock paid to shareholders, usually on a quarterly schedule.

Dogs of the Dow: A contrarian stock selection strategy based upon buying the cheapest stocks of the Dow Jones Industrial Average.

Dow Jones Industrial Average: Unweighted index of 30 of the largest U.S. corporations.

Downtrend: Stock price is heading down.

Due Diligence: The process whereby an in-depth examination of a company's business prospects is conducted.

Dutch Auction: A method of allocating shares in an IPO by which you specify how much you're willing to pay for a certain number of shares.

Earnings per Share (EPS): After-tax annual earnings divided by the number of shares outstanding.

EBITDA: Earnings before interest, taxes, depreciation, and amortization. Adds these items back to reported earnings to more accurately reflect real cash earnings of a company. Similar to operating cash flow, except operating cash flow also considers changes in levels of inventories and receivables.

ECN: Electronic communication (trading) network. ECNs are expected to supplement or even replace conventional stock exchanges over the next one to two years.

EDGAR: Database maintained by the U.S. Securities and Exchange Commission (SEC) containing government-required reports filed by corporations.

Emerging Markets: Developing countries.

EPS: Earnings per share.

Ex-Dividend: The day after dividends are paid.

Execution: A trade completion. For instance, your trade was executed at $12.00.

Expense Ratio: All expenses incurred by mutual fund management in operating and marketing the fund. Includes management and 12b-1 fees. Doesn't include loads or redemption fees. Expense ratios are deducted before computing fund returns.

Extended-Hours Trading: Trades executed outside normal market hours.

Fair Value: The true value of a stock based on criteria of the user's choosing. A stock is said to be overvalued when the share price exceeds the fair value.

Fallen Angel: An IPO trading below its issue price in the aftermarket.

Fed (The): Federal Reserve Board.

Federal Open Market Committee (FOMC): The Fed's monetary policy committee, chaired by Alan Greenspan.

Financials: Financial statements, including operating statement, balance sheet, and statement of cash flows.

Fiscal Year: Any 12-month period designated by a corporation as their accounting year. Once set up, a corporation's fiscal year does not change.

Flipping: The practice of buying IPO shares at the issue price and reselling them on the first day of trading.

Float: Shares outstanding less shares held by insiders. Insiders cannot readily trade shares, so float is considered to be the number of shares available for trading.

Forex: Foreign currency exchange markets.

Free Cash Flow: Operating cash flow minus amounts spent on plants and equipment, and minus dividends.

Full-Service Broker: A stockbroker offering investment advice and other services not usually offered by discount brokers.

Fully Diluted: Number of shares outstanding, including options granted but not yet exercised.

Fundamental Analysis: Analyzing stocks by looking at earnings, sales, profit margins, etc.

GARP: Growth at a Reasonable Price. A strategy of buying stocks whose price/earnings ratio is equal to or less than the estimated annual earnings growth rate.

Geographic Funds: Mutual funds specializing in a specific geographic area, such as Europe.

Good for the Day: Buy or sell limit order will expire at close of trading if not executed.

Good until Canceled: Buy or sell limit order remains active until you cancel it.

Green Shoe: An agreement allowing the lead underwriter to buy additional shares of an IPO at the offering price after the IPO begins trading.

Gross Margin: Profit a company makes on goods and services before considering overhead expenses.

Growth Stocks: Companies with consistent annual earnings and sales growth of at least 15 percent.

Industry Group: Companies in related businesses.

Initial Public Offering (IPO): First sale of stock to the public by a corporation.

Insider Ownership: Number of shares owned or controlled by insiders.

Insider Trading: Shares bought and sold by company insiders. It's legal as long as they follow the SEC's reporting requirements.

Insiders: Officers, directors, and anyone else owning more than 10 percent of stock outstanding.

Institutional Ownership: Shares owned by pension funds, mutual funds, banks, etc.

Interest Coverage: A measure of a company's ability to pay interest on its debts (operating income divided by interest expenses).

Intraday: Stock trading tracked in periods shorter than one day.

Intrinsic Value: A term favored by value-oriented fundamental analysts to express the actual value of a corporation, as opposed to the current value based on the stock price. Usually calculated by adding the current value of estimated future earnings to the book value.

Inventory: Raw materials, work in process, and finished goods that haven't been shipped to customers.

Investment Bank: An organization, usually a stock brokerage firm, involved in taking a new company public (IPO), consulting on mergers and acquisitions, handling corporate borrowing, etc.

January Effect: Refers to the belief that small stocks make a big move up in January.

Large-Cap: Company with market capitalization greater than $8 billion.

Lead Underwriter: Brokerage house in charge of IPO.

LEAP: A long-term put or call option (as long as three years).

Limit Order: Order with broker to buy stock at limit price or less, or to sell stock at limit price or higher.

Liquidity: A measure of the number of shares, or dollar value of shares, traded daily. Mutual funds and other institutional buyers prefer high-liquidity stocks so they can easily move in and out of positions.

Load: A sales commission paid when you buy (front-end) or sell (back-end) a mutual fund.

Lockup Period: Time after IPO, typically 180 days, when insiders are prohibited from selling their shares.

Margin: Borrowing funds from your broker to buy stock.

Margin Account: A brokerage account with approved credit so you can buy stock on margin.

Market Capitalization: Latest stock price multiplied by number of shares outstanding (shares issued).

Market Maker: Intermediary for stocks traded on NASDAQ and for off-hours trading in NYSE stocks. When you trade NASDAQ stocks, you buy your shares from the market maker. When you sell shares, you sell them to the market maker. The market maker keeps the difference between the bid and ask prices.

Market Order: Order with broker to buy or sell stock at current market price.

Median Market Cap: The average market capitalization of stocks owned by a mutual fund.

Message Board: A location on a Web site dedicated to the discussion of a particular topic, usually a single stock or industry sector. Discussions are not real-time. Someone posts a message, and then others respond over a period of hours or days.

Mid-Cap: Company with market capitalization between $2 billion and $7 billion.

Model: A strategy for selecting stocks using screening criteria that have been found to work in the past.

Momentum Analysis: Usually involves looking for stocks in a strong uptrend (high relative strength) with strong earnings growth and increasing earnings forecasts. In today's market, may include relative strength only.

Momentum Stocks: Companies currently in favor by investors (price/sales greater than 10, price/earnings greater than 35 or so).

Money-Center Bank: The largest banks, such as Citigroup and Bank of America.

Money Supply: The amount of money in circulation. The Federal Reserve Board attempts to control the growth of the U.S. economy by regulating the increase in money supply.

Morningstar: Mutual fund rating service.

Most Recent Quarter (MRQ): As of the last date of the last reported fiscal quarter.

NASDAQ: National market for trading stocks.

NASDAQ 100 Index: Index of 100 largest companies on NASDAQ. The NASDAQ trades like a stock under the symbol QQQ.

Net Asset Value: Value of all stock and other assets owned by mutual fund divided by the total number of shares the fund has outstanding.

No-Load Mutual Fund: No sales commission is charged if you buy shares directly from the fund. There may or may not be a commission charged if you buy the fund through a broker.

Non-Operating Expenses: Expenses not due to the basic business of a company.

Non-Operating Income: Income not derived from the basic business of a company.

Open: Trade price of the day's first transaction.

Open-End Mutual Fund: Investors buy shares directly from the fund, and sell shares directly to the fund. Share price is the Net Asset Value (NAV).

Operating Cash Flow: Surplus cash generated from company's basic operations without regard to income tax entries such as depreciation and amortization. Changes in levels of inventories, accounts receivable, and accounts payable also affect cash flow. Also see Free Cash Flow.

Operating Income: Sales minus all expenses except income taxes and other items not related to the basic business.

Operating Margin: Operating income divided by sales.

Over-the-Counter-Market: Older name for stocks traded on NASDAQ. Also refers to bulletin board and Pink Sheet stocks.

Payment for Order Flow: A payment made by a market maker to a broker as a thank you for directing a stock trade to that market maker.

Payout Ratio: Percentage of earnings paid out in dividends.

PEG: Price-to-earnings ratio divided by the forecast annual earnings growth rate. Traditionally, stocks were said to be fairly valued when the P/E and the forecast growth rate were equal.

Phase 1, Phase 2, and Phase 3: The series of FDA-required tests before a new drug can be placed on the market.

Portfolio: A group of stocks, mutual funds, or other securities.

Post-Offering Shares: The number of shares that will be outstanding after an IPO.

Preferred Stock: Debt instruments. Preferred shareholders are paid ahead of common stockholders in the event the corporation is liquidated. Convertible preferred shares can be converted into common stock according to predetermined conditions.

Price-to-Book Ratio (P/B): Latest share price divided by book value stated in latest report.

Price-to-Earnings Ratio (P/E): Latest share price divided by 12-month earnings per share (eps). Also a measure of the market's enthusiasm for a company.

Price-to-Sales Ratio (P/S): Latest share price divided by 12-month sales per share.

Profit Margin: Bottom-line (after-tax) earnings divided by sales.

Prospectus: A document circulated to potential investors prior to an IPO describing a company's business plan.

Put Option: An option to sell 100 shares of a specified company's shares at a predetermined price. Also see LEAPs and Call Options.

Quick Ratio: Cash and cash equivalents plus accounts receivable divided by current liabilities (a.k.a. Acid Test Ratio).

Quiet Period: Time after IPO, typically 25 days, when all parties involved in the IPO are prohibited from commenting on the company's future prospects. Analysts employed by underwriters are free to make buy/hold/sell recommendations after the Quiet Period expiration.

Quote: Information on the last trade and current bid and ask prices. Most quotes are intentionally delayed about 20 minutes.

Range: High and low trade prices for the day, week, or month.

Real-Time Quotes: Stock trading price reports that have not been artificially delayed.

Receivables: See Accounts Receivable.

Redemption Fee: Fee charged when you sell a mutual fund, if you haven't held the fund for the prescribed minimum time.

REIT: Real estate investment trust. A special form of mutual fund investing only in real estate. REITs must pay out most of their earnings as dividends to share owners.

Relative Dividend Yield: Dividend yield of a stock compared to the dividend yield of the S&P 500.

Relative Strength: Stock price performance compared to the S&P 500, or to the entire stock market. Can measure performance over any time span, but most often uses 12 months. Relative strength is different from the RSI (Relative Strength Indicator) used in technical analysis.

Return on Assets: After-tax income divided by total assets.

Return on Equity: After-tax income (latest 12 months) divided by shareholders' equity (from balance sheet).

Return on Investments: After-tax income (latest 12 months) divided by total of shareholders' equity plus long-term debt, plus other long-term liabilities.

Revenues: A company's sales.

Road Show: Presentations made by underwriters and IPO company officials to institutional buyers to create interest in the offering.

Russell 2000 Index: The Russell 3000 is an index of the 3,000 largest U.S. publicly traded corporations. The Russell 2000 is a capitalization-weighted index of the 2,000 smallest companies of the Russell 3000.

S&P 500: Capitalization-weighted index of 500 of the largest U.S. corporations.

Sales: Services and products sold by a company. Sales and revenues mean the same thing.

Sales per Share: Annual sales divided by the number of shares outstanding.

Same-Store Sales: Sales at retail stores or restaurants open at least one year. A chain's same-store sales growth excludes gains due to increases in the number of stores. Same-store sales growth in the 5 percent to 10 percent range is considered good.

Screening: Searching the entire universe of mutual funds or stocks meeting user-specified criteria.

Sector Funds: Mutual funds specializing in a particular industry sector such as computers or health care.

Sell-Side Analyst: An analyst employed by a brokerage house such as Merrill Lynch.

Settlement: The process of paying for stocks you purchase or receiving credit from your broker for the stocks you sell. Most stock transactions must be settled within three business days.

Shareholders Equity: The difference between the total of assets and liabilities shown on a company's balance sheet. Book value is the shareholders' equity divided by the number of outstanding shares.

Shares Outstanding: The total number of shares issued by a corporation.

Sharpe Ratio: An attempt to compare a fund's performance to risk. Higher Sharpe Ratio funds are said to be better performers than lower-ratio funds.

Short Interest: Number of shares borrowed by short sellers.

Short-Interest Ratio: Number of days it would take to cover short interest at average daily volume (short interest divided by average daily volume).

Short Sale: Selling stock you don't own. You hope it drops in price so you can buy it back later at a lower price. You must have a margin account with your broker to sell short.

Short Squeeze: A sharp move up in stock price forcing short sellers to liquidate their positions.

Small Cap: Company with market capitalization less than $1 billion.

Specialist System: A person on a stock exchange floor (specialist) matches buy and sell orders (used on New York and American stock exchanges).

Spider: A security representing one-tenth the value of the S&P 500 index. Spiders trade like a stock. Spiders are a means of owning the index without buying mutual fund shares.

Standard Deviation: A measure of a mutual fund or stock's historical volatility.

Stop Limit Order: A combination of a stop order and a limit order. The limit order becomes effective when the stock hits the stop price.

Stop Order (stop loss): Order with broker to sell stock at market price when it goes down to specified (limit) price.

Surprise: Difference between reported earnings and analysts' consensus forecasts. It's a positive surprise if reported earnings exceed forecasts and a negative surprise when reported earnings come in below forecasts.

Sweep: Movement of funds from a noninterest-bearing account to an interest-bearing account.

Tangible Book Value: Book value minus goodwill and intangible assets.

Technical Analysis: Making buy and sell decisions based entirely on stock price and volume history (same as charting).

Top: A charting term meaning the stock price will be decreasing.

Top-Line: Sales or revenues.

Trailing Twelve Months (TTM): The last four reported quarters.

Triple Witching: The third Friday of March, June, September, and December is the day when index futures, index future options, and certain stock options all expire. Triple-Witching Fridays are know for high volatility.

Turnover Ratio: The frequency with which a mutual fund changes its portfolio holdings. One hundred percent turnover means a fund, on average, changes all the stocks in its portfolio once a year.

Undervalued: A stock trading below its fair value.

Underwriter: Brokerage house participating in an IPO.

Uptrend: Stock price is trending higher.

Value Investor: One who looks for out-of-favor (value-priced) stocks.

Value Stocks: Companies currently out of favor with investors. These companies usually have low valuation ratios (price/earnings < S&P 500, price/sales < 2, price/book < 2).

Venture Capitalist: An investor involved in financing a company's operations before going public in exchange for an ownership percentage.

Volume: Number of shares traded during a specified time, usually one day.

Watch Portfolio: A group of stocks or funds that you are tracking but don't currently own.

Whisper Number: Sometimes analysts publish lower earnings forecasts for companies they follow as a way of reducing chances of a negative surprise but "whisper" their real predictions to their best customers.

Yield: Interest and dividends paid to mutual fund shareholders as a percentage of share price (Net Asset Value). Also, the effective interest rate on a bond. For instance, if a bond pays $1.00 interest annually and is selling for $10.00, the yield is (1.00/10.00) 10 percent.

Index

We Have EVERYTHING!

Available wherever books are sold!

Everything **After College Book**
$12.95, 1-55850-847-3

Everything **Astrology Book**
$12.95, 1-58062-062-0

Everything **Baby Names Book**
$12.95, 1-55850-655-1

Everything **Baby Shower Book**
$12.95, 1-58062-305-0

Everything **Barbeque Cookbook**
$12.95, 1-58062-316-6

Everything® **Bartender's Book**
$9.95, 1-55850-536-9

Everything **Bedtime Story Book**
$12.95, 1-58062-147-3

Everything **Beer Book**
$12.95, 1-55850-843-0

Everything **Bicycle Book**
$12.95, 1-55850-706-X

Everything **Build Your Own Home Page**
$12.95, 1-58062-339-5

Everything **Casino Gambling Book**
$12.95, 1-55850-762-0

Everything **Cat Book**
$12.95, 1-55850-710-8

Everything® **Christmas Book**
$15.00, 1-55850-697-7

Everything **College Survival Book**
$12.95, 1-55850-720-5

Everything **Cover Letter Book**
$12.95, 1-58062-312-3

Everything **Crossword and Puzzle Book**
$12.95, 1-55850-764-7

Everything **Dating Book**
$12.95, 1-58062-185-6

Everything **Dessert Book**
$12.95, 1-55850-717-5

Everything **Dog Book**
$12.95, 1-58062-144-9

Everything **Dreams Book**
$12.95, 1-55850-806-6

Everything **Etiquette Book**
$12.95, 1-55850-807-4

Everything **Family Tree Book**
$12.95, 1-55850-763-9

Everything **Fly-Fishing Book**
$12.95, 1-58062-148-1

Everything **Games Book**
$12.95, 1-55850-643-8

Everything **Get-a-Job Book**
$12.95, 1-58062-223-2

The ultimate reference for couples planning their wedding!

- Scheduling, budgeting, etiquette, hiring caterers, florists, and photographers
- Ceremony & reception ideas
- Over 100 forms and checklists
- And much, much more!

$12.95, 384 pages, 8" x 9 1/4"

Personal finance made easy—and fun!

- Create a budget you can live with
- Manage your credit cards
- Set up investment plans
- Money-saving tax strategies
- And much, much more!

$12.95, 288 pages, 8" x 9 1/4"

For more information, or to order, call 800-872-5627
or visit www.adamsmedia.com/everything

Adams Media Corporation, 260 Center Street, Holbrook, MA 02343